The Oxford English Programme 4A

Liz Lockwood
Anne Powling
Les Stringer

Oxford University Press

Oxford University Press, Walton Street, Oxford OX2 6DP

Oxford   New York
Athens   Auckland   Bangkok   Bombay
Calcutta   Cape Town   Dar es Salaam   Delhi
Florence   Hong Kong   Istanbul   Karachi
Kuala Lumpur   Madras   Madrid   Melbourne
Mexico City   Nairobi   Paris   Singapore
Taipei   Tokyo   Toronto

and associated companies in
Berlin Ibadan

Oxford is a trade mark of Oxford University Press

© Liz Lockwood, Anne Powling and Les Stringer, 1992
First published 1992
Reprinted 1992, 1993, 1994

ISBN 0 19 831176 1

Printed and bound in Italy

Contents

Introduction   vii

Module 1	**Forms of Narrative**	

	Objectives	1

UNIT 1
Diaries, journals, and autobiography

	Coded diaries	2
	Personal diaries	3
	Descriptive journals	5
	Fictional diaries	7
	Autobiography	10

UNIT 2
Letters

	Novels in letters	14
	Ideas in letters	17
	Letters never sent	18

UNIT 3
Travel writing

	A curious life for a lady/Holidays in hell	20
	Far off people and places	22
	Closer to home	24
	Fantasy travel	26

UNIT 4
Myths, legends, and folk-tales

	Early stories	28
	Legends of King Arthur	30
	The birth of Jesus	31
	Modern folk-tales or urban legends	34

UNIT 5
Stories all around us

	Media collage	36
	Picture stories	37
	Family stories	42

UNIT 6
Novels and short stories

	Genre and style	44
	Openings	45
	Plot and theme	46
	Setting	48
	Character	50
	Characters and dialogue	52
	Short stories	54

FEATURE
On trial

	Setting, characters, and story-line	58
	The trial	60

Module 2   Poetry

	Objectives	61

UNIT 1	Mid term break	62
Poetry as picture	Sense images	65
	Personification	70
	Images and feelings	72
	Keeping a poetry journal	75

UNIT 2	Poetry or prose	76
Poem as story	Ballads	78
	Dramatic monologue	84

UNIT 3	A poet's drafts	88
Poem as pattern	Patterns of rhyme	90
	Full rhyme and half rhyme	91
	Internal rhyme	94
	Syllabic verse	98

UNIT 4	Repetition, patterns of imagery,	
Free verse	shape in free verse	100
	Comparing patterns	103
	Relative values	106

UNIT 5	Shakespeare's sonnet 104	112
Poetry and precision	Parody	114
	Comparing two sonnets: Shakespearean	
	and Petrarchan	115

FEATURE	Shaping the anthology	117
Creating your own anthology	So what is poetry?	119

Module 3   Media Scripts

	Objectives	121

UNIT 1
Radio plays

	Radio Times drama listings	122
	Writing for radio	124
	The bogeyman	125
	Follow-up theme: bullying	131

UNIT 2
Screenplay

	Book or film?	134
	My left foot	134
	Same story, different form	138
	Follow-up theme: disability	142

UNIT 3
Devising drama

	Drama techniques	144
	Let her sleep	147
	Nathan's case	151

UNIT 4
Monologue

	A cream cracker under the settee	154
	Follow-up theme: old age	159
	Frangipani House	159
	Elsie	161

UNIT 5
Directing the scene

	Directing a photo story	164
	Romeo and Juliet	164
	Follow-up theme: romance	168
	The lion and the jewel	170
	Directing techniques	172
	Set and costume design	173

FEATURE
Documentary autobiography

	The rock and roll years	174
	A year in the life of Grace Ndiritu	176

	Index of authors	181

Introduction

Books 4A and 4B of *The Oxford English Programme* are designed for use in Years 10 and 11, as you work towards GCSE or Years S3 and S4 for Standard Grade. Using the language of the National Curriculum, they are aimed at Key Stage 4.

The National Curriculum

The National Curriculum thinks of English in terms of three 'Profile Components': Speaking and Listening; Reading; and Writing. It also lists what students should know, understand and be able to do at different 'Levels' of attainment.

The Oxford English Programme at Key Stage 4 has been devised so as to cover all the detailed requirements of the National Curriculum, but at the same time (and just as importantly) offer materials and activities that will be exciting and enjoyable.

The structure of The Oxford English Programme

As there is so much in the English curriculum at this Key Stage, this part of the programme is made up of two books rather than one. We have done this in order to give full and detailed coverage of the areas you need to be familiar with at GCSE or Standard Grade level.

We do not expect that you should begin with Module 1 of Book 4A and work your way through to the end of Book 4B. Nobody develops their ability to use English in such a mechanical, step-by-step way. Moving from module to module, you might be writing a radio play one day, talking about dialects the next and organising a charity event the week after!

The books and the modules

Book 4A gives particular emphasis to literature. In Module 1, **Forms of Narrative**, you will encounter a variety of the ways in which people compose written stories – from diaries to folk-tales; travel writing to short stories – and have the opportunity to experiment with these forms yourself.

Module 2 focuses upon **Poetry**, looking at the different effects that can be achieved through its many features and the forms that it can take.

Media Scripts is the title of Module 3, which offers examples of plays written for radio, film, theatre and television; and encourages you to write and direct your own.

Book 4B directs your attention more towards language. Module 1 is called **Knowledge about Language**. In this you will consider how the English language has changed over the centuries and how it continues to be rich in its variety today.

Module 2 examines **The Process of Writing**, asking you to think about the different purposes of writing (for example, to convey information, or to persuade people) and contains an important unit on planning and drafting.

Newspapers and advertising are a major feature of Module 3, **Non-literary Forms**. It also looks at the types of language used by specialists, such as scientists or historians, when writing for different audiences.

There are cross references between all the modules, to show how work you are involved with in one might be linked to or helped by work in another. For example in Book 4A, work on dramatic monologue in the Poetry module on pages 84-87 would lead well into the unit on scripted monologue on pages 154-158 in the Media Scripts module.

Each module concludes with a special Feature that gives you the opportunity to put into practice in a longer assignment the knowledge, understanding and skills that you have acquired.

Module 1 Forms of Narrative

UNIT 1	Diaries, journals, and autobiography	2
UNIT 2	Letters	14
UNIT 3	Travel writing	20
UNIT 4	Myths, legends, and folk-tales	28
UNIT 5	Stories all around us	36
UNIT 6	Novels and short stories	44
FEATURE	On trial	58

Objectives

The materials and activities included in this module aim to help you learn more about different narrative forms by:

◆ offering a range of reading from many narrative genres which will develop your critical skills
◆ encouraging you to look at different narrative structures and standpoints
◆ presenting you with the chance to experiment in your writing with various forms of narrative

Diaries, journals, and autobiography

Many people have at some point in their lives written their own diaries or journals, sometimes to try to understand themselves and others, sometimes to record facts, observations and reflections.

Certain diaries are written to be shared, others are private and personal and some are entirely imaginary. Who they are written for will affect how they are written, and what is included. All diaries, whether fact or fiction, tend to be written in the first person, giving immediacy and the ring of truth.

Coded diaries

Diaries written solely for the author are sometimes recorded in a special code or shorthand (like the famous diaries of Pepys) or in note form – words or passing impressions jotted down on the spur of the moment. William Allingham wrote in this way, capturing the moods, incidents and fleeting thoughts of his life and friendships between 1824 and 1889.

Allingham's diaries, 1866

Thursday, 30 August

Rail to Winchester, with N., G., and Webb – meet Morris there. All walk by the Close and meadows to St Cross. Old man, dining-hall; men's room, old cloisters, wooden arches – mixed up with leaves and flowers. The Dole. Back by the meadows and streamlets. Dinner at 'The George', tough mutton, parsonic waiter, red-faced grinning Landlady, bill 19s.

Cathedral – west windows, bits of old glass, choir, side aisles, Lady chapel, wall paintings, etc. Morris talked copiously and interestingly on all things, Webb now and again on technicalities (also interesting). Ned enjoyed the general charm and picturesqueness; I also, in my own way – but with the drawback of uncomfortableness which I always feel from the incongruity of the past and present, of old intention and modern significance, in these great and beautiful Edifices...

We went to the College. In the Chapel, bad glass in imitation of old. To Dining Hall by outside stairs, bread and butter on the square slab of wood, beer and tea (a modern innovation). The Boys. I have my usual feeling of no unkindly envy at the discipline and training (the evils, very real, at present invisible). Schoolroom – dormitory. Under gateway and out. Old walls, then clear brisk river, little houses with gardens, bridge, St Giles's with little red-tiled steeple-spire – wide space. High Street, the downs rising beyond. Old Hall, Assize Courts, Arthur's Round Table, View of City and Cathedral, flushed sunset. Fieldpath to Station. Ned, G., and Morris and I back to Lymington – Webb to London. M. being hot wants to sit in draught...

William Allingham

Decoding the events of the day

1 Allingham and a group of friends have visited the town of Winchester. In pairs work out as exactly as you can:
   - who is present in the group and how they spend their day
   - where they go and who they see
   - what their impressions of the day are
   - what they have liked and what they have disliked about the day. (You will need to jot down evidence from the diary for this.)
2 On your own, redraft Allingham's notes and scraps of information into a detailed account of the trip, developing descriptions, including conversations and elaborating on details where meanings are not clear.
3 Compare this with your partner's account. Have you both included all the relevant facts? Have you both developed the same descriptions or are there differences? What sort of effect does the narrative description of the day have when compared with the original diary entry?

Personal diaries

The following diary extracts from *Catherine* by Maureen Dunbar tell the true story of the tragic life of Catherine Dunbar who died in 1984 after a seven-year illness. Because Catherine was a real person, reading about her life and death can be moving and upsetting.

My daughter, Catherine Anne-Marie, died of anorexia nervosa on 2 January 1984, at the age of 22. She was intelligent, sensitive and beautiful, but she only wanted to die.

With hindsight, I think Catherine believed that I accepted her anorexia or, to put it differently, I accepted her own denial of the will to live. I never did: what I did understand, and understood very well, was that this was her anorexia controlling her and not her herself. I constantly tried to explain this to family and friends. To express my deepest feelings about Catherine's illness is impossible. Words fail me. Uppermost in my mind was always the urgent need to infuse in her the desire to live – and I failed....

My hope was always that Catherine would overcome her anorexia and so, with her special knowledge, be able to help others, but she was trapped, trapped in a maze of agony and delusions. She suffered too intolerance and lack of understanding in others: I hope that this book will help to create a climate of compassion, love and support from the families and friends of those unfortunate enough to be anorexic...

Catherine's diary

August 1980
I have never felt as ill and weak as today since last November.
How I survived work I will never know.

28 June 1981
Mood: Depressed
Weight: 30.4
Breakfast: 1½ Kit-Kats, tea
Lunch: Cornish pasty, 2 sausage rolls, cheese dish, tea, 1½ Kit-Kats
Supper: Roast beef, cabbage, boiled new potatoes, Yorkshire pudding,
           gooseberry fool and 1½ Kit-Kats, tea

3

Binge:	I began at 4.00 and finished at 7.30. Bread, sausages, cheese, sugar puffs, sweets, bonbons then a second one on Twiglets, cheese puffs, sweets and crisps.
Laxatives:	145 approx.
Remarks:	This morning I really broke down and sobbed my heart out to Mummy and Daddy. I have just given up hope of ever getting better. Mummy, I am sure, is the only person who can help me. I had a dreadful afternoon bingeing and I have no idea how much food I retained in me, but it feels a lot. I weighed 31.00 kilos after it.

...In January 1982 Dr Foot persuaded her to meet a consultant physician. He came to the house, and Catherine liked him immediately, but she refused to have any kind of treatment. After some weeks Dr Foot and the consultant finally persuaded Catherine to go into hospital... Despite the love, care and kindness given to Catherine she still refused treatment.

Thursday, 6 May 1982

I woke up after a not too good night's sleep. Everything went according to schedule this morning. The doctor came in at 10.00 and we chatted about tube feeding. I felt very calm and placid this morning. In my own mind I know I will never eat without help and that therefore tube feeding is the only way I will survive, but it will be another week or two before I can begin. I know that I can only accept it when I feel ready... I reckon it will be 2-3 weeks, at least, but it is better that way, than before I am ready. It is my mental state, I actually can feel my body packing up now. I know in myself that time is running out...

Thinking about Catherine's diary

In groups of 3 or 4, talk about your reactions to reading about Catherine's life, illness and death.
1 What sort of moods or states of mind can you see in these extracts?
2 What does Catherine's mother feel about this illness?
3 Why in writing this book has Catherine's mother incorporated her account of events along with Catherine's diary?
4 What effect does this have?

Role play and group reflection

1 In these same groups take on the roles of Catherine, her mother, and the doctor trying to treat her. Catherine is trying to explain how she feels and the doctor and her mother are trying hard to understand but also to persuade her to live her life in a different way. Additional group members should observe the role play and note down what results.

2 As a group make a report (written or spoken) on what you have found out about Catherine, her hospital treatment and the reactions of her mother to all the events that occurred.

Writing for advice

1 In groups of 4 to 6, discuss what you think are the most pressing problems and concerns for people of your age in the society of today.
   ● Jot down the areas that concern you most.
   ● Do you think they are likely to be very different from the problems facing young people 50 years ago?
   ● What solutions, if any, can you offer?
2 Select one of these problems and write a letter to the Agony Aunt of a newspaper or magazine, asking for advice. It could be based either on real or imaginary experience.
   You may be able to use this work as part of a piece of coursework at the end of the unit.

Descriptive journals

Other diaries or journals concentrate less on feelings and emotions and more on descriptions of places and surroundings. In this diary the writer describes her village and the countryside around it.

The magic apple tree

Winter

The magic apple tree is bare now. Stand at the top of the seven stone steps. Moon Cottage, and that part of the garden that lies in front of it, are at your feet, and the apple tree is straight ahead, your eyes are level with its lower branches. Through them, you see the rise and fall of the fields beyond, piled upon one another like pillows. The Buttercup field, which is nearest, slopes down to the small brook that runs between four willows; beyond that, the Rise, overlapping with the Dovehouse field, and so gently on, and up, to where the topmost field lies like an arm outstretched, and forms a boundary to one side of the village. On a few, very clear days in winter, you can even see further, right over the top of the apple tree to where the blue hump of the village of Hope – Hope-on-the-Slope – is sometimes visible. But, mostly, there is mist or some other greyness obscuring it, and later in the year it is almost blocked out by the foliage.

The fields within a few acres of this house, the fields you can see through the branches of the apple tree, are all small, and in winter they are empty; these are long-established grazing fields for cattle and horses, never ploughed or planted. They are bounded by hedges of hawthorn and elder, knotted with groups of trees that thicken as the ground rises in the distance, the trees of light, mixed woodlands, sycamore and ash, birch and maple, mingling with all the smaller trees of the village gardens, laburnum and rowan, cherry, plum and pear. But, now, you can identify them only by their outlines. Through them all, and through the magic apple tree, we can see the roofs and walls, gates and fences, of the houses on the east side of the village, the slope which rises above Fen Lane, and those down in its groin; and, after dark, we see their lights. Once their leaves are full again, they too will be concealed and we will feel more isolated. It is a comfort in winter to see those signs of life on the long nights of early dark, we feel drawn towards them. When the leaves shut us off from one another again, and the lights are not lit until nine or ten o'clock, there is warmth outdoors, and light in the sky itself, and then people go for evening walks and meet in the lanes, stand to talk at gates, look over into one another's gardens. But in winter, when we all scurry back into our individual burrows, and no one lingers, we need to be able to see each other's houses and lights, for reassurance.

Whether you stand at the top of the stone steps or at any of the windows, you cannot look from this cottage across to the fields opposite, or to your left, away and down over the whole, flat stretch of the Fen, without also having the apple tree in your sight, it draws your eyes towards it and balances the picture, a point of reference for the whole view. It is only, perhaps, fifteen feet high, and a most beautiful, satisfying shape, it has the dome, falling down to a wider base frill, of the shaggy parasol mushroom...the spirit of the place is in that apple tree.

Susan Hill

Looking at the extract

Susan Hill has painted a picture with words in this journal. Try and draw the scene that she has described and include as many of the details as you can. With a partner talk about:
- which details tell the reader it is winter
- how the writer avoids making her descriptions sound like a list
- what the effect is of the sentence beginning 'Stand at the top...'
- which aspects of her description particularly appeal to you

Writing your own descriptive journal

Try to describe the area where you live or go to school or college in the style of Susan Hill.

Choose a specific time of year, look out of one of the windows and start your description close to hand. Gradually start describing things further and further away from you.

Thinking about where you live

In pairs tell each other about the area where you live, the friends you and your family have and the events and activities you take part in. Then in groups of 4 to 6 choose one of these activities:
1 Prepare a radio programme about where you live or where you go to school.
2 Gather ideas and supporting material to give an illustrated talk about your area to the rest of the class.

For more on assembling leaflets, guides about your area, see The Process of Writing module in Book 4B, page 88.

For more on diaries describing people and events see The Process of Writing module in Book 4B, page 71

Fictional diaries

The following extracts are written as if the characters involved are real people and as if the events described have actually happened but they are, in fact, entirely imaginary...

I'm a health freak too!

5th June

Exams start tomorrow. Resolutions:
I won't panic
I will read the questions
I will look and see how much time I have to answer
I will write short notes first
I will do my best handwriting
I will have all my best pens and pencils and my
   calculator with me
HELP!
P.S. I must remember to take my hayfever spray regularly.

6th June

The English exam was easy but I messed it up. Didn't see the question on the last page. So much for my resolutions... It really made a difference – Mum and Dad being so relaxed with me about the exams. Kate's mum hassles her every time she wants to go out. Even on a Friday night she goes on about 'but what about your homework? Have you thought about the revision you need to do for the exams?' Right in front of her friends. It's really not on – would make me want to do just the opposite. What do they think? That we want to fail our exams? At least Mum and Dad seem to trust me (most of the time anyway). They remind me to have rests from work, and they bring me cups of coffee. Mum makes a special effort to have meals on time and to give me treats.

8th June

Maths OK. But Sheila wasn't. She walked out sobbing – half-way through. Everybody looked at her as she went. Nobody could understand. She's the brain.

Ann McPherson and *Aidan MacFarlane*

'Allo, 'allo   *The war diaries of René Artois*

15 February
For the last few days Colonel Von Strohm and Captain Geering have been lurking in the café dressed as onion-sellers. These disguises were left in the wardrobe in the bedroom of my wife's mother by the escaping British airmen. And it is not even the onion season.
   'Ah, Pierre, Jacques – the onion-sellers,' I greeted them as they sidled into the restaurant. 'Wine for my friends Pierre and Jacques. Sit down here, my friends.'

The British airmen dressed as onion-sellers

Then in a whisper, 'A brilliant disguise, my friends. We will get your uniforms as quickly as possible.'

'You said that yesterday, René,' said the Colonel.

'And the day before, and the day before that,' piped the Captain.

'If we don't get them today, you will be shot,' said the Colonel.

'Up against the wall, with guns,' piped the Captain.

I could tell that they weren't impressed, although even as these harsh threats were uttered I saw tears of compassion in their eyes.

'It is these damned onions,' said the Colonel, but he didn't fool me.

I moved to attend to my other customers as Maria came in with the basket of carrier pigeons, dressed as a small boy.* Thinking quickly, I welcomed her. 'Aha, little Georges, my nephew. It is good to see you, lad.'

'I have got what you want, Uncle,' she said, and I couldn't help noticing she had. Lieutenant Gruber, who was in his favourite position at the bar, noticed too.

'That boy is very well built, René,' he said with approval.

'Ah, it is my wife's cooking.'

'Why is he wearing stockings and suspenders?'

'We have many problems with him.'

* This remains obscure. Why were the carrier pigeons dressed as a small boy?

John Haselden

Comparing the diary extracts

I'm a health freak too! is written from the point of view of a teenage girl but the authors are adults writing with a particular purpose and intention.

Working in pairs

1 Can you see what their intention or purpose might be?
2 What clues can you find that suggest this is not a factual diary but that it is fiction?
3 Examine *'Allo, 'allo* in the same way.
4 Using evidence from both extracts decide why the authors of these fictional pieces have chosen to use the diary form. What differences might there have been if they had written their ideas in the form of novels?
5 What are the obvious differences between these fictional diaries and other factual diaries? (You will need to look at the reasons why the diaries were written as well as the tone used by the author.)

Write a report on your conclusions to share and compare with the rest of the class.

Writing a humorous diary

Write a few pages of your own humorous diary either based on truth, imagination or a mixture of the two. You will need to decide what your intention is, e.g. to inform, to persuade, to entertain, etc. and who you are writing for.

The following extract also reads like a real diary but it is, in fact, from a novel told in diary form. It tells the story of Ann Burden, a sixteen year old girl who thinks she is the only person left alive after a nuclear explosion has devastated the country. A strange man arrives in her valley. The man, Mr Loomis, becomes increasingly sinister and Ann eventually runs away from her home and hides in a cave.

Z for Zachariah

July 1st   After supper, in the cave

Mr Loomis does plan to use Faro to catch me. Yesterday, late in the afternoon, he came outside carrying Faro's plate of food. The dog had stopped crying and gone to sleep, curled up in the grass beside the porch. Mr Loomis did not give him food immediately, but put the plate down on the porch. He untied the leash, the electric cord, from the porch, looped up most of it in his hand like a lasso (it was 25 feet long), and led Faro out to the road still tied to the other end.

Faro, not used to being led, had a hard time at first – he kept trying to run and being brought up short. He learned quickly, however, and in a few minutes was walking along docilely enough, his nose to the road and wagging his tail. He was following my trail again, but this time leading Mr Loomis behind him.

They went in this manner only a few yards up the road, perhaps fifty. Then they turned and came back to the house, Mr Loomis once again limping slightly, Faro trotting beside him, pulling a little to get to his dinner. But in that few yards I began to realise the mistake I had made, and also why Mr Loomis had tied Faro up. If he could teach him to track on a leash, he could find me whenever he wanted to. Not yet, perhaps, but when he could walk farther.

Suddenly I had a feeling he knew I was watching. Or worse, that he hoped I was. Along with it came another feeling which made me feel slightly sick again: that I was in a game of move-counter-move, like a chess game, a game I did not want to be in at all. Only Mr Loomis wanted to be in it, and only he could win it.

After he had tied the dog up and fed him, Mr Loomis walked back to the road, and stood looking, first in the direction they had walked, towards the store: having seen nothing there, he turned slowly in a full circle, inspecting all of the valley that he could see. At one point he stared straight at me, and I had a fearful impulse to put down the binoculars and duck into the cave. But he could not see me, I knew; in a moment his gaze went on past, he completed his circle and went into the house.

Robert C. O'Brien

Looking at the extract

1 Discuss in pairs the advantages of writing a novel in a diary form like this. Are there any disadvantages? Make a note of these.

2 In the extract you have read the events are seen entirely from Anne's point of view. Go through the text listing separately items of 'fact' as opposed to the narrator's opinions or feelings.

Writing from another point of view

The reader has no first-hand knowledge of what Mr Loomis is feeling and thinking. Put yourself in his place and using the same facts that you identified in the last activity, write a diary entry for this same day from his point of view. Include his feelings and opinions and bear in mind that Anne thinks he is trying to hunt and catch her.

Autobiography

Many personal and reflective diaries have been the starting points for jogging the memory and stimulating a person to write more sustained pieces specifically for other people to read. Here, events and narrative are shaped into autobiography.

In the extracts which follow, a variety of people reflect on their early memories, concentrating on describing perhaps an incident, a particular place, a specific person, or feelings and emotions. This piece was written after interviewing a family member about his childhood.

Early memories of school

I first went to school in 1924 to Sunnyhill Road School in Streatham, South London. It had been built by the School Board for London in the previous century but was run by the London County Council. I think it still exists. At that time it was lit by gas and the caretaker had to come round with a gas-lighter's pole to put all the lamps on when the light got bad. Heating was by coal fires in each class. The toilets were outside in the playground and as they had no roofs, nobody lingered there in winter! The school was in three sections: Babies, Mixed Infants and Juniors. Apart from the Babies, who had tables on a flat floor, the other classes all had desks in rows on a series of steps towards the back of the classroom. We seldom had more than 30 pupils to a class.

The Babies were for the under 5 year olds. (I started before I was 4.) We had sand to play with, a rocking horse, a dolls house and bricks. We did learn the ABC there but not I think much more. We all had a sleep in the afternoon, either on fold-up canvas beds or on rush mats on the floor. I still have a class photograph of the Babies when I was in it. The girls wore dresses, some with pinafores over. They had names like Florrie, Gladys, May, Chrissie, Edith, Joan, Mary and Violet. The boys for the most part wore jerseys and short woollen trousers. At least one had his hanky pinned to his jersey. They were called Bertie, Harry, Ted, George, Charlie, Jimmy, Bob, Stanley and Fred.

When we moved up into the Infants we were given a slate with slate pencil and sponge and a small cardboard box with coloured sticks in. We used the sticks to learn to count with and add and subtract. I don't remember how we learned to read and write – it just seemed to happen.

Discipline was strict. There was no talking in class unless spoken to and there was smacking and later caning for those who were deemed to have misbehaved. The teachers were feared rather than liked. They all seemed to me fierce old ladies. There were one or two men teachers in the Juniors but these were sometimes strange. I learnt afterwards that they could have been shell-shocked ex-soldiers.

Fred Rickard

Another member of the same family has written about an event that has remained vivid in his mind.

Free dinners

The dole is a hard task-master. Luckily I have inherited some of my mother's Scottish thrift, so when I was invited by my yuppie sister to a dinner-dance, I got out of my Thatcherite closet, got on my bike and went in search of evening wear. There is a quality second-hand clothes stall in the Thursday market in Central Milton Keynes. I wandered around looking for bargains but there was no stall. There are some interesting specialist stalls – post-cards, toys, also some medals on the bric-a-brac tables that would have looked good with white tie and tails.

Disappointed, I fell back on plan B, the Charity Shops. First the one by The Electra in Newport, is it Age Concern? I did not stay long enough to take it in. The all-pervading atmosphere of poverty was too much. A prematurely middle-aged fat woman with a complexion devastated by a bad diet, struggled to control four children as she tried to squeeze into a shapeless winter coat. The children harried her, like terriers around a chained bear. She scolded and cuffed them as she gave a running commentary on her attempt to get into the coat. The noise, the air of desperation, the lack of a dinner suit, forced me into the street.

I set off for Bletchley. There are – or at least were – three Charity Shops there. It was a crisp Autumn day and even if I was unsuccessful, the cycling was keeping me fit. Railway walk to Linford, then all the way down the canal to Fenny, and the NSPCC Shop on the corner of Denmark Street. This was clean and neat, staffed by pleasant, helpful ladies doing good work. The clothes were well sorted and individually priced, but it was an undistinguished selection – no suit.

Not one to give up a free evening's entertainment lightly, I pressed on to the Oxfam Shop... There I saw it, double-breasted, all wool – it felt thick enough to stop a bullet. And the trousers. They were all that trousers should be, voluminous pockets, so roomy that without braces they would not stay up. With the waist-band at waist level the legs fell into uncontrollable concertina bellows. Snuggly fitted under the arm-pits, the creases were as sharp as Neil Kinnock's wit. They were perfect. I knew then that there must be a God.

On the night I felt like a million dollars, like Bogart in *Casablanca* (only taller). I danced, drank, sweated, danced, drank, sweated and the heat built up. The weight of the material began to tell. I began to fear that the suit's previous owner had died with it on of a horrible, putrifying disease – as after spending money on buying it, I did not have enough left to get the suit cleaned!

Ken Rickard

Developing your own memories

1 Although these pieces both recall specific incidents in the past, they are written in very different styles. Using evidence from these accounts compare what the two authors aim to communicate. Are they concerned solely with facts or is there something more?

2 In pairs or small groups talk about days or events that stand out in your own memories. You will probably remember several incidents from when you were young. Jot down several key images from your most vivid memories.

Laurie Lee also focuses on specific incidents and emotions coupled with vivid description in the opening of his autobiography, *As I walked out one midsummer morning*.

London Road

The stooping figure of my mother, waist-deep in the grass and caught there like a piece of sheep's wool, was the last I saw of my country home as I left it to discover the world. She stood old and bent at the top of the bank, silently watching me go, one gnarled red hand raised in farewell and blessing, not questioning why I went. At the bend of the road I looked back again and saw the gold light die behind her; then I turned the corner, passed the village school, and closed that part of my life for ever.

It was a bright Sunday morning in early June, the right time to be leaving home. My three sisters and a brother had already gone before me; two older brothers had yet to make up their minds. They were still sleeping that morning, but my mother had got up early and cooked me a heavy breakfast, had stood wordlessly while I ate it, her hand on my chair, and had then helped me pack up my few belongings. There had been no fuss, no appeals, no attempts at advice or persuasion, only a long and searching look. Then, with my bags on my back, I'd gone out into the early sunshine and climbed through the long wet grass to the road.

It was 1934. I was nineteen years old, still soft at the edges, but with a confident belief in good fortune.

Laurie Lee

Writing about a memorable day

Concentrating on facts and emotions and aiming to develop descriptive detail, write about a memorable day in your life – it might be a time when you were ill, when you were afraid, when you moved house or changed school, or when you were part of a serious or funny family incident.

The notes you made of key moments from early memories on page 11 may be a good starting point for your account.

Family interview

Set up an interview with a relative on the subject of their early or adolescent memories. Record the interview on tape and later make a transcript of everything that was said (including references to any accent or dialect that might have been used). Using the transcript turn this information into a narrative account of one or several of the events described.

In this extract the writer concentrates on her memories of a specific person.

I know why the caged bird sings

Bailey was the greatest person in my world. And the fact that he was my brother, my only brother, and I had no sisters to share him with, was such good fortune that it made me want to live a Christian life just to show God that I was grateful. Where I was big, elbowy and grating, he was small, graceful and smooth. When I was described by our playmates as being dirt colour, he was praised for his velvet-black skin. His hair fell down in black curls, and my head was covered with black steel wool. And yet he loved me.

When our elders said unkind things about my features (my family was handsome to a point of pain for me), Bailey would wink at me from across the room, and I knew that it was only a matter of time before he would take revenge...

His movements, as he was later to describe those of an acquaintance, were activated with oiled precision. He was also able to find more hours in the day than I thought existed. He finished chores, homework, read more books than I and played the group games on the side of the hill with the best of them. He could even pray out loud in church, and was apt at stealing pickles from the barrel that sat under the fruit counter and Uncle Willie's nose.

Maya Angelou

Analysing characters

A reader gains information about character in a number of ways. Analyse this extract and chart how information is built up:
- through action
- through physical description
- through reflection

Writing about a person you know well

Decide which of the above methods of describing character you will choose to write about a friend or a member of your family. Concentrate on what this person looks like, and the sorts of things this person says and does.

For more on character see Unit 6, pages 50-53.

Assignments

1 Write your own autobiography.
   a) Using any of the ideas and material you have already written about in this unit – such as descriptive diaries, memories of people and places – assemble your work into the opening of your own autobiography. You can also include other written work e.g. from Unit 4 of the Poetry module.
   You will need to think about:
   - the facts and details, the emotions and feelings you will include
   - how to make characters seem real
   b) Write an account of the stages you went through to complete this first part of your autobiography:

   - how did you select your material?
   - how did your ideas develop?
   - how true are your accounts?
2 Write about the problems of growing up. You may be able to develop the notes you took when discussing *Catherine's diary* and could include the letter that you wrote and extracts from your own humorous diary.
3 Select and read an autobiography. Write a review of it commenting on:
   - the events the author writes about
   - the details that make characters seem realistic
   - how direct speech adds to this
   - how successful the story has been in capturing your interest

As well as being a means of communication, letters are also a way of writing about important personal feelings – sometimes these are feelings to share and sometimes they are private.

Novels in letters

Here is a letter from the book *An accidental man*. Letters between the central characters are interspersed with narrative and dialogue in this novel, to reveal interesting contrasts between their private and public lives.

Dearest Gracie,
This is just a routine apology for what happened at the party. I don't flatter myself that my untoward behaviour will have knocked even the smallest apple off your cart. The main hurt is to my own vanity. However, we have known each other all our lives and this momentary rise in temperature prompts me to tell you, what you already know, that in some totally unfrenzied but deep sense of the word I love you and always will and would always help at need, always. That's a lot of alwayses from an unattached young fellow with his life before him, but I know you understand me as you (dear me, here comes that word again) always have. I greatly esteem your fiancé and I am sure you will be very happy; and as for you and me, it was just one of those things. I gather you are still in Ireland where I trust the customary rain is in abeyance.

Your friend
Sebastian

Iris Murdoch

Thinking about the letter

In pairs talk about what you have found out from this letter. Although it is short, there is quite a lot of information you can deduce.

● What have you learned about the writer and Gracie?
● What sort of lives do they have?
● What do you discover about their backgrounds?
● What do you think the rest of the story might be about?

Some of the earliest writers of novels in English chose to tell their stories through a succession of letters. *Pamela*, written in 1740, was one of the first. In this story the heroine is in constant moral danger as the man in whose house she is working tries to seduce her. The following letter is part of her parents' answer to Pamela's first letter to them.

Dear Pamela,

   Your letter was a great trouble, and some comfort, to me and your poor mother. We are troubled for your good lady's death, who took such care of you, and gave you learning, and for three or four years past has always been giving you clothes and linen, and everything that a gentlewoman need not be ashamed to appear in. But our chief trouble is, and a very great one, for fear you should be brought to anything dishonest or wicked, by being so set above yourself. Everybody talks how you have come on, and what a genteel girl you are; and some say you are very pretty... But what avails all this, if you are to be ruined and undone? My dear Pamela, we begin to be in great fear for you; for what signify all the riches in the world, with a bad conscience, and to be dishonest? We are, it is true, very poor, and find it hard enough to live; though once, as you know, it was better with us. But we would sooner live upon the water, and if possible, the clay of the ditches I dig, than live better at the price of our child's ruin.

   I hope the good squire has no design; but when he has given you so much money, and speaks so kindly to you, and praises your coming on; and oh! that fatal word, that he would be kind to you, if you would do as you should do, almost kills us with fears...

   ...We accept kindly of your dutiful present; but, till we are out of pain, cannot make use of it, for fear we should partake of the price of our poor daughter's shame: so have laid it up in a rag among the thatch, over the window, for awhile, lest we should be robbed. With our blessings, and our hearty prayers for you, we remain, your careful, but loving father and mother,

John and Elizabeth Andrews

Samuel Richardson

Discussing the letter

1 In pairs, work out what events you think have taken place before the writing of this letter.
2 Then list the emotions and feelings of the four main characters in relation to these events.
3 Decide between you exactly what you think has happened.

For writing

On your own write the letter you think that Pamela may have written to her parents. There are a lot of clues in their answer relating to some of the things she must have mentioned in this original letter. For example:

● things that would trouble her parents
● things that would comfort them
● the 'good lady's death'
● what the squire has been doing

If you can, try to write in the same style, tone and language as the original letter.

   Alternatively, write a modern version of the letter, bringing the subject matter, style and language up to date.

The following letter comes from the book *So long a letter*. It was written in Senegal and is a cry from the heart of a Muslim woman living in a changing society. After 30 years of marriage and love for her husband, the writer of the letter, Ramatoulaye, feels betrayed when he takes a second wife. He chooses a teenage friend of their young daughter and although this is permitted by Islam, to Ramatoulaye it is a denial of their marriage and she passionately refuses to accept a polygamous life.

Dear Aissatou,
I have received your letter. By way of reply, I am beginning this diary, my prop in my distress. Our long association has taught me that confiding in others allays pain.

Your presence in my life is by no means fortuitous. Our grandmothers in their compounds were separated by a fence and would exchange messages daily. Our mothers used to argue over who would look after our uncles and aunts. As for us, we wore our wrappers and sandals on the same stony road to the koranic school; we buried our milk teeth in the same holes and begged our fairy godmothers to restore them to us, more splendid than before.

If over the years, and passing through the realities of life, dreams die, I still keep intact my memories, the salt of remembrance.

I conjure you up. The past is reborn, along with its processions of emotions. I close my eyes. Ebb and tide of feeling: heat and dazzlement, the woodfires, the sharp green mango, bitten into in turns, a delicacy in our greedy mouths. I close my eyes. Ebb and tide of images: drops of sweat beading your mother's ochre-coloured face as she emerges from the kitchen, the procession of young wet girls chattering on their way back from the springs.

We walked the same paths from adolescence to maturity, where the past begets the present.

My friend, my friend, my friend. I call on you three times.

Yesterday you were divorced. Today I am a widow.

Mariama Bâ

Looking at the letter

1 This piece of writing builds up a number of descriptions that give the reader clues about the life-style and culture of the author. What details can you find about the following:
   ● the people being described
   ● the type of place where they live
   ● the feelings being described
   What conclusions can you draw about the writer of the letter?
2 Collect images from magazines, newspapers, etc. and make a collage to illustrate the main visual details of the passage. Try to include some way of showing the writer's mental state and the tone and atmosphere of the letter.

Ideas in letters

The previous letters have all been fictional but most commonly letters are written to be sent, to convey a message to someone or outline an idea. The poet John Keats was a prolific letter writer, and in many of his letters attempted to explain his theories and beliefs about poetry. In a letter written to Richard Woodhouse on Tuesday 27 October 1818 he is grappling with an idea about his identity:

My dear Woodhouse,
Your Letter gave me a great satisfaction; more on account of its friendliness, than any relish of that matter in it which is accounted so acceptable in the 'genus irritabile'. The best answer I can give you is in a clerklike manner to make some observations on two principal points, which seem to point like indices into the midst of the whole pro and con, about genius, and views and achievements and ambition...

First. As to the poetical Character itself...it is not itself – it has no self – it is everything and nothing – it has no character – it enjoys light and shade; it lives in gusto, be it foul or fair, high or low, rich or poor, mean or elevated... A Poet is the most unpoetical of any thing in existence; because he has no Identity – he is continually in for – and filling some other Body – The Sun, the Moon, the Sea and Men and Women who are creatures of impulse are poetical and have about them an unchangeable attribute – the poet has none; no identity – he is certainly the most unpoetical of all God's creatures... It is a wretched thing to confess; but is a very fact that not one word I ever utter can be taken for granted as an opinion growing out of my identical nature – how can it, when I have no nature?...

In the second place I will speak of my views, and of the life I purpose to myself – I am ambitious of doing the world some good... I will assay to reach to as high a summit in Poetry as the nerve bestowed upon me will suffer... But even now I am perhaps not speaking from myself; but from some character in whose soul I now live. I am sure however that this next sentence is from myself. I feel your anxiety, good opinion and friendliness in the highest degree, and am
    Yours most sincerely

John Keats

Analysing the letter

Work in pairs or small groups on the content of this letter.
- Why has this letter been written?
- What are the ideas about a poet's identity that Keats is suggesting to Woodhouse?
- How does Keats hope to do the world some good?
- What are the main differences between a letter like this and a fictional letter like those earlier in the unit?

Writing your own

Write a letter to a real or imaginary friend where you try and decide 'Who am I? What am I like?' Try not to concentrate on what you look like. Instead explain how you think, what you feel and what makes you who you are. Keats says he is anxious to do the world some good. Continue your letter with your ideas of how you hope to do the world some good.

For more on letter writing see Unit 5 in The Process of Writing module, in Book 4B, page 108.

Letters never sent

The letter below was written by a holiday-maker after a disastrous trip abroad. Some letters, like this one, are never sent but help to give vent to strong emotions.

Dear Sir/Madam

Thank you for sending me as a 'treasured client' a copy of your brochure for villa holidays in the Algarve next year so soon after our return. In the circumstances you may care to know how we fared this year.

First, I would like to congratulate your photographer on the way the illustration in your earlier brochure gave 'our' villa an appearance of exclusivity in what turned out to be a very high-density development and an impression of grandeur to such a handkerchief-sized swimming pool. Do you happen to know if such cameras with rose coloured lenses are generally available?

We were tired and hungry on our arrival. As the shops were all shut, your free bag of groceries was a godsend. An egg and a roll each was just about right for us after being so long without food. We saw nothing anywhere during our stay to match the 50p box of red wine you supplied. It fizzed slightly in the metal sink when we poured it away. I think it would have turned blue litmus paper red.

You will be pleased to know that we were not too tired to appreciate the orthopaedic qualities of the beds. The lack of pillows gave the exciting air of a lottery to our preparations for sleep and the thin blankets ensured that we did not overheat during the long, chilly night.

The next morning was one of the three in our fortnight when the sun shone so we were able to get out early to the shops. Although we made the house secure, closing the windows, bolting the shutters and locking all the doors, we found on our return that we had been burgled – a common experience we subsequently learned. Your representative was most helpful and obviously well versed in all the necessary procedures. The bolts on the shutters and the locks on the windows were very good; it is a pity the wood turned out to be so rotten. Fortunately the company with which you had insured us paid up promptly on our return but we were not as well covered as we had thought. Our own fault for not reading the small print. Still, half the value of the £1000 worth of goods we lost was better than nothing.

The large contractors' lorries passing the villa from early morning to late at night, seven days a week, unerringly found the pothole nearest the window of my parents' bedroom. However, it gave my elderly father something to listen for when he was laid low by gastritis for four days after our visit to the 'ethnic' restaurant. We left the rest of the disinfectant in the bathroom.

We were impressed by the solar heating panels and applaud such attempts to use natural energy. There was always enough lukewarm water for one of the six of us to have a bath each day. For the rest we managed with the small electric kettle and the electric stove – how lucky that we are all seasoned campers. Had we known the oven would catch fire so readily we would never have turned it on. We managed to put the fire out relatively easily but repairing the fuse blown by the fire, while in pitch darkness, was a little more difficult. The matches just lasted out. It was a good job we bought candles the next day to give us light when the 25 watt bulb in the hall exploded. Each time we replaced the fuse it blew again. Inspection by daylight showed a lot of bare wire in the fitment. We made it as safe as we could.

The resort itself will be delightful when it is finished in a year or two and the quaint ideas relating to safety on building sites made our walks through the town a real adventure. From what we could see of the beaches under the debris they looked sandy and it was interesting from an ecological point of view to note that the sewage outfall pipe ran a good 200 metres out to sea. No doubt the roughness of the waves quickly sorts things out.

The day we left was the hottest of the holiday – in fact nearly hot enough to dry out the mud and puddles at the side of the road where we were deposited with all our luggage when the coach taking us to the airport broke down. It took no more than an hour or so to have a mechanic on the spot and only a further hour and a half for another coach to be organised when his efforts failed.

We missed our flight of course and it took a long time to find out exactly what would become of us. On this occasion your representatives showed vanishing powers worthy of Paul Daniels. During the seven hours wait for another plane we quickly exhausted the delights of the airport but we were able to get some food in a smart and extremely expensive restaurant there. We were not told that passengers were being issued with meal vouchers for food at the cafeteria until we had started eating. An aircraft did take us home eventually and one good thing about arriving at Gatwick at three o'clock in the morning is that you go quickly through customs once someone has been found to unload the baggage.

I hope this letter will explain why we shall not be booking another holiday with you next year despite your generous offer of a 10% discount if we book and pay 6 months in advance.

Yours faithfully,

Cecil Morrison

Analysing the letter

The letter you have just read is really a short story in disguise. (For more on short story structure see Unit 6, page 47.) This one happens to be based on fact but it could easily have been fiction. With a partner talk about:
- what the actual facts of the holiday are
- how the humour in the letter has been created
- how it would have been different if it had been written as a story

For writing

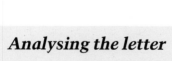

Write your own letter about a visit or holiday. Either base your letter on fact or make your trip a fictitious one.

Assignment

Convert a story or play you have read recently into a series of letters. You will need to decide which characters and themes you will develop in your letter sequence. There will probably be letters between friends and family members, formal letters, postcards, invitations, letters of enquiry, etc. Make these realistic in the way you write them and in your choice of stationery.

Travel writing is often a form of personal journal which records experiences and journeys to ordinary, far-away or even imaginary places where the writer tries to recreate the place visited in the minds of the readers. This usually means close observation of all surrounding detail: of landscape, buildings, people, atmosphere, weather, depending on what the writer is concentrating.

Before reading the extracts which follow, talk in pairs or small groups about the reasons why people travel and explore – often in dangerous and difficult places. Jot down the reasons you come up with and then read on.

A curious life for a lady

'In 1872 a quiet, intelligent-looking dumpy English spinster sailed to Australia in a desperate search for physical and mental health...'

A curious life for a lady by Pat Barr tells the story of Isabella Bird, the daughter of a Victorian country parson, who began her journeys to some of the most inhospitable corners of the world at the age of forty. Isabella wrote letters to her sister Henrietta from all corners of the world, ranging from The Sandwich Isles, The Rocky Mountains, Persia, Kashmir and Tibet, in an effort to make her younger sister see what she had seen, and share in what she was doing.

In one of her early letters home she describes the exhilaration of adventure and danger after what had been a life of sickness, pain, and the feeling of growing old, unused and unfulfilled. She set sail from New Zealand to California in an ancient paddle-steamer: there was a hurricane on the second day that nearly wrecked them, a 'constant threat of permanent engine failure... The cabins were alive with rats, food squirmed with ants and weevils and was served in a dining-room usually awash with spray from the leaking deck above', and Isabella seemed to come alive.

'It is so like living in a new world, so free, so fresh, so vital, so careless, so unfettered, so full of interest that one grudges being asleep; and instead of carrying cares and worries and thoughts of the morrow to bed with one to keep one awake, one falls asleep at once to wake to another day in which one knows that there can be nothing to annoy one – no door-bells...no dirt, no bills, no demands of any kind... Above all, no nervousness, and no conventionalities, no dressing. If my clothes drop into rags they can be pinned together... I am often in tempestuous spirits. It seems a sort of brief resurrection of a girl of twenty-one.'

Holidays in hell

In a similar way but in very different circumstances it is danger and adventure, described in this extract, that stimulate the journalist, P. J. O'Rourke.

He writes, 'What I've really been is a Trouble Tourist – going to see insurrections, stupidities, political crises, civil disturbances and other human folly because...because it's fun... I'm bored by ordinary travel. See the Beautiful Grand Canyon. OK, I see it. OK, it's beautiful. Now what?... The planet I've got a chance to visit is Earth, and Earth's principal features are chaos and war. I think I'd be a fool to spend years here and never have a look.'

In 1984 he visited Lebanon for a holiday. Read this extract to a partner in a cynical tone of voice.

'Everybody with a gun has a check-point in Lebanon. And in Lebanon you'd be crazy not to have a gun. Though, I assure you, all the crazy people have guns, too... The gun barrels all have the bluing worn off the ends as though from being rubbed against people's noses. The interesting thing about staring down a gun barrel is how small the hole is where the bullet comes out, yet what a difference it would make in your social schedule. Not that people shoot you very often, but the way they flip those weapons around and bang them on the pavement and poke them in the dirt and scratch their ears with the muzzle sights... Gun safety merit badges must go begging in the Lebanese Boy Scouts.

On the other hand, Lebanon is notably free of tour groups and Nikon-toting Japanese. The beaches, though shell-pocked and occasionally mined, are not crowded. Ruins of historical interest abound; in fact, block most streets. Hotel rooms are plentiful. No reservation is necessary at even the most popular restaurant (though it is advisable to ask around and find out if the place is likely to be bombed later). And what could be more unvarnished and authentic than a native culture armed to the teeth and bent on murder, pillage and rape?'

Looking at the extracts

The writers of these two extracts have very different reasons for writing and travelling.
1 Talk about what you think these differences are.
2 What is there that connects these experiences?
3 Does a life of adventure appeal to you? Try to explain your reasons why it might or why it might not.
4 Look at the styles in which these pieces are written. How do they differ?

Developing ideas

Develop your own piece of travel writing. Write about quite an ordinary trip – perhaps to the supermarket, or to school or on a bus. Try to invest this journey with some danger or write as if you are a traveller for whom this is a new experience.
For more on travel writing see The Process of Writing module in Book 4B, pages 84-86.

Far off people and places

The following extract from *Into the heart of Borneo* is an account of a serious natural history journey into the interior of a tropical jungle filled with dangers, set-backs and humour.

Into the heart of Borneo

It was time to go to bed. We washed our mess tins in the river, kicked out the fire on the beach, and stoked up the smoking-house fire with more wet logs. Slinging my soaking clothes from a tree with parachute cord, I rubbed myself down with a wet towel and, naked, opened my Bergen to pull out my set of dry kit for the night. Every nook and cranny in the bag was alive with inch-long ants. Deciding that anything so huge must be the Elephant ant, and not the Fire ant, which packs a sting like a wasp, I brushed the first wave off my Y-fronts. Glancing up, I was astonished to see my wet clothes swarming with ants, too; a procession of dark ants poured down one side of the rope and up the other, and, all over my wet trousers, hundreds of different moths were feeding. Darkness seemed to rise from the leafy mush of the forest floor; and I rummaged quickly in the outside Bergen pocket for my army torch. As my fingers closed on it, everyone else's little fingers seemed to close on my arm. I drew it out fast and switched on: Elephant ants, this time with massive pincers, were suspended from hand to elbow.

…Slipping under the mosquito net, I fastened myself into the dark-green camouflage SAS tube. It seemed luxuriously comfortable. You had to sleep straight out like a rifle; but the ants, swarming along the poles, rearing up on their back legs to look for an entry, and the mosquitoes, whining and singing outside the various tunes of their species in black shifting clouds, could not get in.

'Eeeeeee-ai-yack yack yack yack yack!' Something screamed in my ear, with brain-shredding force. And then everyone joined in.
'Eeeeeee-ai-yack yack yack yack yack to yooo!' answered every other giant male cicada, maniacally vibrating the tymbals, drumskin membranes in their cavity amplifiers, the megaphones built into their bodies.

'Shut up!' I shouted.

'Wah Wah Wah Wah Wah!' said four thousand frogs.

'Stop it at once!' yelled James.

'Clatter clitter clatter,' went our mess-tins over the shingle, being nosed clean by tree shrews.

…The river grew louder in the darkness. Something hooted. Something screamed in earnest further off. Something shuffled and snuffled around the discarded rice and fish bits flung in a bush from our plates. A porcupine? A civet? A ground squirrel? The long-tailed giant rat? Why not a Clouded leopard? Or, the only really dangerous mammal in Borneo, the long-clawed, short-tempered Sun bear?

I switched off the torch and tried to sleep. But it was no good. The decibel level was way over the limit allowed in discotheques. And, besides, the fire-flies kept flicking their own torches on and off; and some kind of phosphorescent fungus glowed in the dark like a forty-watt bulb.

Redmond O'Hanlon

In *Behind the Wall*, Colin Thubron tells of his recent journeys through China. One of the first places he visited was Beijing.

Behind the wall

I abandoned the avenues and slipped down side-streets into a maze-world of alleys and courtyards. These hutongs are still the living flesh of Beijing, and once you are inside them it shrinks to a sprawling hamlet. The lanes are a motley of blank walls and doorways, interspersed by miniature factories and restaurants. Each street is a decrepit improvisation on the last. Tiled roofs curve under rotting eaves. The centuries shore each other up. Modern brick walls, already crumbling, enclose ancient porches whose doors of beaten tin or lacerated pinewood swing in carved stone frames. Underfoot the tarmac peels away from the huge, worn paving-slabs of another age, and the traffic thins to a tinkling slipstream of pedicabs and bicycles.

Sometimes, as I stepped under one of the porches, I found its door ajar and peered into a courtyard littered with panniers, potted shrubs, bicycles, bird-cages. Three or four families would be living there. Their windows offered grime-dimmed visions of bare living-rooms and kitchens. Their walls of glass and latticed wood were thin as paper. I imagined a gust of wind clearing the whole *mise-en-scène* away. But in August the wind scarcely found them. Instead, smells of urine and rotted fish hovered in a sultry air.

…The alleys flood into Tiananmen Square as streams vanish into the sea. No urban space I had ever seen struck me with the same sense of aridity. Even the Chinese groups here were whittled to meandering centipedes. Its paving slabs were painted with numbers for the regimentation of official demonstrations, more than five hundred to a row. It could hold half a million. It was less a square than a stone field – a hundred acres of emptiness, distantly fringed by the scarps of public buildings…

…As I lingered near one of the deep entrances, I was approached by a sad-looking man whose eyes peered at me so myopically from behind their spectacles that I thought he must have mistaken me for somebody else. His English came halting and quaint.

'Excuse me, sir.' He delved into his pockets. 'Do you wish a purchase?' Even when standing still he looked dangerously uncoordinated; his legs seemed on the point of buckling. 'I wish to study in America.' He pulled out a trio of coins, joined with grubby string through their perforated centres. 'These are Tang dynasty,' he said. 'Do you buy antiques?'

'They provenate from Luoyang in Henan province.' His face came close to mine, death-white. 'They come from old tombs.'

I stared back at him. He looked all but broken. Beneath their bones his cheeks were cratered into two starved crescents. He was thirty-eight, perhaps, but already old.

I said gently, 'I can't buy them.' I didn't want them (and their export was illegal).

He thrust his face closer to mine. His breath was asphyxiating. 'I must go to America. There's a special course there. I need $250. I need… These coins are genuine.' He juggled them miserably in his fingers. 'The peasants dig them up. The peasants are my friends.'

23

...'But I haven't got any dollars.'

There was growing on his face a beaten, defensive look which reminded me of Western drop-outs. But in China nobody voluntarily dropped out. It was the system which had dropped out from under him. I glanced down at his baggy trousers and frayed sandals. I had a few Chinese coins on me, but felt ashamed to offer them. 'Perhaps you can find an American...'

Colin Thubron

Looking closely at the extract

1 Make a chart using the following ideas and any others that you think might help you examine how these descriptions have been built up. For both pieces jot down what you can find out about:
   - the setting and landscape
   - natural detail
   - buildings and people
   - atmosphere
   - any dialogue used
   - what appeals to the senses are made
   - the character of the narrator
   - the different purpose of each piece

2 Work on these notes and redraft them into a written account and comparison of style in each extract. End your account with an explanation of which piece you prefer in terms of how it has been written, what the subject matter is and what you think the author is trying to share with you.

Closer to home

Journeys of discovery do not have to be to exotic or far-away places. The Ordnance Survey Pathfinder Guides give details of walks the length and breadth of Britain. The extract below gives details of a walk along the North Cornish Coast.

A

There is a fine view back across Widemouth Bay. This would be a taxing walk in a strong westerly. There is a triangulation pillar above Dizzard Point with a spot-height of 538 ft (164m). Soon after this look for a stile where the scrub ends; this leads the path to the cliff edge. The view to the east is even better. The cliff-edge vegetation is now of stunted oaks with a few examples of gorse, which always seems to be able to show a flower even in the bleakest months.

The first great test of stamina is now to be faced. At Chipman Point the path plunges down a precipitous cliff-face (up to now the cliffs, though high, have been gently sloping). Note the contorted strata far below, and the daunting climb up the opposite side of this valley. Fortunately steps have been made up much of it. The stream descends to the shore as a waterfall. At the top the tower of St Gennys church can be seen peeping above the flank of the hill. Another steep descent/ascent soon follows though not as severe as the previous one. Quite close to us on the left is the farmhouse of Cleave and the scant remains of the medieval village of Tresmorn – a few grassy hillocks may be seen.

From Cleave the path goes right out onto the headland before dropping down to the valley. This is National Trust land. It is possible to glimpse Boscastle from here, beyond Cambeak which guards the entrance to Crackington Haven. The steep climb up the southern side of this valley is unassisted by steps; it must be very tricky to descend in wet weather. At the top pause to regain breath and admire the view of Cambeak and Crackington Haven. If you need refreshment it is easy to walk down to the village from here.

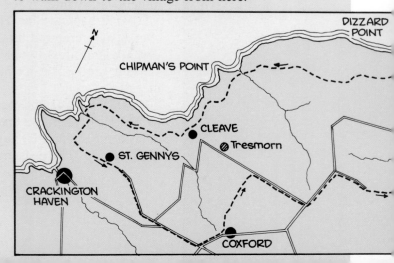

The following extract from *500 mile walkies* describes one walker's quite different impressions of the same stretch of coastal footpath.

B Still my pasty denied entry. Eventually I broke it over my knee and found inside a steaming mass of yellow and white stuff vaguely reminiscent of school dinners, I took a bite and the thing hit me back. Home-made Pasties On Sale Here was obviously a cleverly worded lie that should have read: Mass-produced Pasties, That Bear No Resemblance Whatsoever To The Real Thing, On Sale Here. Still, they could only get better. I had a feeling I'd be eating a lot of these during my time in Cornwall.

We continued past the beach huts and caravans that straggled along Widemouth Bay, but soon the wild cliffs resumed; wild and steep; wild and very steep; wild, very steep and after a day of them, tedious. I wanted to reach Crackington Haven that night as I knew there was a pub there – probably a fishermen's haunt, an old smugglers' dive, with nutty beer and full of garrulous Cornish characters with tales of the sea. Every hilltop I reached I imagined I was going to see the village nestling in the valley below. But the path just plunged in familiar fashion down to another combe and then climbed up another identical hill and I walked on, realising that I was beginning to hate those bloody little pink flowers.

The North Cornish coast is positive proof that the sun sets in the west. As we climbed the last hill before Crackington Haven, it was already well on its way to the horizon, a shimmering red and yellow vessel sinking into the sea, dragging its golden sail under with it. The sky turned red, making all the local shepherds really happy, and Boogie and I caught our first sight of the Coombe Barton Hotel.

In contrast to the seafarers' tavern I'd envisaged, the pub had big windows, pool tables, fizzy beer and eight flavours of crisps. I stumbled in with a dirty face, dirty trousers, dirty boots and a dirty dog and ordered a pint of the first liquid I saw. The barman very kindly filled up Boogie's bowl and we drank deeply, with all eyes on us.

Mark Wallington

Comparing the descriptions

Work in groups of four and divide into two pairs. One pair will study extract **A** and the other will study extract **B**. Read the passages carefully and jot down your answers to the following questions. Compare your answers with those of the other pair.

1 What actual places are mentioned?
2 What opinions, if any, does the author have about each place you have listed?
3 What does the author feel about the walk as a whole? List all the evidence that you can find.
4 Why do you think this was written and what sort of person has it been written for?

Now the whole group should reread both passages. Why are these descriptions so different?

Assignment

Using and adapting the ideas you have been working with in this unit, describe in two contrasting styles a walk or journey you know well. Your first description should concentrate on facts and directions for others to follow in the style of the Pathfinder Guide. Your second description should be your own version of the journey, concentrating on events, feelings and more personal details unlikely to appear in a guide.

Finish your description with a reflection on what you have tried to do in your writing and to what extent you think you have been successful.

For more on writing for direction and instruction see The Process of Writing in Book 4B, pages 87-91.

Fantasy travel

Imaginary journeys can seem just as real and vivid as actual ones. The fantasy epic, *Lord of the rings,* describes an amazing journey fraught with danger and full of adventure.

Lord of the rings

Their way wound along the floor of the hollow, and round the green feet of a steep hill into another deeper and broader valley, and then over the shoulder of further hills, and down their long limbs, and up their smooth sides again, up onto new hill-tops and down into new valleys. There was no tree nor any visible water: it was a country of grass and short springy turf, silent except for the whisper of the air over the edges of the land, and high lonely cries of strange birds. As they journeyed the sun mounted, and grew hot. Each time they climbed a ridge the breeze seemed to have grown less. When they caught a glimpse of the country westward the distant Forest seemed to be smoking, as if the fallen rain was steaming up again from leaf and root and mould. A shadow now lay round the edge of sight, a dark haze above which the upper sky was like a blue cap, hot and heavy.

About midday they came to a hill whose top was wide and flattened, like a shallow saucer with a green mounded rim. Inside there was no air stirring, and the sky seemed near their heads. They rode across and looked northwards. Then their hearts rose, for it seemed plain that they had come further already than they had expected. Certainly the distances had now all become hazy and deceptive, but there could be no doubt that the Downs were coming to an end. A long valley lay below them winding away northwards, until it came to an opening between two steep shoulders. Beyond, there seemed to be no more hills. Due north they faintly glimpsed a long dark line...

J. R. R. Tolkien

Looking for details

1 After reading the passage from *Lord of the rings* pick out as many details as you can that are natural and seem real.
2 Now pick out any details that suggest a fantasy world is being described.
3 Why do you think the landscape has been described in such naturalistic and realistic terms? What is gained by this? The following extract describes another adventure journey which takes place in a more obvious fantasy landscape.

The never ending story

Desire, hunger and thirst pursued Atreyu. It was two days since he had left the Swamps of Sadness, and since then he had been wandering through an empty rocky wilderness. What little provisions he had taken with him had sunk beneath the black waters with Artax. In vain, Atreyu dug his fingers into the clefts between stones in the hope of finding some little root, but nothing grew there, not even moss or lichen.

At first he was glad to feel solid ground beneath his feet, but little by little it came to him that he was worse off than ever. He was lost. He didn't even know what direction he was going in, for the dusky greyness was the same all around him. A cold wind blew over the needlelike rocks that rose up on all sides, blew and blew.

Uphill and downhill he plodded, but all he saw was distant mountains with still more distant ranges behind them, and so on to the horizon on all sides. And nothing living, not a beetle, not an ant, not even the vultures which ordinarily follow the weary traveller until he falls by the wayside.

Doubt was no longer possible. This was the Land of the Dead Mountains. Few had seen them, and fewer still escaped from them alive. But they figured in the legends of Atreyu's people. He remembered an old song:

> Better the huntsman
> Should perish in the swamps,
> For in the Dead Mountains
> There is a deep, deep chasm,
> Where dwelleth Ygramul the Many,
> The horror of horrors.

Even if Atreyu had wanted to turn back and had known what direction to take, it would not have been possible. He had gone too far and could only keep on going.

Michael Ende

Thinking about style

1 Which details in this extract suggest a fantasy world?
2 Can you find any naturalistic or realistic descriptions here?
3 What is the effect of this?
4 How does it compare with what you found in the Tolkien passage?

Who tells the story?

The other extracts in this unit have been written in the first person but these last two have been written in the third person.

- In pairs, talk about what difference this makes to the pieces of writing.
- What would the effect be if they had been written in the first person?

Assignment

Write your own adventure journey, based either on fact or fiction, describing a place you know well or can imagine clearly.

1 Try to look at this place in a new and different way and aim to describe it using images that will enable another person to visualise it as vivdly as you can.
2 Include a short introduction to this explaining your choice of topic. Bear in mind these points about travel writers that have come out of this unit:
   - they all set out to visit or explore something
   - they observe their surroundings closely
   - they write down what they see
   - they write about who or what they meet
   - they share their observations in an individual style
3 Decide whether you will use the first person or the third person in your writing.
4 Conclude your writing with reflections on what you discovered and what you think you achieved.

Myths, legends, and folk-tales

Stories have existed for as long as man has been able to speak. Long before people could write they told each other stories and sometimes drew pictures that told stories as well. Parents told stories to their children who in turn told them to their own children.

Read the myths and legends which follow. They come from different ages, different cultures and different traditions.

Early stories

This first story tells of Pandora's box – and originated in Ancient Greece. There are several different stories of Pandora and her box, but all of them tell how her curiosity brought troubles to mankind. The second story on page 29 is from Bangladesh.

Pandora's box

Zeus, the Lord of the Gods of Olympus, sent Pandora down to earth with Hermes after she had received a gift from each of the gods. But before Hermes took her to earth, she was given one last gift – a beautiful box, fastened by a golden viper. Hermes warned her never to open this box, because it would only lead to disaster. First of all she was taken to the home of Prometheus, to be his bride, but he was suspicious of Zeus and refused to accept her. However, his brother fell in love with her and they were married. Some say that it was her new husband who persuaded Pandora to open the box while others say that she could not resist her own curiosity when the snake uncoiled. Whatever the reason, she lifted the lid and out flew all the evils that were to plague the world. Pandora cried and wept but as she cried a white bird flew out from the bottom of the box – it was Hope, to help mankind stand up to all his misfortunes.

Working with the story

The story you have just read about Pandora is little more than a basic outline. Write it out in much more detail in a way that would be suitable for a child aged 10 to read. You will need to think about:

- how to describe the background settings of the story – both Earth and Mount Olympus
- how to describe the characters so that they seem more realistic
- what the characters will say to each other and how they will say it
- what illustrations to include

As an alternative you could rework this story as a play and develop a script that would be suitable for young children to read and enjoy.

The boatman and the scholar

A learned scholar was being rowed across the River Ganges. The boat was small and the river was wide. The boatman rowed very slowly. For a time the two men were silent, but the learned man could not remain silent for very long. At last he said to the boatman,

'Have you read any history?'

'No, master,' said the boatman. He continued to row slowly along.

'That is a great pity,' said the scholar. 'Don't you know of the interesting things we can read about in the history books? There are stories of the ancient kings and famous battles. History books tell us about the people of long ago. We learn how they lived, what they ate and how they dressed. Why haven't you read any history?'

'Master, I have never learnt to read,' said the boatman. 'I do not know any history.'

After a little time, the scholar spoke again.

'Have you studied geography?' he asked.

'No, master,' the boatman replied.

'Geography tells us that the world is round; it tells us where the continents, mountains and rivers are. We learn from geography how people live in far-off lands, and where metals, spices and precious stones are found,' said the scholar.

'I do not know about these things,' said the boatman.

'So you know nothing about history or geography,' said the scholar. 'Your life is hardly worth living... You know nothing. Your life is useless; in fact you might as well be dead!'

Black clouds were now gathering in the sky. A storm was coming, and the little boat was only halfway across the great river. They would not get to the bank before the storm started.

'Look at those black clouds!' said the boatman to the scholar. 'A storm is coming. Can you swim?'

Trembling with fear, the scholar said, 'Oh dear! I cannot swim!'

'Oh!' said the boatman. 'You say my life is useless because I know no history, geography or science. But you did not learn to swim, so now your life will be useless!'

The storm started. The little boat sank. The boatman swam safely to the bank, but the scholar was drowned in the great River Ganges.

Thinking about childhood stories

One of the most common kinds of story gives warnings particularly to children, telling them how to behave sensibly. This sort of story can be found all over the world. They are usually full of monsters, witches, and highly improbable events.

1 Look again at the myths you have just read and write one sentence to sum up the message of each tale.
2 Working in pairs or small groups, choose at least two folk-tales or myths you remember from childhood and in chart form plot:
   ● who the major characters are and what they are like
   ● what happens to them
   ● what sort of settings these events take place in
   Finally decide what the 'message' of the story is.

Writing your own myth or folk-tale

Using your own characters, story and setting, try to create your own myth or folk-tale. Your notes on key characters and events in folk-tales should help you to structure your story.

Remember to decide on the age of your audience or reader as this will have an effect on the sort of story, language and characters that you choose to write about.

Legends of King Arthur

Writers throughout history have used and adapted well-known stories for many different reasons – to sing them as ballads, recite them as narrative poetry, to retell them to different audiences.

The stories of King Arthur are among the best known British legends. Early in the Twelfth century Geoffrey de Monmouth wrote a romantic but not very accurate history of the Britons. He developed the story of King Arthur, a story based on the last British hero to make a stand against the invading Saxons of the Fifth century. Arthur was not a king by royal descent but a warlord.

Minstrels later added the Breton stories of Merlin and the legends of Lancelot, Tristram and Gawayne, and the savagery of the earlier versions became romanticised into tales of knightly grace and chivalry.

The legend was told, retold, embroidered and embellished down the ages until, early in the Fifteenth century, Sir Thomas Malory collected all legends of King Arthur and put them together in one volume: *Le mort d'Arthur*. After his last great battle, Arthur, grievously wounded, is left alone with Sir Bedivere, one of his knights.

Le mort d'Arthur

My time hieth fast, said the king. Therefore, take thou Excalibur, my good sword, and go with it to yonder water side, and when thou comest ther, I charge thee throw my sword in that water, and come again, and tell me what thou there seest.

My lord, said Bedivere, your commandment shall be done, and lightly bring you word again. So Sir Bedivere departed, and by the way he beheld that noble sword, that the pommel and haft was all of precious stones; and then he said to himself, If I throw this rich sword in the water, thereof shall never come good, but harm and loss. And then Sir Bedivere hid Excalibur under a tree. And as soon as he might he came again unto the king, and said he had been at the water, and had thrown the sword in the water. What sawest thou there? said the king. Sir, he said, I saw nothing but waves and winds. That is untruly said of thee, said the king; therefore go thou lightly again, and do my commandment; as thou art to me lief and dear, spare not, but throw it in...

Missing section for you to work on

30

Now put me in the barge, said the king; and so he did softly; and there received him three queens with great mourning... And so they then rowed from the land, and Sir Bedivere beheld all those ladies go from him. Then Sir Bedivere cried: Ah, my lord Arthur, what shall become of me now ye go from me, and leave me here alone among mine enemies?

Comfort thyself, said the king, and do as well as thou mayest, for in me is no trust for to trust in. For I will into the vale of Avalon, to heal me of my grievous wound: and if thou hear never more of me, pray for my soul...

Sir Thomas Malory

Working with the story

One important section of this story has been left out. Talk with a partner about what happens in the parts of the story that you do have and between you decide what facts you think have been left out. Try to write the missing paragraphs, keeping as close as you can to the original style. You will need to discuss:
● in what ways the language is archaic. Look at phrases used by each character to address one another for example.
● in what ways the sentence structure is different from modern English

What effect do these features have on the piece as a whole?

The birth of Jesus

The following verses, based on historical fact, come from the Authorised King James Version of the Bible.

Now the birth of Jesus Christ was on this wise: When as his mother Mary was espoused to Joseph, before they came together, she was found with child of the Holy Ghost. Then Joseph her husband being a just man, and not willing to make her a publick example, was minded to put her away privily. But while he thought on these things, behold, the angel of the Lord appeared unto him in a dream, saying, Joseph, thou son of David, fear not to take unto thee Mary thy wife: for that which is conceived in her is of the Holy Ghost.

And it came to pass in those days, that there went out a decree from Caesar Augustus, that all the world should be taxed... And all went to be taxed, every one into his own city. And Joseph also went up from Galilee, out of the city of Nazareth, into Judea, unto the city of David, which is called Bethlehem: (because he was of the house and lineage of David:) To be taxed with Mary his espoused wife, being great with child.

And so it was, that, while they were there, the days were accomplished that she should be delivered. And she brought forth her first born son, and wrapped him in swaddling clothes, and laid him in a manger; because there was no room for them in the inn.

And there were in the same country shepherds abiding in the field, keeping watch over their flock by night. And, lo, the angel of the Lord came upon them, and the glory of the Lord shone round about them: and they were sore afraid. And the angel said unto them, Fear not: for, behold, I bring you good tidings of great joy, which shall be to all people. For unto you is born this day in the city of David a Saviour, which is Christ the Lord. And this shall be a sign unto you; Ye shall find the babe wrapped in swaddling clothes, lying in a manger. And suddenly there was with the angel a multitude of the heavenly host praising God, and saying, Glory to God in the highest, and on earth peace, goodwill toward men. And it came to pass, as the

31

angels were gone away from them into heaven, the shepherds said one to another, Let us now go even unto Bethlehem, and see this thing which is come to pass, which the Lord hath made known unto us. And they came with haste, and found Mary, and Joseph and the babe lying in a manger.

Now when Jesus was born in Bethlehem of Judea in the days of Herod the king, behold, there came wise men from the east to Jerusalem, saying, Where is he that is born King of the Jews? for we have seen his star in the east, and are come to worship him. When Herod the king had heard these things, he was troubled, and all Jerusalem with him... And he sent them to Bethlehem, and said, Go and search diligently for the young child; and when ye have found him, bring me word again, that I may come and worship him also.

When they had heard the king, they departed; and, lo, the star, which they saw in the east, went before them, till it came and stood over where the young child was... And when they were come into the house, they saw the young child with Mary his mother, and fell down, and worshipped him: and when they had opened their treasures, they presented unto him gifts; gold, and frankincense, and myrrh.

And being warned of God in a dream that they should not return to Herod, they departed into their own country another way. And when they were departed, behold, the angel of the Lord appeareth to Joseph in a dream, saying, Arise, and take the young child and his mother, and flee into Egypt, and be thou there until I bring thee word: for Herod will seek the young child to destroy him. When he arose, he took the young child and his mother by night, and departed into Egypt. And was there until the death of Herod.

Read this next extract to yourself. It is from a narrative poem by Charles Causley about the same event. Now try reading the poem out loud in groups of 5, choosing people for the different parts.

Ballad of the bread man

Mary stood in the kitchen
  Baking a loaf of bread.
An angel flew in through the window.
  'We've a job for you,' he said.

'God in his big gold heaven,
  Sitting in his big blue chair,
Wanted a mother for his little son.
  Suddenly saw you there.'

Mary shook and trembled,
  'It isn't true what you say.'
'Don't say that,' said the angel.
  'the baby's on its way.'

Joseph was in his workshop
  Planing a piece of wood.
'The old man's past it,' the neighbours said.
  'That girl's been up to no good.'

'And who was that elegant fellow,'
  They said, 'in the shiny gear?'
The things they said about Gabriel
  Were hardly fit to hear.

Mary never answered,
  Mary never replied.
She kept the information,
  Like the baby, safe inside.

It was election winter.
  They went to vote in town.
When Mary found her time had come
  The hotels let her down.

The baby was born in an annexe
  Next to the local pub.
At midnight, a delegation
  Turned up from the Farmer's Club.

Looking at the Bible story

Discuss in pairs or small groups whether you think there is any point in Charles Causley changing the Bible story like this.

- Has the story-line changed in any way?
- How and why have the characters been altered?
- Why do you think Charles Causley has chosen the ballad form?
- What is the effect of changing the Bible story like this?

Changing stories

1 Use a different traditional story that you know well – perhaps a folk-tale or another Bible story – and try to tell it in a different way. You could rewrite it either as a ballad or as a film script or screenplay.

2 When you have completed this write a commentary to help you reflect on what you have done and how your story has changed:

- What are the differences between the piece of work you started off with and your own finished poem or script?
- Which parts of the story have you had to leave out and why?
- What extra information have you decided to include and why?
- Can you draw any conclusions about how the language of poetry works when compared with the prose that you would use in telling a story or writing a script?

For more on ballad form see the Poetry module, page 78. Guidance on the layout for screenplay is given in the Media Scripts module, pages 138-141.

They talked about an explosion
  That made a hole in the sky,
Said they'd been sent to the Lamb & Flag
  To see God come down from on high.

A few days later a bishop
  And a five-star general were seen
With the head of an African country
  In a bullet-proof limousine.

'We've come,' they said, 'with tokens
  For the little boy to choose.'
Told the tale about war and peace
  In the television news.

After them came the soldiers
  With rifle and bomb and gun,
Looking for enemies of the state.
  The family had packed and gone.

Charles Causley

Modern folk-tales or urban legends

These are the sorts of story that we have all heard plenty of by word of mouth. They are usually horrifying in some way, and extremely difficult to prove true. What all stories like this have in common is that they are supposed to have happened to a friend of a friend.

In his book, *The vanishing hitchhiker*, Professor Jan Harold Brunvand has gathered many of these stories together and in its introduction he writes:

'Urban legends...are realistic stories concerning recent events (or alleged events) with an ironic or supernatural twist... The story-tellers assume that the true facts of each case lie just one or two informants back down the line with a reliable witness, or in a news media report. The mass media themselves participate in the dissemination and apparent validation of urban legends, just as they sometimes do with rumour and gossip, adding to their plausibility. But...urban legends are folklore, not history.'

You have probably all heard of versions similar to the following stories. No doubt you know plenty more.

The couple in the car

This happened just a few years ago on the road that turns off 59 highway by the Holiday Inn. This couple were parked under a tree out on this road. Well, it got to be time for the girl to be back in the dorm, so she told her boy-friend that they should start back. But the car wouldn't start, so he told her to lock herself in the car and he would go down to the Holiday Inn and call for help. Well, he didn't come back and he didn't come back, and pretty soon she started to hear a scratching noise on the roof of the car. 'Scratch, scratch...scratch, scratch.' She got scareder and scareder, but he didn't come back. Finally when it was almost daylight, some people came along and helped her out of the car, and she looked up and there was her boy-friend hanging from the tree, and his feet were scraping against the roof of the car. This is why the road is called 'Hangman's Road'.

Dangers of the microwave oven

I once heard of an elderly lady who used to breed pedigree cats and exhibit them at shows. She specialised in Persian cats and their long hair always made it a difficult task to clean and groom them for showing. In order to cut down the effort involved the old lady had evolved the practice of first washing the cat, towelling it dry and then, finally, giving it a very brief warming in her electric oven.

One Christmas her cooker developed a fault and so her son, by way of a Christmas present, bought her a brand new microwave oven. On the day of the next cat show, not understanding the basic difference in the technology between an ordinary electric cooker and a microwave oven, the old lady industriously washed her prize-winning Persian cat and popped it into the oven for a few seconds. There really was no miaow, nor any noise at all from the cat, for the poor creature exploded the instant the oven was switched on.

The least successful animal rescue

The firemen's strike of 1978 made possible one of the great animal rescues attempts of all time. Valiantly, the British Army had taken over emergency fire-fighting and on 14 January they were called out by an elderly lady in South London to retrieve her cat which had become trapped up a tree. They arrived with impressive haste and soon discharged their duty. So grateful was the lady that she invited them all in for tea. Driving off later, with fond farewells completed, they ran over the cat and killed it.

Working on urban legends

Discuss possible reasons why we share and pass on stories like these. What role do they play in our culture?

In pairs or small groups, share all the stories like this that you know. Gather these together and begin a class collection.

Note down any details that you think the stories have in common and try to work out some of their main features using the chart below to help you record them.

Choose one of the stories that particularly appeals to you and rework it as a narrative ballad.

For more on writing ballads see the Poetry module, page 81.

Sequence of events	No. of people	Setting	Fears	Coincidences	Factual details	Moral

Stories all around us

Stories help to make sense of the world around us. We are surrounded by stories in the newspapers, on radio, TV and film; stories about famous people, national scandals, about personal tragedies, or political struggles. We tell each other such stories every day:

- in conversations with our families and friends
- in our places of work or at school
- in many of our leisure activities
- to express ourselves
- to amuse ourselves
- to control our fears

Stories like these are not necessarily fictional but can be about things that have happened to us or to other people.

Telling our own stories

1 What do you tell stories about? Choose a story to share with others in your group of 5 or 6. It might be about:
  - you
  - someone or something you've heard about
  - someone you know
  - something you've read
  - something you've made up

2 Tell your story to the person you are sitting next to. Ask them to suggest ways your story should change. When you are happy with changes retell the story to the whole group.

3 Try writing your story in at least two of the following forms:
  - a newspaper report (either exaggerated or serious)
  - a news item for TV
  - a music video
  - an advert
  - a playscript

  If possible use a word processor, camera, video camera or cassette recorder to help you. Finish your work with a written reflection about the different effects each type of presentation has had on your story.

'This girl my friend knows...'

The curious case of the shrinking pygmies

My search for my G.I. dad

'It sounds awful, I'm only glad it didn't happen to me!'

Wave of relief sweeps the West

British way of life 'is in peril'

Felicity silent on 'love rift' rumour

'You'll never guess what happened to...'

Picture stories

Stories do not always need words. When children are very young some of the first stories they are introduced to are in the form of pictures and only gradually are words introduced. Visual clues are all-important in telling the reader what is going on. Even so, many of the features of picture stories, like the ones on pages 37-39, will be the same as those found in stories which rely more on words.

The lost teddy

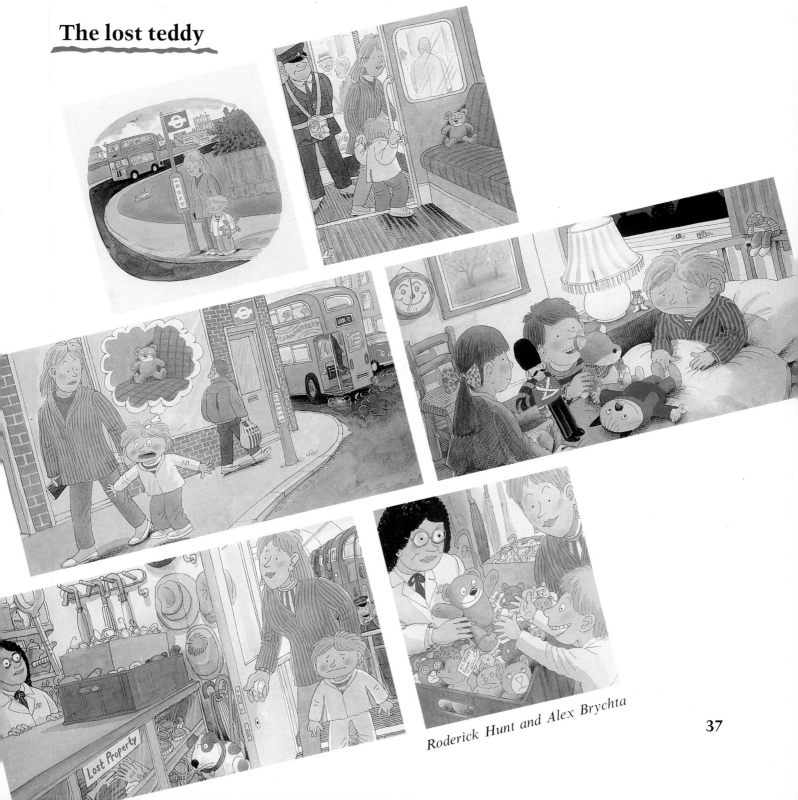

Roderick Hunt and Alex Brychta

37

A porcupine named Fluffy

When Mr. and Mrs. Porcupine had their first child, they were delighted. Now he needed a name.

Should they call him Spike?
No. Spike was too common.

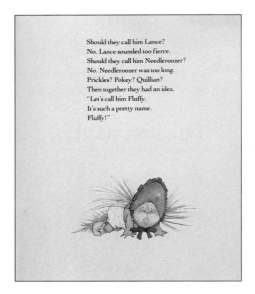

Should they call him Lance?
No. Lance sounded too fierce.
Should they call him Needleroozer?
No. Needleroozer was too long.
Prickles? Pokey? Quillian?
Then together they had an idea.
"Let's call him Fluffy.
It's such a pretty name.
Fluffy!"

But soon there came a time when Fluffy began to doubt that he was fluffy.

He first became suspicious when he backed into a door and stuck fast.
That was not a fluffy thing to do.

One afternoon Fluffy set out for a walk, trying to think of ways to become fluffy.

Before long he met a very large rhinoceros.

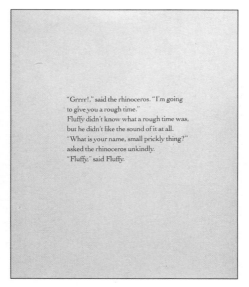

"Grrrr!," said the rhinoceros. "I'm going to give you a rough time."
Fluffy didn't know what a rough time was, but he didn't like the sound of it at all.
"What is your name, small prickly thing?" asked the rhinoceros unkindly.
"Fluffy," said Fluffy.

"A porcupine named Fluffy!" howled the rhinoceros.

Discussing the children's stories

In pairs or small groups, discuss the impact of stories told largely through pictures.

1   What appeal do these stories have for young children?
2   Work out the basic plots of the two stories
3   What is the message being communicated in each?
4   What have you learned about the main characters in the stories?
5   What is the effect of *The lost teddy* being told entirely in pictures?
6   Has the addition of simple sentences in *A porcupine named Fluffy* added to or detracted from the impact of the story?

Helen Lester

Fluffy was embarrassed, but he tried to be polite. "And what is *your* name?" he inquired.

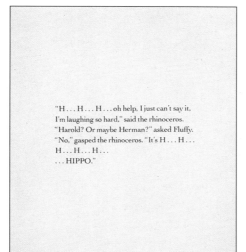

"H...H...H...oh help, I just can't say it, I'm laughing so hard," said the rhinoceros. "Harold? Or maybe Herman?" asked Fluffy. "No," gasped the rhinoceros. "It's H...H... H...H... ...HIPPO."

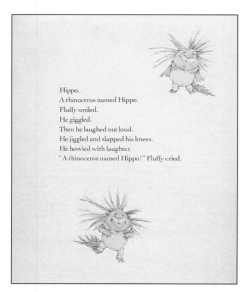

Hippo.
A rhinoceros named Hippo.
Fluffy smiled.
He giggled.
Then he laughed out loud.
He jiggled and slapped his knees.
He howled with laughter.
"A rhinoceros named Hippo!" Fluffy cried.

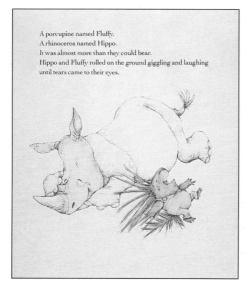

A porcupine named Fluffy.
A rhinoceros named Hippo.
It was almost more than they could bear.
Hippo and Fluffy rolled on the ground giggling and laughing until tears came to their eyes.

At last they lay exhausted on the ground.
From that time on they were the best of friends.

But stories told largely through pictures are not just for young children. Stories for teenagers and adults are told in this way in cartoons, photo stories and adverts. The following cartoons are representations of part of two classic texts, T. S. Eliot's *The wasteland* and Shakespeare's *Romeo and Juliet*. In this cartoon *The wasteland* is cast in the genre of detective fiction and features Philip Marlowe.

For more on photo-stories see the Media Scripts module, page 164, where a scene from *Romeo and Juliet* becomes a photo story. For more on genre see Unit 6, page 44.

The wasteland

Martin Rowson

Romeo and Juliet

William Shakespeare

Analysing adult picture stories

In pairs or small groups discuss the ways in which these stories are presented:

1 How have the artists made the stories visually interesting?
2 Why have different kinds of speech bubbles and print been used in *The wasteland*?
3 In what ways do the illustrations in *The wasteland* set the scene and the atmosphere?
4 What is the effect of converting Shakespeare into cartoon form?
5 Do the pictures make the story or the language easier to understand?

Developing your own picture story

1 Choose a story you know well or select a poem or a chapter from the book you are reading at the moment and try to recreate the story in picture form.
2 Before you begin you will need to decide on the age group you will be writing for.
3 Make sure you choose a story with an interesting but simple plot and with characters that will encourage a reader to find out more.
4 Your space will be limited so you will need to choose words and dialogue with care. You will find it easier if you write down the words of the story before making the picture.

   If you would prefer not to draw 'finished' cartoons, you could present your story as a story-board.
5 Finish your picture story with a written reflection on:
   ● what you set out to do
   ● why you chose the pictures you did
   ● whether you stressed different parts of the story from the original
   ● what you tried to communicate with the words you selected
   ● how successful you think your final piece of work was
   ● what are the advantages and disadvantages of stories told in this way

Family stories

Every family has its own wealth of picture stories usually in the form of photo albums. Look at the pictures and documents below and talk about what you think they are. Try to put them into a sequence that tells the story of Fred and Louisa.

A

B

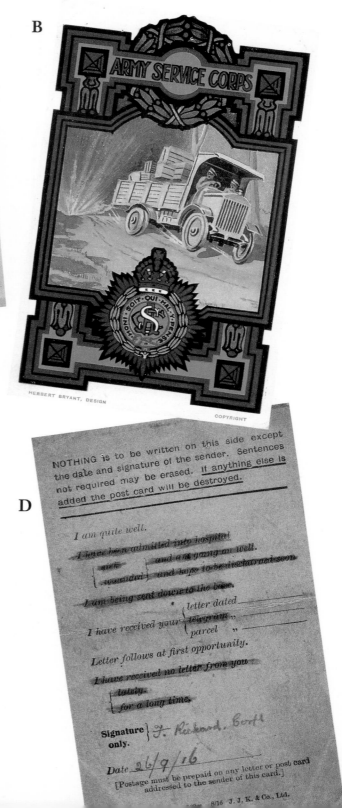

C

D

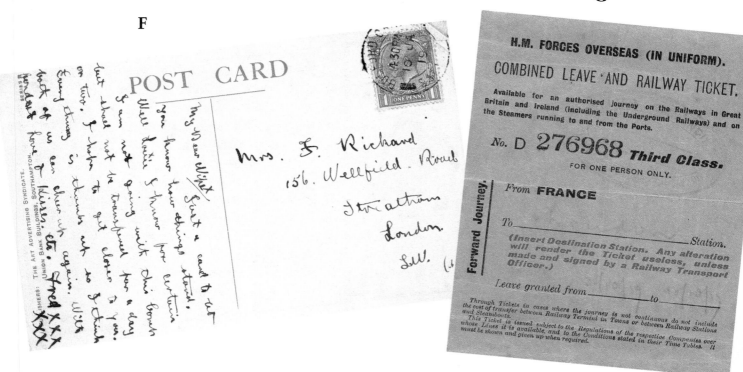

E — Certificate of Marriage

F — Post Card

G — H.M. Forces Overseas (In Uniform) Combined Leave and Railway Ticket

Imagining the story

Once you have ordered the pictures and documents see if you can construct and write a story around them. Fill in any gaps with documents of your own. For example, you could add:

- letters written between the couple
- a scripted scene from the trenches
- a newspaper report about the wedding

Using your own material

Collect your own personal pictures and documents from a specific time in the past – they could be from your own childhood or from that of your parents or grandparents. Include any other images of the time, such as posters, advertisements, local newspaper features, and weave all of these into your own story.

43

Novels and short stories

Genre and style

In short stories and novels elements of plot, character, setting and theme are closely linked with how ideas are organised, and how an individual style is developed.

Authors choose their words and phrases deliberately in order to create a particular effect, emphasis or mood and to portray the subject matter to the reader in a chosen way. There are many different types or genres of fiction which are written in widely varying styles. Here are just a few:

Crime	Romance	Horror
Westerns	Science Fiction	War
Adventure	Fantasy	Thrillers

Brainstorm

In a group of 3 or 4 think of some more fiction genres to add to this list.

Looking at and designing covers

1 Look at these covers that have been included without their accompanying blurbs.
   a) Decide what types of fiction each cover has been designed for and write the appropriate blurbs.
   b) Outline in each blurb what you think the story will be about, using clues in the cover illustrations to help you.
2 In a small group choose an existing book jacket.
   a) Discuss how the cover should be up-dated for a new readership, e.g. for today's reader or a more adult audience.
   b) Redesign the picture and rewrite the blurb.
   c) Include a report/analysis of what you set out to change and why.

A

B

C

D

Openings

The opening of a novel or short story is also important as a way of catching the imagination and tempting the reader into the book. It sets up certain questions in the reader's mind and introduces themes which may be developed later in the plot. Look at the following openings from different genres of fiction.

1

The call had come at 6.12 precisely. It was second nature to him now to note the time by the illuminated dial of his electric bed-side clock before he had switched on his lamp, a second after he had felt for and silenced the raucous insistence of the telephone. It seldom had to ring more than once, but every time he dreaded that the peal might have woken Nell. The caller was familiar, the summons expected. It was Detective-Inspector Doyle. The voice, with its softly intimidating suggestion of Irish burr, came to him strong and confident, as if Doyle's great bulk loomed over the bed.

2

Somewhere above, hidden by the eternal clouds of Wesker's World, a thunder rumbled and grew. Trader John Garth stopped when he heard it, his boots sinking slowly into the muck, and cupped his good ear to catch the sound. It swelled and waned in the thick atmosphere, growing louder.

'That noise is the same as the noise of your sky-ship,' Itin said, with stolid Wesker logicality, slowly pulverising the idea in his mind and turning over the bits one by one for closer examination. 'But your ship is still sitting where you landed it. It must be, even though we cannot see it, because you are the only one who can operate it. And even if anyone else could operate it we would have heard it rising into the sky. Since we did not and if this sound is a sky-ship sound, then it must mean...'

3

When the east wind blows up Helford river the shining waters become troubled and disturbed, and little waves beat angrily upon the sandy shores. The short seas break above the bar at ebb-tide, and the waders fly inland to the mud flats, their wings skimming the surface, and calling to one another as they go. Only the gulls remain, wheeling and crying above the foam, diving now and again in search of food, their grey feathers glistening with the salt spray.

4

Wars came early to Shanghai, overtaking each other like the tides that raced up the Yangtze and returned to this gaudy city all the coffins cast adrift from the funeral piers of the Chinese Bund.

Jim had begun to dream of wars. At night the same silent films seemed to flicker against the wall of his bedroom in Amherst Avenue, and transformed his sleeping mind into a deserted newsreel theatre. During the winter of 1941 everyone in Shanghai was showing war films. Fragments of his dreams followed Jim around the city; in the foyers of department stores and hotels the images of Dunkirk and Tobruk, Barbarossa and the Rape of Nanking sprang loose from his crowded head.

5

Hale knew, before he had been in Brighton three hours, that they meant to murder him. With his inky fingers and his bitten nails, his manner cynical and nervous, anybody could tell he didn't belong – belong to the early summer sun, the cool Whitsun wind off the sea, the holiday crowd.

Looking at the openings

In small groups talk about each of the extracts on page 45:

1 What kinds of stories would you expect to follow?
2 Use evidence from each opening to try and explain why. You will need to think about:
   - what is being written about (the subject)
   - specific words the author has chosen (the diction)
   - the way the writer calls up pictures in the reader's mind (imagery)
   - what the writer's attitude to the story is (the tone)
   - what effect different sentence lengths and structures have
   - the effect of the order in which ideas are introduced

3 Write a paragraph about the style of each opening, highlighting their similarities and differences.

Writing your own openings

'It had been two days since he had stopped drinking but...'

1 Use this sentence as the opening of a story. Choose the genre of fiction that appeals to you most and continue writing in the appropriate style.
2 Include with your work reflections and comments outlining the specific effects you were trying to create.
3 Try the same exercise using a different genre.

Plot and theme

The opening is the way in to a story – a story which the author has shaped into a plot and which focuses on one or more issues or themes. Read the following short story.

Standing up

The passengers were stunned to silence by the woman's audacity.

The bus filled up as it neared the city centre and the narrow aisle was soon jammed.

An old man stood next to the seated woman, his white hand clutching claw-like to the hanging-strap.

'Perhaps you'll leave the seat now,' said a blonde mother behind her. 'There's a gentleman here who needs it.'

The woman turned and spoke, half over her shoulder. 'Maybe one of your kids would oblige.'

'Well, really!' the mother protested and, turning for support, she declared, 'Did you hear that?'

There were gasps and shocked mutterings of assent.

'Don't worry, lady, I'll deal with her!' called a man in a check suit, squeezing along the aisle.

The woman looked up at the frail figure of the old man.

'Excuse me, sir, but would you care to sit down?'

Everyone looked, waiting for him to support them on his behalf.

'No, no,' he said reedily. 'I've never taken a seat from any lady.'

'She ain't just any lady,' blustered the check-suited man. 'You're entitled to that seat, she's not!'

'It's no bother,' said the old man. 'I'm getting off a couple of blocks from here.'

'You sit there! She's not getting away with this.'

The woman spoke: 'I'm staying right here.'

'Oh no, you're getting to the back where you belong!'

As the younger man lunged towards her, the old man shuffled across in his way.

The two men eyed each other. The woman looked fixedly ahead, her black hands clasping the sides of the seat.

Bob Taylor

Working with the story

1 In small groups discuss the differences between plot and themes in the story:
   a) What are the outline facts of the story?
   b) How are these facts organised into a plot so that our curiosity is aroused?
   c) What specific details can you find that give us clues as to what the story might be about e.g. 'his white hand'?
   d) What possible themes or issues is the author raising here?
2 Once you have agreed on what are the main facts and themes in the story, devise a story-board sequence to show the main stages of *Standing up*.

Even in a story as short as this a certain sequence is followed:
a situation is set up (**exposition**),
a conflict takes place (**complication**),
the main events of the story unfold (**climax**)
and some sort of solution is reached (**resolution**).

3 In pairs, analyse *Standing up* and try to work out where these four stages occur. Using a chart like the one below, fill in the details for each stage.

Exposition	Complication	Climax	Resolution
The story is introduced with the explanation that...	The complication begins at the point when...	The climax of the story is reached where...	Some sort of solution is arrived at when...

Setting

Setting plays an important part in every story. A strong idea of place is often the starting point for an author's work and the initial means of creating a mood and atmosphere.

In the opening to *Brighton rock* which you have already seen, Graham Greene goes on to fill in details of the sea-side setting:

Hale knew, before he had been in Brighton three hours, that they meant to murder him. With his inky fingers and his bitten nails, his manner cynical and nervous, anyone could tell he didn't belong – belong to the early summer sun, the cool Whitsun wind off the sea, the holiday crowd. They came in by train from Victoria every five minutes, rocked down Queen's Road standing on the tops of the little local trams, stepped off in bewildered multitudes into fresh and glittering air: the new silver paint sparkled on the piers, the cream houses ran away into the west like a pale Victorian water-colour; a race in miniature motors, a band playing, flower gardens in bloom below the front, an aeroplane advertising something for the health in pale vanishing clouds across the sky.

In the opening to *Silas Marner*, George Eliot sets a scene in the countryside:

In the days when the spinning-wheels hummed busily in the farm-houses – and even the great ladies, clothed in silk and thread-lace, had their toy spinning wheels of polished oak – there might be seen in districts far away among the lanes, or deep in the bosom of the hills, certain pallid, undersized men, who, by the side of the brawny country-folk, looked like the remnants of a disinherited race. The shepherd's dog barked fiercely when one of these alien-looking men appeared on the upland, dark against the early winter sunset; for what dog likes a figure bent under a heavy bag? – and these pale men rarely stirred abroad without that mysterious burden. The shepherd himself, though he had good reason to believe that the bag held nothing but flaxen thread, or else the long rolls of strong linen spun from that thread, was not quite sure that this trade of weaving, indispensable though it was, could be carried on entirely without the help of the Evil One.

Working with both passages

In both *Brighton rock* and *Silas Marner* particular settings are described into which an 'outsider' is introduced.

1   In pairs, pick out all the key words and phrases that tell us what these settings are like.
- What sort of atmosphere is being created?
- What is the relationship between the main character and each setting?

2   Compare the key words and phrases which describe these settings and those which describe the characters as 'outsiders'.

3   On your own use the information you have gathered in a written comparison of the styles of Graham Greene and George Eliot, concentrating on explaining how the settings have been constructed so that the characters are highlighted.

Michael Ende in *The never ending story* gives his readers the imaginary setting of Fantastica:

While gliding soundlessly over the flowery maze, the night-hob sighted all sorts of animals. In a small clearing between lilacs and laburnum, a group of young unicorns was playing in the evening sun, and once, glancing under a giant bluebell, he even thought he saw the famous phoenix in its nest… At the centre of the Labyrinth there now appeared, shimmering in fairy whiteness, the Ivory Tower, the heart of Fantastica and the residence of the Childlike Empress.

The word 'tower' might give someone who has never seen it the wrong idea. It had nothing of the church or castle about it. The Ivory Tower was as big as a whole city. From a distance it looked like a pointed mountain peak twisted like a snail shell. Its highest point was deep in the clouds. Only on coming closer could you notice that this great sugarloaf consisted of innumerable towers, turrets, domes, roofs, oriels, terraces, arches, stairways and balustrades, all marvellously fitted together. The whole was made of the whitest Fantastican ivory, so delicately carved in every detail that it might have been taken for the latticework of the finest lace.

Looking back

1 How would you describe the mood and atmosphere being created here? Which words and phrases in particular would you pick out as emphasising this atmosphere?
2 What sort of creatures might live here? Discuss what you think possible inhabitants of this world might be like in looks and behaviour, on the basis of the setting and atmosphere that are described here.

Assignment

1 In pairs, list all the different settings you can think of, e.g. town, country, house, garden, hospital, another planet, etc. Then make a separate list of some of the possible qualities of these settings, such as desolation, mystery, quiet, beauty, magic, destruction, etc.
2 On your own, choose one of these and try to get a picture of it in your mind. Now list all the words and phrases that you can think of that give more specific details about your chosen setting.
3 Now write a description of your chosen place – either in the third person (i.e he/she) or the first person (i.e. I) – and try to capture the atmosphere and mood of what you have been imagining. Try to write it so that the reader will see this place as clearly as you can. Include a picture or map if it seems appropriate.

Character

In any novel a character will react to the setting, and in turn the mood of the character may influence how the reader reacts to the setting. In *Brighton rock* Hale's identity is gradually revealed and with it we get a sense of the person himself in contrast with the place he finds himself in. His character is revealed not just by direct description but by what he does and how he does it.

It had seemed quite easy to Hale to be lost in Brighton. Fifty thousand people besides himself were down for the day, and for quite a while he gave himself up to the good day, drinking gins and tonics wherever his programme allowed. For he had to stick closely to a programme: from ten till eleven Queen's Road and Castle Square, from eleven till twelve the Aquarium and Palace Pier, twelve till one the front between the Old Ship and West Pier, back for lunch between one and two in any restaurant he chose round the Castle Square, and after that he had to make his way all down the parade to the West Pier and then to the station by the Hove streets. These were the limits of his absurd and widely advertised sentry go.

Advertised on every *Messenger* poster: 'Kolly Kibber in Brighton today'. In his pocket he had a packet of cards to distribute in hidden places along his route: those who found them would receive ten shillings from the *Messenger*, but the big prize was reserved for whoever challenged Hale in the proper form of words and with a copy of the *Messenger* in his hand: 'You are Mr Kolly Kibber. I claim the *Daily Messenger* prize.'

This was Hale's job, to do sentry go, until a challenger released him, in every seaside town in turn: yesterday Southend, today Brighton, tomorrow –

He drank his gin and tonic hastily as a clock struck eleven, and moved out of Castle Square. Kolly Kibber always played fair, always wore the same kind of hat as in the photograph the *Messenger* printed, was always on time... It was his duty today to be spotted – and it was his inclination too. There were reasons why he didn't feel too safe in Brighton, even in a Whitsun crowd.

Examining character

1 When trying to understand a character a reader needs to get as full a picture as possible, such as:
  - what the character says about him/herself
  - what the author/narrator says about the character
  - what other characters say
  - what the character looks like/wears
  - what the habits and mood of the character are like
  - how the character acts and reacts to others
  - what the character's social position and education are

  In pairs, using the ideas in the list above, make a chart like the one opposite of all the details you can find about Hale's character and situation.

2 In the earlier extract Hale is very much an outsider who stands out in the seaside setting and holiday atmosphere.
  a) In what ways has the setting changed here
  b) How are the facts of Hale's movements built up?
  c) How would you describe the pace of the extract?
  d) How does his mood/attitude change?
  e) How does this link with the way the setting changes?

Information needed	Evidence
a) What does each character say about him/herself?	Quote from the text
b) What does the author say about the character?	Quote from the text

In *Nicholas Nickleby* Charles Dickens describes the character of Squeers in a much more direct way:

Mr Squeers's appearance was not prepossessing. He had but one eye, and the popular prejudice runs in favour of two. The eye he had was unquestionably useful, but decidedly not ornamental, being of a greenish-grey, and in shape resembling the fan-light of a street door. The blank side of his face was much wrinkled and puckered up, which gave him a very sinister appearance, especially when he smiled, at which times his expression bordered on the villainous. His hair was very flat and shiny, save at the ends, where it was brushed stiffly up from a low protruding forehead, which assorted well with his harsh voice and coarse manner. He was about two or three and fifty, and a trifle below the middle size; he wore a white neckerchief with long ends, and a suit of scholastic black, but his coat sleeves being a great deal too long, and his trousers a great deal too short, he appeared ill at ease in his clothes, and as if he were in a perpetual state of astonishment at finding himself so respectable.

Working with details

1 With a partner examine how this description has been built up. Pick out:
  - all the vivid comparisons
  - all the physical characteristics
  - details about clothes
  - details that make this a caricature rather than a realistic description

2 On your own write a 'snapshot' description of a character: one in a grotesque, deliberately exaggerated style like Dickens uses, and one in your own style, aiming at realistic description.

Characters and dialogue

The words a character speaks will always tell the reader something more of what that character is like and the writer is usually as concerned with *how* the character speaks as with *what* the character says.

Look at what Miss Bates says and how she speaks in Jane Austen's *Emma*. The company has been talking about the announcement of a marriage between Mr Elton, whom they know, and a Miss Hawkins, who is a stranger to them. They have just agreed that Mr Elton is 'the standard of perfection' in the local community and Miss Bates continues:

'He is the very best young man – But, my dear Jane, if you remember, I told you yesterday he was precisely the height of Mr Perry. Miss Hawkins, – I dare say, an excellent young woman. His extreme attention to my mother – wanting her to sit in the vicarage-pew, that she might hear the better, for my mother is a little deaf, you know – it is not much, but she does not hear quick. Jane says that Colonel Campbell is a little deaf. He fancied bathing might be good for it – the warm bath – but she says it did him no lasting benefit. Colonel Campbell, you know, is quite an angel. And Mr Dixon seems a very charming young man, quite worthy of him. It is such a happiness when good people get together – and they always do. Now, here will be Mr Elton and Miss Hawkins; and there are the Coles, such very good people; and the Perrys – I suppose there never was a happier or a better couple than Mr and Mrs Perry. I say, sir,' turning to Mr Woodhouse, 'I think there are few places with such society as Highbury. I always say, we are quite blessed in our neighbours. My dear sir, if there is one thing my mother loves better than another, it is pork – a roast loin of pork...'

Examining the speech

1 What does this style of writing tell a reader about the character who is speaking?
2 What do the details in Miss Bates' speech reveal about her life-style?

As well as giving the reader information about themselves in conversation, characters often reveal new information about the plot, views, themes and ideas. Look at the way dialogue is used in the following extract.

My brilliant career

By the generosity of relatives and the goodness of neighbours as kind as ever breathed, our furniture was our own again, but what were we to do for a living? Our crops were withering in the fields for want of rain, and we had but five cows – not an over-bright outlook. As I was getting to bed one night my mother came into my room and said seriously, 'Sybylla, I want to have a talk with you.'

'Talk away,' I responded rather sullenly, for I expected a long sing-song about my good-for-nothingness in general – a subject of which I was heartily tired.

'Sybylla, I've been studying the matter over a lot lately. It's no use, we cannot afford to keep you at home. You'll have to get something to do.'

I made no reply, and my mother continued, 'I am afraid we will have to break up the home altogether. It's no use; your father has no idea of making a living. I regret the day I ever saw him. Since he has taken to drink he has no more idea of how to make a living than a cat. I will have to give the little ones to some of the relatives; the bigger ones will have to go out to service, and so will your father and I. That's all I can see ahead of us. Poor little Gertie is too young to go out in the world (she was not twelve months younger than I); she must go to your grandmother, I think.'

I still made no reply, so my mother inquired, 'Well, Sybylla, what do you think of the matter?'

'Do you think it absolutely necessary to break up the home?' I said.

'Well, you suggest something better if you are so clever,' said mother, crossly. 'That is always the way; if I suggest a thing it is immediately put down, yet there is never anyone to think of things but me. What would you do? I suppose you think you could make a living on the place for us yourself.'

'Why can't we live at home? Blackshaw and Jansen have no bigger places than we, and families just as large, and yet they make a living. It would be terrible for the little ones to grow up separated; they would be no more to each other than strangers.'

Miles Franklin

Looking at the extract

1 a) In pairs, look at this conversation and find all the information you can about what is happening in the story
   b) Discuss what you have learned about Sybylla, her mother and their relationship.

2 a) On your own, rewrite the passage as a description of events without any dialogue.
   b) Compare your version with your partner's to check you have included all the necessary facts.
   c) What has been gained or what has been lost by not using any dialogue?

Short stories

In a short story a writer does not have the space a novelist does to develop plot, ideas, characters, settings, etc. Economy with words and ideas is all important and instead of detailed descriptions the author will concentrate on a few striking details or some fragments of dialogue from which the reader can build up the whole picture. Read the story below by Jean Rhys which is set in Dominica, in the Caribbean.

I used to live here once

She was standing by the river looking at the stepping stones and remembering each one. There was the round unsteady stone, the pointed one, the flat one in the middle – the safe stone where you could stand and look around. The next wasn't so safe for when the river was full the water flowed over it and even when it showed dry it was slippery. But after that it was easy and soon she was standing on the other side.

The road was much wider than it used to be but the work had been done carelessly. The felled trees had not been cleared away and the bushes looked trampled. Yet it was the same road and she walked along feeling extraordinarily happy.

It was a fine day, a blue day. The only thing was that the sky had a glassy look that she didn't remember. That was the only word she could think of. Glassy. She turned the corner, saw that what had been the old pavé had been taken up, and there too the road was much wider, but it had the same unfinished look.

She came to the worn stone steps that led up to the house and her heart began to beat. The screw pine was gone, so was the mock summer house called the ajoupa, but the clove tree was still there and at the top of the steps the rough lawn stretched away, just as she remembered it. She stopped and looked towards the house that had been added to and painted white. It was strange to see a car standing in front of it.

There were two children under the big mango tree, a boy and a little girl, and she waved to them and called 'Hello' but they didn't answer her or turn their heads. Very fair children, as Europeans born in the West Indies so often are: as if the white blood is asserting itself against all the odds.

The grass was yellow in the hot sunlight as she walked towards them. When she was quite close she called again, shyly: 'Hello'. Then, 'I used to live here once,' she said.

Still they didn't answer. When she had said for the third time 'Hello' she was quite near them. Her arms went out instinctively with the longing to touch them.

It was the boy who turned. His grey eyes looked straight into hers. His expression didn't change. He said 'Hasn't it gone cold all of a sudden. D'you notice? Let's go in.' 'Yes let's,' said the girl.

Her arms fell to her sides as she watched them running across the grass to the house. That was the first time she knew.

54

Looking back

1 In pairs, talk about and jot down:
   ● what are the basic facts of the story
   ● whether the ending is a surprise
   ● what was it the main character knew?
   ● what details you can find which build on the theme, the setting, and the main figure
2 Analyse the structure of this story identifying the key transition points in terms of exposition, complication, climax, and resolution; see page 47.

A Corsican bandit

The road sloped gently upwards through the forest of Aitone. The lofty pine trees spread a moaning archway above our heads, and seemed to wail sadly and continuously, while to the right and left their slender upright trunks were like an army of organ pipes playing the monotonous music of wind in the trees.

After walking for three hours the multitude of tall, entangled tree trunks began to clear. Here and there an enormous umbrella pine, separate from the others, spread out like a huge parasol its dark green dome. Then suddenly we reached the edge of the forest, a few hundred metres below the pass which led to the wild Niolo valley.

Up on the two narrow peaks which dominate this pass, a few old misshapen trees seemed to have made their way with difficulty, like scouts sent on ahead of the huge dense mass of trees behind them. We turned round and saw the whole forest stretched out beneath us, like an enormous green bowl with edges made of sheer rock that seemed to touch the sky.

We set off again, and ten minutes later we reached the pass.

It was then that I caught my first glimpse of a startling landscape. Beyond yet another forest was a valley, but a valley such as I had never seen before, a desert of stone some three miles long, hollowed out of mountains more than three thousand feet high, with no trace of greenery, without a single tree. The Niolo valley, home of Corsican liberty, the impregnable fortress whose men of the mountains could never be driven out by the island's invaders.

My companion said to me, 'That is also where all our bandits have sought refuge.' Soon we were in the middle of that wild but indescribably beautiful place.

Not a single plant; not a blade of grass; granite, nothing but granite. As far as the eye could see, a desert of glittering granite, heated like an oven by an intensely hot sun which seemed to hover directly above the valley of stone. I looked up to the mountain tops, and stopped in wonder before a dazzling sight. They looked deep red, and lacy-edged, like coral, for all the peaks were of purplish volcanic rock, and the sky above was lilac-coloured, pale against those strange mountains. Further down, the granite was grey and sparkling, and under our feet it seemed crushed, like crystals. We were walking on a kind of gleaming dust. To our right a tumultuous river noisily ran its long and tortuous course. And we staggered and swayed in the heat and brightness of that wild, burning valley. The turbulent water cutting across it seemed to flee hastily, unable to bring any cultivation to those crags, lost in that furnace which drank it up greedily without ever being refreshed, without a drop seeping through.

Then suddenly we saw to our right a little wooden cross buried in a heap of stones. A man had been killed there, and I said to my companion,

'So tell me about your bandits.'

He replied, 'I knew the most famous, the most terrible of them all, Sainte Lucie. I will tell you his story.

'They say his father was killed in a quarrel by a young man from the same area, and Sainte Lucie was left alone with his sister. He was a weak, spineless boy, slight in build, often ill, with no energy or drive. He did not declare a vendetta against his father's murderer. All his relatives sought him out and pleaded with him to seek revenge. He ignored all their threats and entreaties.

'So, following an old Corsican custom, his outraged sister took away all his black clothes so that he could not wear mourning for a death that was not avenged. He seemed unmoved by this drastic action, and instead of taking down his father's still loaded gun, he shut himself away and never went out, not daring to face the scornful glances of the local young men. Many months went by. He seemed to have actually forgotten the murder, and lived with his sister, behind closed doors.

'Then, one day, the man suspected of the murder got married. Sainte Lucie did not seem affected by this news, but, to taunt him no doubt, the bridegroom went past the house of the two orphans on his way to Church. Brother and sister were at their window eating little fried cakes when the young man saw the wedding party going past his home. Suddenly he began to tremble, he got up without a word, crossed himself, took down the gun which was hanging over the hearth, and went out.

'When he spoke of all this later, he said, "I don't know what came over me. There was a sudden fire in my blood. I felt I had to do it, that in spite of everything I would not be able to stop myself, and I went to hide the gun in the bushes on the road to Corte."

'An hour later he returned, empty-handed, looking the same as usual, sad and tired. His sister thought he had put it all out of his mind.

'But at nightfall he disappeared. His enemy, meanwhile, set off on foot towards Corte that very evening, with two wedding guests. They were going along the road singing when Sainte Lucie appeared before them, and, staring straight at the murderer he shouted,

'"Now is the moment!"

'Then, at point-blank range, he shot him in the chest. One of the wedding guests fled, the other stared at the young man, saying repeatedly,

'"What have you done, Sainte Lucie?"

'He tried to run to Corte to get help. But Sainte Lucie shouted,

'"If you take one more step I'll blow your leg off."

'The other knowing him to be, until then, weak and cowardly, said,

'"You wouldn't dare!" and he set off. But he collapsed immediately, his thigh shattered by a bullet. And Sainte Lucie, coming over to him, said,

'"I'll take a look at your wound. If it isn't serious, I'll leave you here. If it's fatal, I'll finish you off."

'He examined the wound, decided it was fatal, slowly reloaded his gun, invited his victim to say a prayer, and then shattered his skull.

'By the next morning he was up in the mountains.

'And do you know what Sainte Lucie did next?

'His whole family was arrested by the Police. His uncle, a priest, who was suspected of inciting him to seek revenge, was himself put in prison and accused of the murder by the relatives of the dead man. But he escaped, took a gun in his turn, and joined his nephew in the maquis.

'Then Sainte Lucie killed one after the other, those who had accused his uncle, and he ripped out their eyes as a warning to others never to swear to something they had not seen with their own eyes.

'He killed all the relatives and friends of his enemy's family. In his lifetime he killed fourteen policemen, set fire to the houses of all his enemies, and was, until his death, the most terrible bandit in living memory.'

The sun was setting behind Mount Cinto, and the huge shadow of the granite mountain fell on the granite of the valley. We hurried onward, anxious to reach before nightfall the little village of Albertacce, a distant huddle of stones clinging to the sheer rock face of the rugged valley. And I said, thinking of the bandit,

'What a terrible custom your vendetta is!'

My companion replied, in a tone of resignation,

'What do you expect? We must live by the Code!'

25th May 1882

Guy de Maupassant (translated by Linda Rougale)

Examining the story

1 On your own look at the following list of statements about the story and come to a decision about which you agree with and which you do not:
   ● Sainte Lucie is shown as justified in seeking revenge.
   ● As shown in the story Sainte Lucie and his sister have the option of relying on the law to punish the murderer.
   ● Sainte Lucie is shown to be just as much of a murderer as the man who killed his father.
   ● His way of seeking revenge is not seen as justifiable in the story.
   ● The reader is meant to pity Sainte Lucie.
   ● The reader is meant to see Sainte Lucie as a monster.
   ● The reader is expected to accept the events as inevitable.
2 Agree a group decision about each of the statements. You must be able to back up your decisions with evidence from the story.
3 Look closely at the language, content and style of the story. Why do you think so much emphasis has been given to setting the scene and describing the surroundings?

Assignment

Write a review of *A Corsican bandit*, discussing how all the elements of the story you have considered contribute to its overall effect. Make sure you:
● give a brief summary of the plot
● look at the setting and atmosphere
● describe the main characters
● look at the style of the story
● identify any themes or messages

Does the story have an unexpected ending which tells the reader more about the overall purpose of the story?

Try to think about why the story has been written how it has and give reasons about whether you liked the story or not.

On trial

An incident has occurred one summer night which will end up with a hearing in Court. Before the trial takes place you have to gather all the evidence available from all points of view. Discuss all information and ideas in small groups but compile your own written evidence.

Setting

A lonely country lane which leads just to 3 houses – The Manor House, Manor Cottage and The Old Rectory. The lane ends in a small pond surrounded by a wooded area.

Characters

1

Mr James Brown, aged 56, owner of The Manor House

2

Mrs Jane Brown, aged 55, wife of James Brown

3

Mr David White, aged 18, driver of the red XR3i Cabriolet

4

Miss Laura Smith, aged 17, girl-friend of David White and passenger in the red car

In addition, there are the families who live in the neighbouring two houses and the young people who were in the car which followed behind David's red open-top XR3i. Any or all of these may have witnessed the events.

Although not present at the incident Mr Eric Pointer, Membership Secretary of the local Gun Club, could give information about Mr Brown. He had to compile a Confidential File on Mr Brown when the latter applied to join the Gun Club three years earlier.

Likewise, Detective Inspector Jennifer Forward has been compiling a Confidential File on David White whose movements she has been watching closely for several months.

Story-line

Mr David White has accused Mr James Brown of shooting him with intent to wound. Mr James Brown maintains he is innocent of that charge. He does admit, however, that he did fire a shotgun in the air to warn suspected poachers off his property. He maintains he has had continuous problems throughout the summer with 'lager louts' vandalising his property and intimidating his wife and family, and with poachers stealing his pheasants and deer.

The alleged incident occurred on July 28th between 1 and 2am – the early hours of a Sunday morning. Mr and Mrs Brown were woken up by the noise of cars, music and voices. On investigation Mr Brown saw figures moving through the trees near to where he keeps his pheasants. He took his shotgun with him and shotgun pellets ended up embedded in David White's car and in his back.

In your groups start to work out the details of the plot. The following questions will help to focus your investigations.

- What has led to these incidents?
- What was David White really doing outside the Manor House?
- How does he come to be driving an expensive car?
- Why might he be the subject of an on-going police investigation?

- Can you really believe Mr Brown's story that this was an accident?
- Is there some previous connection between the two men or are they strangers?
- What was the outcome of Mr Pointer's investigations?
- Was Mr Brown able to join the Gun Club?

Confidential files

A great deal of information is available about both these men in the confidential files compiled by Mr Pointer and by Detective Inspector Jennifer Forward.

Write the files held on both James Brown and David White. You will need to set out your basic information on two separate sheets of paper. Additional documents you might want to include could be letters, diary extracts, transcripts of conversations, newspaper cuttings, maps, photographs or illustrations. Use your own stationery, word-processed articles and illustrations to create something really special.

Mr Brown's story

Mr Brown is asked to give a detailed statement of what has happened to the Police. A detailed description of the setting and perhaps a map or a picture must be included with this. The police also need to know about the previous incidents that Mr Brown says have been going on all summer. Write the story that Mr Brown gives. (There is always a possibility that he will not tell the truth if he has something to hide.) Remember to keep the style of writing in keeping with the sort of person he is and the impression he is trying to make.

David White's story

In a similar way write the story that David gives the Police. Again, details of the setting as well as events leading up to the incident as well as the incident itself should be included. (It is also possible that David has something to hide from the police.) You must also write this statement in a style that is in keeping with this character.

Witnesses' accounts

Write the transcripts of interviews between the police and the witnesses to the incident. Remember that a transcript is a written version of the actual words spoken. (The witness statements may differ yet again from the stories given by James Brown and David White. It will be the task of the Jury to try and decide where the truth lies.)

Everyone should end up with slightly different written accounts of the story, characters and witnesses, written in a variety of different styles for a number of purposes which can be submitted as coursework. Before the trial begins, prepare a statement on how you think the case will turn out, giving your reasons.

The trial

You will need to set up a Court Scene with the following characters, as James Brown is now being tried for malicious wounding of David White:

Judge
Prosecuting Lawyer
Mr James Brown
D.I. Forward
Defence Lawyer
Mr Pointer
David White
Mrs Jane Brown
Miss Laura Smith

Other witnesses from the neighbouring houses, the other car, or the police may be added as necessary.

The rest of the class should act as the jury and write notes about what they hear each character say in order to come to a reasoned conclusion and verdict at the end.

The layout of your courtroom should look something like the diagram below.

Procedure

1 The Judge opens the case and conducts all proceedings.
2 The Prosecuting Lawyer outlines the facts of the case against Mr James Brown and questions the relevant witnesses:
    David White, Laura Smith, the occupants of the other car, the police and possibly D.I. Forward.
3 The Defence Lawyer cross-examines these witnesses.
4 The Defence Lawyer questions the witnesses for the defence:
    James Brown, Jane Brown, the neighbours, the police and possibly Mr Pointer.
5 The Prosecuting Lawyer cross-examines these witnesses.
6 The Judge sums up the evidence.
7 The Jury retires to consider its verdict.

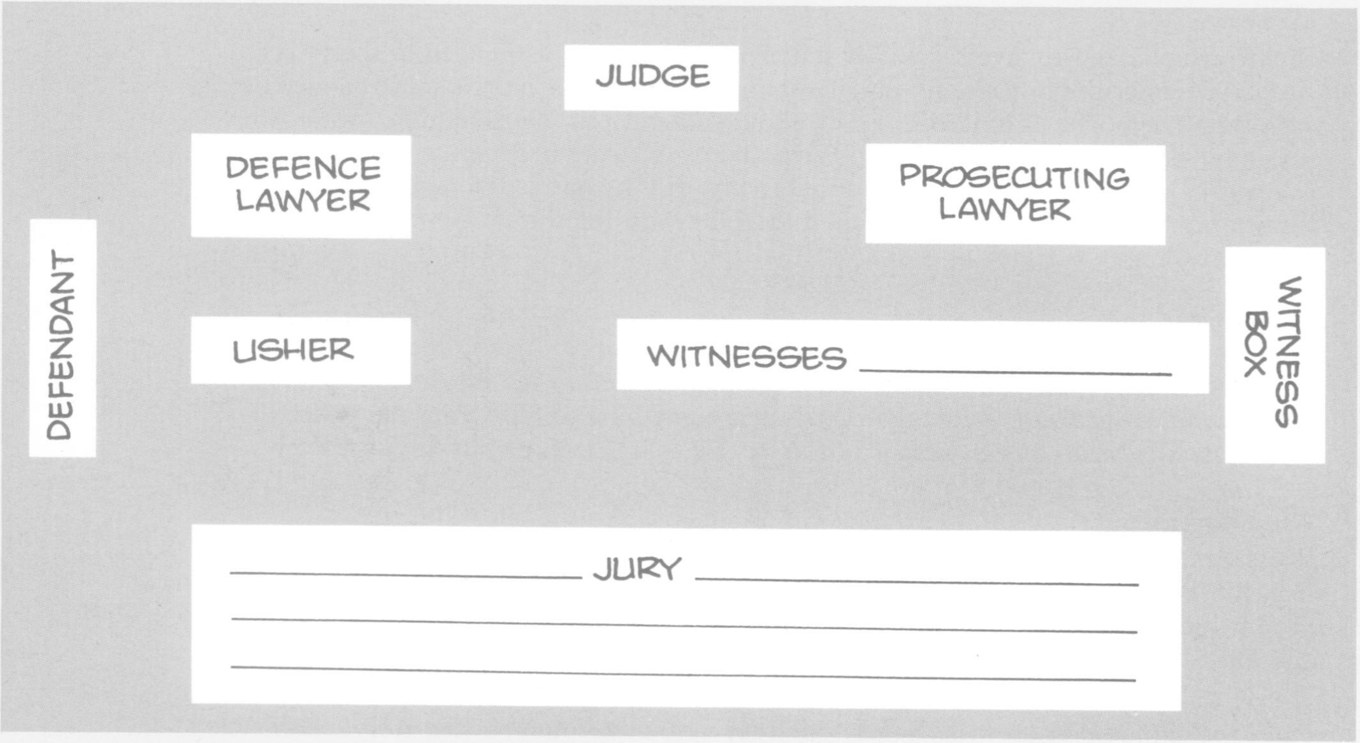

JUDGE

DEFENCE LAWYER

PROSECUTING LAWYER

DEFENDANT

USHER

WITNESSES _____

WITNESS BOX

_____ JURY _____

Look back at the statement you wrote before the trial began. How have your views changed? Rewrite your statement in the light of these changes.

At the end of the proceedings write up a newspaper report of the trial and verdict.

Module 2   Poetry

UNIT 1	Poetry as picture	62
UNIT 2	Poem as story	76
UNIT 3	Poem as pattern	88
UNIT 4	Free verse	100
UNIT 5	Poetry and precision	112
FEATURE	Creating your own anthology	117

Objectives

The materials and activities included in this module
aim to help you learn more about different forms of
poetry by:

◆ providing a lively collection of poems that should
  invite and encourage you to develop your
  individual response
◆ giving opportunities for you to explore these poems
  through performance, discussion and creative
  writing.
◆ looking closely at the structure of a variety of
  poetic forms to discover how they work

Reading the words of a piece of writing or a poem you often find yourself building a series of pictures or images to fit the words on the page in front of you. A poet will often work to create these word pictures like Roger McGough has below:

Vinegar

Sometimes
i feel like a priest
in a fish and chip queue
quietly thinking
as the vinegar runs through
how nice it would be
to buy supper for two

A good poem with strong images can help you picture it clearly.
Read the poem below and see if you can picture the sequence of images it suggests.

Mid term break

I sat all morning in the college sick bay
Counting bells knelling classes to a close.
At two o'clock our neighbours drove me home.

In the porch I met my father crying –
He had always taken funerals in his stride –
And Big Jim Evans saying it was a hard blow.

The baby cooed and laughed and rocked the pram
When I came in, and I was embarrassed
By old men standing up to shake my hand

And tell me they were 'sorry for my trouble',
Whispers informed strangers I was the eldest,
Away at school, as my mother held my hand

In hers and coughed out angry tearless sighs.
At ten o'clock the ambulance arrived
With the corpse, stanched and bandaged by the nurses.

Next morning I went up into the room. Snowdrops
And candles soothed the bedside; I saw him
For the first time in six weeks. Paler now,

Wearing a poppy bruise on his left temple
he lay in the four foot box as in his cot
No gaudy scars, the bumper knocked him clear.

A four foot box, a foot for every year.

Seamus Heaney

Creating a film script

As we have seen, *Mid term break* can suggest a series of images or pictures. With a partner or in a group of 3, look at the poem again and try and visualise a series of film shots. As you read, you may find that music and/or sound effects suggest themselves too, but these are not essential.

1 First look through the kinds of shot a film director might use, and the film script layout sheet shown on page 64.

2 With a partner, use the layout sheet to begin drafting ideas for your shoot. It may help to make notes around the poem to decide which sections will go with which shot.

I sat all morning in the college sick bay,
Counting bells knelling classes to a close.

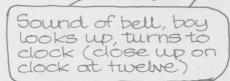

Sound of bell, boy looks up, turns to clock (close up on clock at twelve)

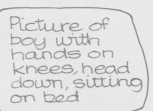

Picture of boy with hands on knees, head down, sitting on bed

3 You need to give a clear picture of each shot in the left-hand column of the layout sheet. You can do this with words but an outline sketch would be better. You do not need to be a superb artist to do this.

4 In the middle column give clear details to explain each shot, e.g. whether it is a close-up or long shot.

5 Remember you can have more than one shot for each line of the poem. Some lines may suggest two or three camera angles.

6 Vary shots to fit the mood of the line, e.g. you might use close-ups for very intense moments and a panning effect to show the response of others.

7 In the right-hand column write in the lines that will go with each shot and decide how you will read the poem. Which words will you emphasise, where will you pause, and where will you go faster? How many speakers will you have and for which lines?
  You may also want to add ideas for sound effects and/or music to be heard in the background.

Finished work can be displayed so groups can compare interpretations. Did any lines give you particular difficulties? If so, why?

Camera angles

Wide angle

Close-up

Long shot

Extreme close-up

Medium range

In addition, the following terms can be used in instructions on the layout sheet.

Zoom: camera moves in quickly to close-up or back from close-up to long shot

Pan: camera moves across the scene from one side to the other

Track: camera follows a moving object like a person or vehicle

Film script layout sheet

Shot no.	Picture (sketch/caption)	Detail of camera movement	Sound (lines of poem/sound effects)

Sense images

Images in poems don't just make us think of pictures, they can also suggest sounds, smells, feelings, tastes. Listen to the following poems read aloud and then discuss with a partner which lines helped you see, hear, feel and smell the scenes.

In Mrs Tilscher's class

You could travel up the Blue Nile
With your finger tracing the route
While Mrs Tilscher chanted the scenery
Tana. Ethiopia. Kartoum. Aswan.
That for an hour, then a skittle of milk
and the chalky Pyramids rubbed into dust.
A window opened with a long pole
The laugh of a bell swung by a running child.

This was better than home. Enthralling books.
The classroom glowed like a sweet shop.
Sugar paper. Coloured shapes. Brady and Hindley
faded like the faint, uneasy smudge of a mistake.
Mrs Tilscher loved you. Some mornings, you
   found
She'd left a gold star by your name.
The scent of a pencil, slowly, carefully shaved.
A xylophone's nonsense heard from another form.

Over the Easter term, the inky tadpoles changed
from commas into exclamation marks. Three frogs
hopped in the playground freed by a dunce,
followed by a line of kids, jumping and croaking
away from the lunch queue. A rough boy
told you how you were born. You kicked him, but
   stared
at your parents, appalled, when you got back home.

That feverish July, the air tasted of electricity.
A tangible alarm made you always untidy, hot,
fractious under the heavy, sexy sky. You asked her
how your were born and Mrs Tilscher smiled,
then turned away. Reports were handed out.
You ran through the gates, impatient to be grown,
as the sky split open into a thunderstorm.

Carol Ann Duffy

Cold

Tonight the brittle trees
rattled and snapped in wind and the stars broke
trembling like shattered ice.
Logs and frozen heather creaked
and starlight shook under our feet.

My son and I went on to the moor,
walking under drapes of a low sky.
A skull cracked underfoot;
a tarred roof winked; a snowball fell;
then quiet that seemed to glow.
We came indoors when we had stared at snow.

Now we change our places at the hearth
like penguins on an ice floe. Draughts
enter through wall and roof: the swords
of cold sneak through our warmth
like poison threading liquid in a glass.

Glyn Hughes

From the night window

The night rattles with nightmares.
Children cry in the close packed houses,
A man rots in his snoring.
On quiet feet, policemen test doors.
Footsteps become people under streetlamps.
Drunks return from parties,
Sounding of empty bottles and old songs.
The young women come home,
The pleasure in them deafens me.
They trot like small horses
And disappear into white beds
At the edge of night
All windows open this hot night,
And the sleepless, smoking in the dark,
Making small red lights with their mouths,
Count the years of their marriages.

Douglas Dunn

Looking at the poems

Using three different symbols (e.g. underline, ring, star) annotate your own copies of the poems marking lines that:
- helped you picture events/scenes
- helped you hear them
- helped you use senses of touch, taste and smell

66

Collage

Poems like these invite illustration. Either use one of the three poems on pages 65 and 66 or choose another from your own reading that describes places or events as vividly. First, write out the lines or phrases that you want to focus on. Then, using a collection of magazines and newspapers, carefully match pictures to these lines. Try to create a collage of pictures and line snippets from the poem to represent the images you see in it.

Footsteps become people under streetlamps

lose-packed houses

On quiet feet policemen test doors

Count the years of their marriages

The young women come home

the sleepless, smoking in the dark

They trot like small horses

Writing your own

Write your own poem or descriptive piece depicting a place/time you recall clearly. You may use ideas and places similar to the ones suggested in the poems on pages 65-66, i.e. a classroom memory or sounds late at night, but the details should be original. You may instead prefer to work from an old photograph.

Be prepared to make several drafts as Judith Nicholls does for her piece, *Orang-utan*, since this is how you get ideas just as you want them. Try to include imagery that appeals to all five senses and use comparisons to help your reader picture the scene.

For another writer's views on drafting see The Process of Writing module in Book 4B, pages 79-83. See also Unit 3, page 88 for Yeats' drafts of his poem, *After long silence*.

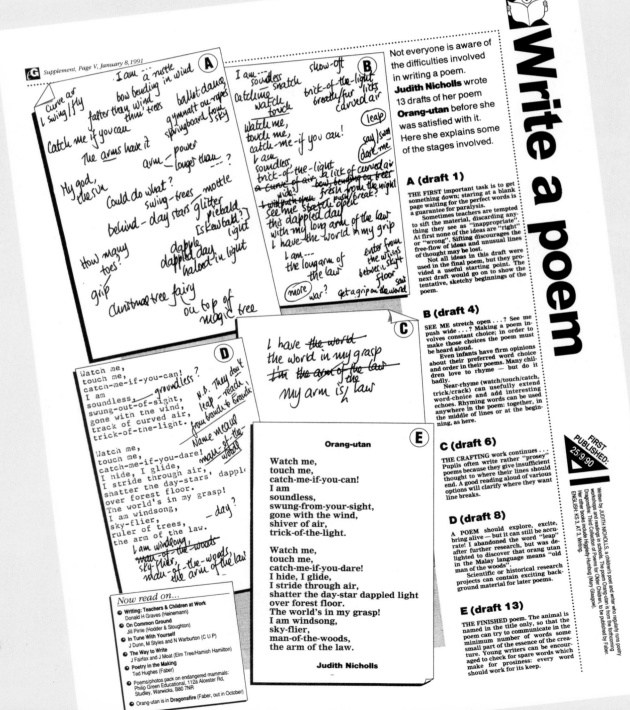

Write a poem

Not everyone is aware of the difficulties involved in writing a poem. **Judith Nicholls** wrote 13 drafts of her poem **Orang-utan** before she was satisfied with it. Here she explains some of the stages involved.

A (draft 1)

THE FIRST important task is to get something down; staring at a blank page waiting for the perfect words is a guarantee for paralysis.

Sometimes teachers are tempted to sift the material, discarding anything they see as "inappropriate". At first none of the ideas are "right" or "wrong". Sifting discourages the free-flow of ideas and unusual lines of thought may be lost.

Not all ideas in this draft were used in the final poem, but they provided a useful starting point. The next draft would go on to show the tentative, sketchy beginnings of the poem.

B (draft 4)

SEE ME stretch open . . . ? See me push wide . . . ? Making a poem involves constant choice; in order to make those choices the poem must be heard aloud.

Even infants have firm opinions about their preferred word choice and order in their poems. Many children love to rhyme — but do it badly.

Near-rhyme (watch/touch/catch, trick/crack) can usefully extend word-choice and add interesting echoes. Rhyming words can be used anywhere in the poem: together, in the middle of lines or at the beginning, as here.

C (draft 6)

THE CRAFTING work continues . . . Pupils often write rather "prosey" poems because they give insufficient thought to where their lines should end. A good reading aloud of various options will clarify where they want line breaks.

D (draft 8)

A POEM should explore, excite, bring alive — but it can still be accurate! I abandoned the word "leap" after further research, but was delighted to discover that orang utan in the Malay language means "old man of the woods".

Scientific or historical research projects can contain exciting background material for later poems.

E (draft 13)

THE FINISHED poem. The animal is named in the title only, so that the poem can try to communicate in the minimum number of words some small part of the essence of the creature. Young writers can be encouraged to check for spare words which make for prosiness: every word should work for its keep.

FIRST PUBLISHED: 25.9.90

Written by JUDITH NICHOLLS, a children's poet and writer who regularly runs poetry workshops and readings in schools. The poem Orang-utan is from the forthcoming Dragonsfire: Third Collection of Poems for Older Children, to be published by Faber. Her other books include Higgledy-Humbug (Mary Glasgow). ENGLISH, KS 3, AT 3, Writing.

Orang-utan (E) (draft 13)

Watch me,
touch me,
catch-me-if-you-can!
I am
soundless,
swung-from-your-sight,
gone with the wind,
shiver of air,
trick-of-the-light.

Watch me,
touch me,
catch-me-if-you-dare!
I hide, I glide,
I stride through air,
shatter the day-star dappled light
over forest floor.
The world's in my grasp!
I am windsong,
sky-flier,
man-of-the-woods,
the arm of the law.

Judith Nicholls

Now read on . . .

● Writing: Teachers & Children at Work
Donald H Graves (Heinemann)

● On Common Ground
Jill Pirrie (Hodder & Stoughton)

● In Tune With Yourself
J Dunn, M Styles and N Warburton (C U P)

● The Way to Write
J Fairfax and J Moat (Elm Tree/Hamish Hamilton)

● Poetry in the Making
Ted Hughes (Faber)

● Poems/photos pack on endangered mammals:
Philip Green Educational, 112a Alcester Rd,
Studley, Warwicks. B80 7NR

● Orang-utan is in Dragonsfire (Faber, out in October)

The warm and the cold

Freezing dusk is closing
Like a slow trap of steel
On trees and roads and hills and all
That can no longer feel.
But the carp is in its depth
Like a planet in its heaven
And the badger in its bedding
Like _____
And the butterfly in its mummy
Like _____
And the owl in its feathers
Like _____

Freezing dusk has tightened
Like _____
On the starry aeroplane
Of the soaring night
But the trout is in its hole
Like a chuckle in a sleeper
The hare strays down the highway
Like _____
The snail is dry in the outhouse
Like _____
The owl is pale on the gatepost
Like _____

Moonlight freezes the shaggy world
Like a mammoth of ice
The past and the future
Are the jaws of a steel vice.
But the cod is in the tide-rip
Like _____
The deer are on the bare-blown hill
Like smiles on a nurse.
The flies are behind the plaster
Like _____
Sparrows are in the ivy-clump
Like _____

Such a frost
The flimsy moon
Has lost her wits.

A star falls.

The sweating farmers
Turn in their sleep
Like _____

Ted Hughes

In this poem, Ted Hughes describes the onset of a freezing night in a series of sense images. To paint a vivid picture of the way different animals keep warm he uses a number of **similes** – comparisons where one thing is compared to another using the words 'like' or 'as'.

Unscrambling the images

In groups of 3 or 4, fit the jumbled comparisons below into the right places. Try looking for points of similarity in the images, and working out which lines in the poem rhyme to help you.

oxen on spits	a loaf in the oven
a root going deeper	a doll in its lace
a clock on its tower	like a viol in its case
a key in a purse	the lost score of a jig
money in a pig	a seed in a sunflower
a nut screwed tight	

Personification

The following poems both provide pictures of the wind – a walking, talking, thinking wind, since these pieces describe the wind as though it is a person. This technique of giving a non-human thing human feelings and actions is known as **personification**.

Brainstorm

What kind of person do you visualise as you read these? List a few key words that characterise each wind.

The song of the broken reeds

The wind from the Torwana mountains
has her lap full of moss
She carries a sleeping child
She recites from the stars
with the voice of broad waters
against the white skeletons of the day

The wind from the Torwana mountains
shoreless without horizon without seasons
has the face of all people
has the bitter-aloe of the world at her breast
has the lamb of all joy over her shoulder
and the hangman of every daybreak in her eyes

The wind from Torwana mountains
with her lap full of moss
carries a sleeping child
carries a night of thistles
carries a death without darkness

and blows through the broken reeds

Ingrid Jonker

(translated by Jack Cope and William Plomer)

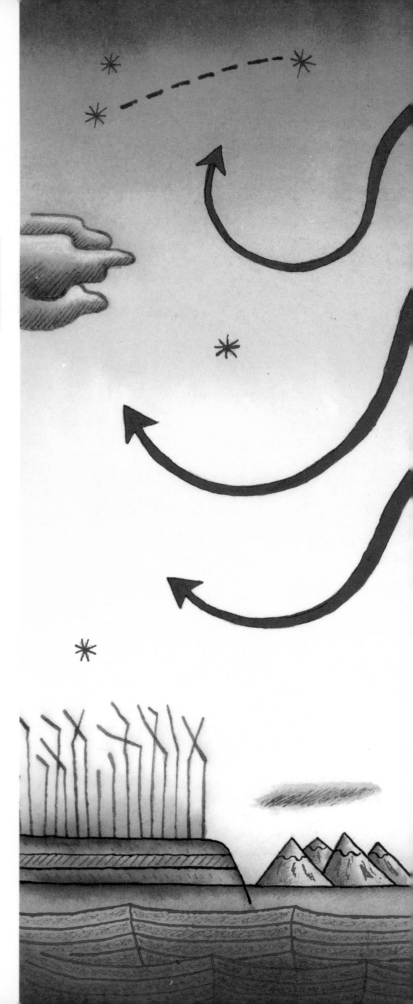

70

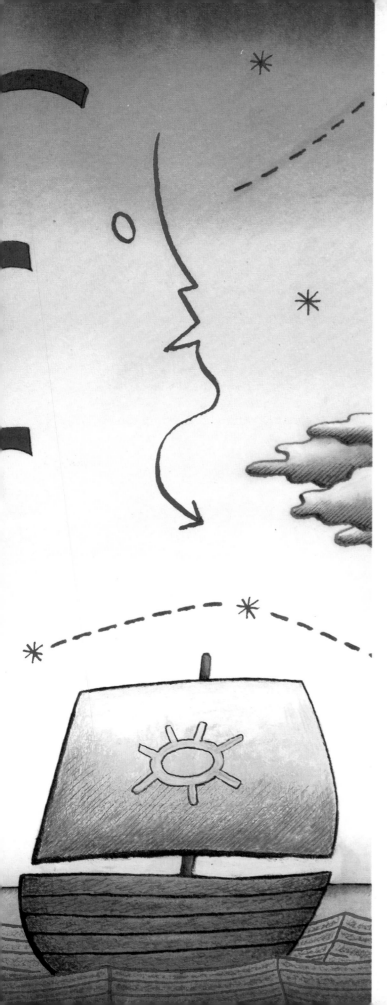

Wind

I pulled a hummingbird out of the sky one day
  but I let it go,
I heard a song and carried it with me
  on my cotton streamers
I dropped it on an ocean and lifted up a wave
  with my bare hands
I made a whole canefield tremble and bend
  as I ran by
I pushed a soft cloud from here to there
I hurried a stream along a pebbled path
I scooped up a yard of dirt and hurled it in the air,
I lifted a straw hat and sent it flying
I broke a limb from a guava tree
I became a breeze, bored and tired
and hovered and hung and rustled and lay
  Where I could.

Dionne Brand

Poetry in performance

Either individually or in a group, prepare a
presentation of one or both of these poems.
As long as ideas match the content of the
poem, you can do what you want in terms
of sound effects. But try to use your voice
to bring out the different tones in the poem.
For more about poetry in performance see
Unit 3, page 97.

For writing

Using the structure of the poem, *Wind,* make
one of the following into a person and
describe the actions that 'person' performs:

- fog
- fire
- sunlight
- frost
- hunger
- achievement
- despair

Images and feelings

In both of these poems the writers paint a word-picture of their parents. The images they use to portray them also reveal the feelings of each poet.

[handwritten annotations: driving car (circled: Boy driving), forcing (pointing to driving), sins (pointing to confession), R. Catholic church]

Boy driving his father to confession

[handwritten annotation: four pictures (pointing to Four times)]

Four times now I have seen you as another
Man, a grown-up friend, less than a father;
Four times found chinks in the paternal mail
To find you lost like me, quite vulnerable.
There was the time when my child brother died
And in the porch, among the men, you cried.
Again, last year, I was shocked at your tears
When my mother's plane took off. In twelve years
you had not been apart for one whole day
Till this long-talked-of, two week holiday:
I left you lonely at the barrier,
Was embarrassed later when you stood a beer.
The third time you made a man of me
By telling me an almost smutty story
In a restaurant toilet. We both knew
This was an unprecedented breakthrough.

Today, a sinner, and shy about it,
You asked me to drive up to church, and sit
Morose as ever, telling me to slow
On corners or for potholes that I know
As well as you do. What is going on
Under that thick grey skull? What confession
Are you preparing. Do you tell sins as I would?
Does the same hectic rage in our one blood?
Here at the churchyard I am slowing down
To meet you, the fourth time, on common ground.
You grunt, and slam the door. I watch another
Who gropes as awkwardly to know his father.

Seamus Heaney

Writing about poems

Organising your ideas and thoughts on a poem needs preparation. The following stages will help you plan and write.

1 **Reading**   Either, listen to the poems read aloud to you, or read them silently to yourself. You may want to repeat this process to clarify ideas.

2 **Recording ideas**   On the two poems above, the reader's ideas about the first lines have been recorded in the form of jottings around the poems themselves. This can be done by making a copy of the poem to work around. To help you record these ideas, a set of possible questions you could ask yourself has been included on page 74 under the heading

'Jotting around a poem'. Keep these jottings safe because you can use them in your poetry journal. They will help you chart your own progress in tackling poems. (For more on putting together your own poetry journal see page 75.)

3 **Discussion**   In pairs or in groups of 3 or 4, compare and discuss your ideas. Illustrate your point of view with examples from the poems.

4 **Structuring**   Organise your notes so you can record and write:
● your first main impressions on what the poems say and how

Praise song for my mother

You were *[handwritten: Is she dead? Is there regret there?]*
water to me
deep and bold and fathoming *[handwritten: Always break new ground – like waves on dry beach]*
[handwritten: Had many layers/sides] *[handwritten: Understood how I felt?]*
You were *[handwritten: Knowledge]*
moon's eye to me
pull and grained and mantling

You were
sunrise to me
rise and warm and streaming

You were
the fishes red gill to me
the flame trees spread to me
the crab's leg/the fried plantain smell
                    replenishing replenishing

Go to your wide futures, you said

Grace Nichols

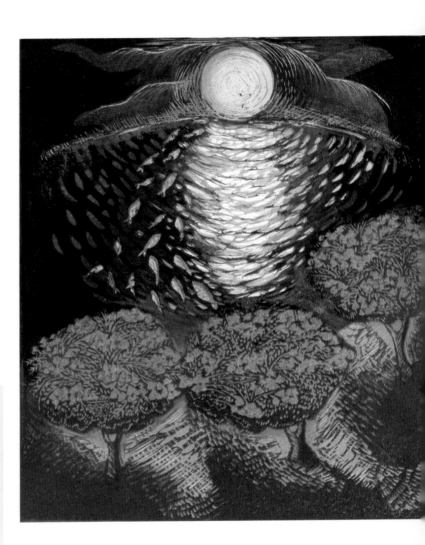

- several paragraphs on the first poem, looking at ideas in detail
- several paragraphs on the second poem, looking at ideas in detail
- paragraphs looking at similarities and contrasts
- a concluding paragraph on your preference.

5 **Drafting**: You may well go through several drafts of your notes before reaching your final version.

 For more on drafting techniques see Unit 2 in The Process of Writing module in Book 4B, pages 79-82.

Assignment

Compare the two portraits. What pictures do you have of each parent? How did they get on with their children? How did you decide this? Which piece did you prefer and why?

 Follow stages 1 to 5 opposite as you prepare this piece of writing.

Jotting around a poem

The questions below are intended as possible starting points when reading or discussing a poem. It is useful to have your own copy of the poem so that you can jot your ideas around the edge.

First impressions

◆ Listen to the poem read aloud.

◆ Do any lines or images conjure up thoughts or feelings?

◆ Do you have any questions you would like to ask?

◆ What are your first impressions?

What the poem says

◆ Does the title suggest anything to you?

◆ Who is 'speaking' in the poem?

◆ What is the speaker's attitude to the ideas raised and to you as the reader?

◆ Think of a word to suggest the mood or tone of the poem, e.g. sad, defiant.

◆ Who is the poem spoken to? Is it the world in general, the writer, you, another character?

◆ Does the poem develop an argument or a line of thought?

◆ Do the last lines make this argument clearer?

◆ What is the poem trying to do? Does it attack someone or something else? Does it describe something? Does it recall an incident or person?

How the poem works

◆ Look at the shape of the poem on the page. Is it a shape you recognise like a haiku or a sonnet?

◆ Is it split into regular verses?

◆ Does it have long or short lines? Do lines run on into each other?

◆ The poet will have deliberately chosen this shape. How does it match the poem's message?

◆ Are there any lines, words or images which you particularly like or find strange?

◆ Ring any parts of the poem that seem to form a pattern.

◆ Are any lines, words or images repeated?

◆ What is the pace of the poem? Do any words or phrases sound light or heavy and slow?

◆ Is there a lot of punctuation? Does this speed up the poem or slow it down?

◆ What do you think of the poem?

Keeping a poetry journal

One way of recording your impressions, ideas and work on the poems you have studied is to keep a poetry journal.

Here are some alternatives for how you might present material in your journal.

- Stick in the jottings you make around a poem when you first meet it.
- Underneath this you could record any questions you want to ask about the piece or note the parts that puzzle you.
- Sometimes a poem brings back to you a particular moment or memory. You could recall these memories in a short paragraph.
- As shown in the 'Poetry as picture' unit, poems can bring vivid pictures to mind; you may want to draw or stick in pictures that seem to match the piece.
- Some lines in poems are particularly moving or memorable. You could use your journal to just note these lines down.
- You could include early drafts and final drafts as you write your own poems.
- You could write down your impressions of particular lessons/activities that worked well for you.
- You can look back through the poems you have used and written and choose the ones you like best and recall why they are your particular favourites. Look back over your favourites – are there any links between them?

The journal will be your record, to be shared only if you wish to. As you collect together all your responses to different poems, you will be able to look back and reflect on progress you have made.

Poetry or prose

Often within poems there is a strong story-line which catches and engages our interest and invites us to read on. Both these poems develop a short 'story'.

Miracle on St David's Day★

*★St David Patron Saint of Wales whose Saint's day is 1st March

'They flash upon that inward eye
Which is the bliss of solitude'
        'The Daffodils' by W. Wordsworth

An afternoon yellow and open-mouthed
with daffodils. The sun treads the path
among cedars and enormous oaks.
It might be a country house, guests strolling,
the rumps of gardeners between nursery shrubs.

I am reading poetry to the insane.
An old woman, interrupting, offers
as many buckets of coal as I need.
A beautiful chestnut-haired boy listens
entirely absorbed. A schizophrenic

on a good day, so they tell me later.
In a cage of first March sun a woman
sits not listening, not seeing, not feeling.
In her neat clothes the woman is absent.
A big, mild man is tenderly led

to his chair. He has never spoken.
His labourer's hands on his knees, he rocks
gently to the rhythms of the poems.
I read to their presences, absences
to the big, dumb labouring man as he rocks.

He is suddenly standing, silently,
huge and mild, but I feel afraid. Like slow
movement of spring water or the first bird
of the year in the breaking darkness,
the labourer's voice recites 'The Daffodils'.

The nurses are frozen, alert; the patients
seem to listen. He is hoarse but word-perfect.
Outside the daffodils are still as wax,
a thousand, ten thousand, their syllables
unspoken, their creams and yellows still.

Forty years ago, in a Valleys school,
the class recited poetry by rote
Since the dumbness of misery fell
he has remembered there was a music
of speech and that once he had something to say.

When he's done, before the applause, we observe
the flowers' silence. A thrush sings
and the daffodils are flame.

Gillian Clarke

The conquerors

By sundown we came to a hidden village
Where all the air was still
And no sound met our tired ears, save
From the sorry drip of rain from blackened trees
And the melancholy sound of swinging gates.
Then through a broken pane some of us saw
A dead bird in a rushing cage, still
Pressing his thin tattered breast against the bars,
His beak wide open. And
As we hurrried through the weed-grown street
A gaunt dog started up from some dark place
And shambled off on legs as thin as sticks
Into the woods, to die at least in peace.
No one had told us victory was like this;
Not one amongst us would have eaten bread
Before he'd filled the mouth of the grey child
That sprawled, stiff as stone, before the shattered door.
There was not one who did not think of home.

Henry Treece

Piecing the story together

1 You are a relative of the big Welsh
labourer and you sit watching the recital
and scene that surrounds it. There are
parts of the story untold that may be
included in your version of it.
  • What caused this man to lose his
    voice and mind, e.g. an accident?
    war?
  • How does he react to what happens?
  • How do you, the nurses, the poet
    react?
Use your own words to describe the
setting, scenery, other patients, the poet,
the recital.
2 You are one of the 'conquerors' entering the village. That night you sit with
other soldiers around a camp fire and
write a letter home describing the village,
the scenes that affected you there and
your feelings about them.
  Again, there are parts of the story that
remain untold which you may wish to
draw out.
  • Who has entered the village?
  • Why are there no adults there?
  • What is the setting for this conquest?
  • What will happen next?

Writing a prose version

Choose the poem that makes the biggest
impact on you and write a prose version of
what happens from one of the viewpoints
suggested above. Aim for an account of
between 250 and 500 words.

Group discussion

In groups of 3 or 4, read the poem aloud
and then share your stories with each other.
1 What do you feel you have gained from
  turning the poem into a prose story?
2 What do you feel you have lost?
3 In what ways is the poem different from
  your piece of writing?
4 What has a poem got that a piece of
  prose has not?
5 Which form do you prefer?

Comparing your writing to the poems of Gillian Clarke and Henry Treece, one of the most obvious differences between the two was probably shape. A glance at a poetry anthology is enough to tell you that, like prose, poems come in all shapes and sizes. They may extend over four pages or come in four line sections; they may be two lines long or come in fourteen line blocks; lines may be long or just a few words in length. These patterns are called the poem's **form** and a poet will choose this carefully to fit his/her ideas.

But it's not just shape that we notice in a poem, it is also sound. Many poems will resonate with **rhyme**. This may be a strong rhyme at the end of lines that carries us along and helps us remember the piece; or it may be a more subtle similar sound, or repetitions within a line.

Rhyme is matched by the **rhythm** of a piece. This may be a strong regular beat such as 'rapping', or it may be fast or slow to fit with the mood of the poem.

As you look at the next verse story form – the ballad – notice how the shape, rhyme and rhythm help carry the meaning.

Ballads

Ballads are a popular form of telling stories in verse that date back to the Middle Ages. Ballads were created to be sung or told aloud, with a definite pattern of rhyme and rhythm so the singer or speaker could easily recall the story.

Stories within ballads dealt with an heroic way of life, where loyalty to family and loyalty in love were often in conflict. Each verse would depict either a vivid scene in the story or certain dialogue that carried the story along.

Read this ballad, if possible aloud, and then use the guidelines that follow to help decide what 'makes' a ballad.

Sir Patrick Spens

The king sits in Dunfermline town
Drinking the blood red wine:
'O where will I get a good sailor,
To sail this ship of mine?'

Up and spake an elder knight,
Sat at the king's right knee:
'Sir Patrick Spens is the best sailor
That ever sailed the sea.'

The king has written a braid letter
And sealed it with his hand.
And sent it to Sir Patrick Spens
Was walking on the strand.

'To Noroway, to Noroway,
To Noroway o'er the foam;
The King's own daughter of Noroway,
'Tis though must bring her home!'

The first line that Sir Patrick read
A loud loud laugh laughed he:
The next line that Sir Patrick read
The tear blinded his ee.

'O who is this has done this deed
This ill deed unto me;
To send me out this time o' the year
To sail upon the sea?

'Make haste, make haste, my merry men all,
Our good ship sails the morn.'
'O say not so my master dear,
For I fear a deadly storm.

I saw a new moon late yestere'en
With the old moon in her arm;
And if we go to sea, master,
I fear we'll come to harm.'

They had not sailed a league, a league
A league but barely three
When the sky grew dark, the wind blew loud,
And angry grew the sea.

The anchor broke, the topmast split,
T'was such a deadly storm.
The waves came over the broken ship
Till all her sides were torn.

O long, long, may the ladies sit
With their fans into their hand,
Or ere they see Sir Patrick Spens
Come sailing to the strand.

O long, long may the maidens stand
With their gold combs in their hair
Before they'll see their own dear loves
Come home to greet them there.

O forty miles off Aberdeen
'Tis fifty fathom deep.
And there lies good Sir Patrick Spens
With the Scots Lords at his feet.

Scots traditional ballad

Thinking about the poem

In pairs devise a ballad recipe. The following
questions may help you consider some key ideas.

- What has happened in the story?
- The story is told using just key incidents.
  (These break down into the following verse
  blocks: verses 1 to 3, verses 4 to 6, verses
  7 and 8, verses 9 and 10, verses 11 to 13.)
  What happens in each scene?
- What is the rhyme pattern of each verse?
- How many strong beats do you get in each line?

The ballad of Charlotte Dymond

Many ballads, particularly the 'broadside' ballads of the Seventeenth and Eighteenth centuries, told tales of terrible crimes and violence. The piece below was written by a modern poet, Charles Causley, but tells of a well-known murder that took place on Bodmin Moor, Sunday 14 April 1844.

In a groups of 5 or 6, rearrange the following verse sections to discover the full story. The first two verses have been provided for you in sequence.

1   It was on a Sunday evening
    And in the April rain
    That Charlotte went from our house
    And never came home again

    Her shawl of diamond redcloth
    She wore a yellow gown
    She carried the green gauze handkerchief
    She bought in Bodmin town.

2   Why do you sit so sadly
    Your face the colour of clay
    And with a green gauze handkerchief
    Wipe the sour sweat away?

3   I've come to take you, Matthew,
    Unto the magistrate's door.
    Come quiet now, you pretty poor boy
    And you must know what for.

4   Charlotte she was gentle
    But they found her in the flood
    Her Sunday beads among the reeds
    Beaming with her blood.

    Matthew, where is Charlotte?
    And wherefore has she flown?
    For you walked out together
    And now are come alone.

5   'She is pure,' cried Matthew,
    'as is the early dew,
    her only stain it is the pain
    That round her neck I drew!'

    'She is guiltless as the day
    She sprang forth from her mother.
    The only sin upon her skin
    Is that she loved another.'

6   And your steel heart search, Stranger,
    That you may pause and pray
    For lovers who come not to bed
    Upon their wedding day.

    But lie upon the moorland
    Where stands the sacred snow
    Above the breathing river,
    And the salt sea-winds go.

7   As Matthew turned at Plymouth
    About the tilting Hoe
    The cold and cunning constable
    Up to him did go:

8   Why do you mend your breastplate
    With a rusty needle's thread
    And fall with fears and silent tears
    Upon your single bed?

9   About her throat her necklace
    And in her purse her pay:
    The four silver shillings
    She had at Lady Day.

    In her purse four shillings
    And in her purse her pride
    As she walked out one evening
    Her lover at her side.

10   They took him off to Bodmin
    They pulled the prison bell,
    They sent him smartly up to heaven
    And dropped him down to hell.

    All through the granite kingdom
    And on its travelling airs
    Ask which of these two lovers
    The most deserves your prayers.

11   Out beyond the marshes
    Where the cattle stand,
    With her crippled lover
    Limping at her hand.

12   Charlotte walked with Matthew
    Through the Sunday mist
    Never saw the razor
    Waiting at his wrist.

13   Has she gone to Blisland
    To seek an easier place,
    And is that why your eye won't dry
    And blinds your bleaching face?

    'Take me home!' cried Charlotte,
    'I lie here in the pit!
    A red rock rests upon my breasts
    And my naked neck is split!'

14   Her skin was soft as sable
    Her eyes were wide as day,
    Her hair was blacker than the bog
    That licked her life away.

    Her cheeks were made of honey
    Her throat was made of flame
    Where all around the razor
    Had written its red name.

Thinking about the poem

When you have decided on your sequence of events, prepare a group performance of the poem for a Year 8 or Year 9 form.

There are a number of voices in this poem: Lady Barrington's (Charlotte's employer), Matthew's, Charlotte's, a narrator's, the constable's and friends'. First agree which lines are most appropriate for each character. Then, each take a part to make your group reading more dramatic.

Role play

After the performance, as a group, take on the role of the constable and answer any questions posed by the audience. Discuss what you believe has happened, explaining why the guilty party did it.

In the light of this role play, would you change the way you originally sequenced the verses?

Your own writing

1 Write the newspaper report concerning the event that appears in *The Bodmin Courier* the day after Matthew is hanged. Include quotes from witnesses, friends of Charlotte, etc.
2 Write the constable's report of the crime, outlining evidence, who he interviewed and what conclusions he reached.

A ballad recipe

Looking at these two ballads you will find they contain most of the following basic ingredients:

Ballads:
◆ usually tell a story of heroism or tragedy
◆ are broken into four line stanzas which provide short scenes for the story
◆ use dialogue that gives a picture of the character who is talking
◆ have verses with a rhyme scheme of **a b c b**
◆ have a a regular rhythm, usually with a beat pattern of **4 3 4 3** in each verse

Miss Moses

The next three pages contain factual details, a ballad and pictures that depict aspects of the life of Harriet Tubman, also known as Miss Moses, a negress, who not only escaped from slavery herself, but risked her own life to help many others to freedom.

Writing a ballad

Read through all the material and study the pictures, then either write your own version of Harriet's story as a ballad, or working in a group of 2 or 3 divide up her life story and write a series of verses that will link together to make a group ballad. You may want to collaborate on the early drafts of your verses so that in the final version they flow well.

A rhyming dictionary may help you to put the stanzas together.

Harriet Tubman   1820–1913

1820 Born to Benjamin and Harriet Ross, both slaves on a plantation in the State of Maryland in America. Her childhood was hard, since she was expected to do an adult's work in the fields, hoeing crops and chopping wood.

However, she was surrounded by slaves who discussed rebellions in other parts of the country. Often, if they learnt they had been sold and would be separated from their families, slaves would run away to freedom, although the punishment for this was torture or hanging.

1833 Harriet helped an escaping slave by obstructing the chasing overseer. He turned on her and hit her with a heavy weight, gashing her head. Throughout her life she would suffer terrible headaches and concussion because of this injury.

1840s She married a freeman, John Tubman, whose status made her more determined to escape. When she heard her sisters had been sold and it was

rumoured she had been too, she decided she had to go. She went to a white woman who had offered her help, and through her discovered a secret route or network of safe houses and people that could lead her to freedom.

Nicknamed the Underground Railroad, these routes, run by blacks and whites, carried many slaves to their freedom.

1849 Harriet reached Philadelphia in the North and freedom. Here she got a job as a cook and began to work for her family's liberty.

She joined the Vigilance Committee, a group run by free blacks and whites to help slaves escape. After memorising the routes, she made many dangerous journeys back to the slave plantations in the South to free her family and others.

Slaves knew she was near because she would sing *Go down Moses* outside their cabins and then they knew a lucky few would soon be guided to safety. When escaping mothers needed to bring babies she would dope them with a syrup mixture to keep them quiet. In addition, she carried pepper to throw bloodhounds off their scent and a gun to threaten any slave who lost his or her nerve.

Owners got so angry at her success they put a $40 000 reward on her head but she still led over three hundred slaves to safety and was never caught.

In the Civil War, where North fought South over slavery, she fought for the North, acting as spy, scout and nurse.

1913 She died in Auburn, New York on March 10th. As a sign of respect the town announced a day of mourning and erected a plaque in front of the courthouse to commemorate her bravery.

Harriet Tubman

'Miss Moses' people called her,
For she was very brave.
She opened the doors of freedom
To help the hopeful slave.

She led her folks from bondage
On many, many trips;
A gun beneath her cloak but
A prayer on her lips!

Sometimes they grew so frightened
Their bodies quaked with fears.
She nudged them with her gun and
Then wiped away their tears!

She slipped behind the Rebel lines;
A Union spy was she,
She burned their crops and freed their slaves.
Then left to set more free!

Eloise Crosby Culver

Dramatic monologue

In the poems in this section, the story of a central character will unfold as you listen to that person's spoken thoughts in what is known as a **monologue**. You can explore this dramatic form further in Unit 4, in the Media Scripts module.

Thinking about the poem

Listen to a prepared reading of *Porphyria's lover* given by a member of the class and around your own copy of the poem, note down any clues you have as to what has happened. Ask for a repeat performance if necessary.

1 In pairs, make a note of the lines that give you clues about:
   a) the background, personality and feelings of Porphyria.
   b) the background and feelings of the narrator.

2 With your partner prepare a set of questions that you can ask the narrator. These should be phrased to help you understand the background of each character more clearly; to help you understand the motives behind the narrator's actions; to help you understand his intentions and thoughts at the end of the piece.

3 Ask your questions and note down the responses given by your narrator.

4 When you have all the information you need to understand the situation, discuss the following questions in groups of 4 to 6:
   a) What is the narrator's background? Why is he so agitated at the start?
   b) What can you deduce about Porphyria's background and character?
   c) Describe the way you see their relationship.
   d) What are the narrator's feelings after Porphyria has told him of her love?
   e) Given these feelings why does he kill her?
   f) How does he feel once he has killed her?

   g) Using the clues given by his language and actions describe the narrator's character as fully as you can.

5 As a class, discuss the following issues:
   a) How far can Porphyria be held responsible for what happens?
   b) Do you accept the testimony of the narrator?

Role play

Develop a conversation that happens prior to the killing in which Porphyria explains to a friend what she gains from this relationship.

Written work

Imagine you are Porphyria's lover and write your confession for the magistrate while you are awaiting trial. Look back at the ideas you have discussed and include:
- points about you and your background
- how you committed the crime
- details of your relationship with Porphyria
- why you committed the crime
- how you feel now

Considering form

Now you have written Porphyria's lover's confession, look back at your own work and the poem.
- Which parts of the confession come from your imagination and which parts are drawn from the poem itself?
- What further information could Browning have included if this story had been written as a playscript with Porphyria's entrance as the start of the scene?
- How is dramatic monologue different from other forms of story?

Porphyria's lover

The rain set early in tonight,
The sullen wind was soon awake,
It tore the elm-tops down for spite,
And did its worst to vex the lake:
I listened with heart fit to break.
When glided in Porphyria; straight
She shut the cold out and the storm,
And kneeled and made the cheerless grate
Blaze up, and all the cottage warm;
Which done, she rose, and from her form
Withdrew the dripping cloak and shawl
And laid her soiled gloves by, untied
Her hat and let the damp hair fall
And, last, she sat down by my side
And called me. When no voice replied,
She put my arm about her waist
And made her smooth white shoulder bare.
And all her yellow hair displaced,
And, stooping, made my cheek lie there,
And spread o'er all, her yellow hair.
Murmuring how she loved me – she
Too weak, for all her heart's endeavour,
To set its struggling passions free
From pride, and vainer to dissever
And give herself to me forever.
But passion sometimes would prevail,
Nor could tonight's gay feast restrain
A sudden thought of one so pale
For love of her and all in vain:
So, she was come through wind and rain.

Be sure I looked up at her eyes
Happy and proud; at last I knew
Porphyria worshipped me; surprise
Made my heart swell, and still it grew
While I debated what to do.
That moment she was mine, mine, fair,
Perfectly pure and good: I found
A thing to do, and all her hair
In one long yellow string I wound
Three times her little throat around,
And strangled her. No pain felt she:
I am quite sure she felt no pain
As a shut bud that holds a bee,
I warily oped her lids: again
Laughed the blue eyes without a stain.
And I untightened next the tress
About her neck; her cheek once more
Blushed bright beneath my burning kiss:
I propped her head up as before
Only, this time my shoulder bore
Her head, which droops upon it still:
The smiling rosy little head,
So glad it has its utmost will,
That all it scorned at once is fled,
And I, its love, am gained instead!
Porphyria's love: she guessed not how
Her darling one wish would be heard.
And thus we sit together now,
And all night long we have not stirred,
And yet God has not said a word.

Robert Browning

Who am I?

As seen in the last poem, dramatic monologue forces the reader to do a lot of the work. In the following poems, two very different characters describe their occupations.

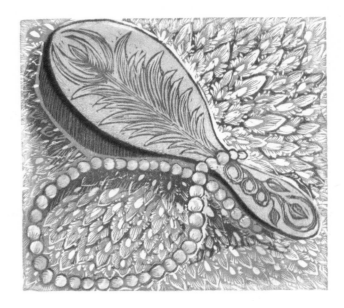

Next to my own skin, her pearls. My mistress
bids me wear them, warm them, until evening
when I'll brush her hair. At six, I place them
round her cool white throat. All day I think of her,
resting in the Yellow Room, contemplating silk
or taffetta, which gown tonight? She fans herself
whilst I work willingly, my slow heat entering
each pearl. Slack on my neck, her rope.

She's beautiful. I dream about her
in my attic bed; picture her dancing
with tall men, puzzled by my faint, persistent scent
beneath her French perfume, her milky stones.

I dust her shoulders with a rabbit's foot,
watch the soft blush seep through her skin
like an indolent sigh. In her looking glass
my red lips part as though I want to speak.

Full moon. Her carriage brings her home. I see
her every movement in my head... Undressing,
taking off her jewels, her slim hand reaching
for the case, slipping naked into bed, the way

She always does... And I lie here awake
knowing the pearls are cooling even now
in the room my mistress sleeps. All night
I feel their absence and I burn.

Carol Ann Duffy

Read each poem on your own and make a note of any information you gain on:
- the time the action takes place in terms of year/time of day
- the place(s) in which the action takes place
- the kind of world the characters live in
- the demands of their job and how they feel about what they do
- the kind of language they use

Share your ideas in a group of 4 or 5. Justify your ideas with quotations from the two poems and, based on your decision, supply a title for each poem that indicates the role of the narrators.

Writing your own

1 Without directly stating the occupation of your chosen character, write your own dramatic monologue. Remember the surroundings, actions, attitudes and the kind of language you give your narrator will give your reader hints about their background.

a) Once you have chosen the character you will write as, you could use these prompt points for each line to give you some initial images to work with.

Verse 1

Lines 1 & 2 You are looking through a window, what do you see?

Lines 3 & 4 You turn back into the room, what surrounds you?

Verse 2

Lines 5 & 6 Other people are in or enter the room – what relation are they to you?

Lines 7 & 8 How do you react to them? What do you do?

It was winter. Wilson had just said
We should have one in The Dog. So we did,
running through the blue wet streets
with our heads down, to get there,
down doubles in front of our drenched reflections.
The barmaid caught my eye in the mirror. Beautiful.

We had a job to do, but not till closing time
hard men knocking back the brandy, each of us
wearing revenge like a badge on his heart. Hatred
dresses in cheap anonymous suits, the kind
with an inside pocket for a small gun. Good Health.
I smiled at her. Warm rain, like blood, ran down my back.

I remembered my first time, my trembling hand
and Big Frank Conell hissing Get A Grip.
Tonight, professional, I walked with the boys
along a filthy alley to the other pub, the one
where it happened, the one where the man
was putting on his coat, ready for home

Home. Two weeks in a safe house and I'd be there,
glad of familiar accents and my dull wife.
He came out of a side door, clutching a carry-out.
Simple. Afterwards, Wilson was singing dada da da
Tom Someone, hang down your head and cry.
Too bad. I fancied that barmaid alright.

Carol Ann Duffy

Verse 3

Lines 9 & 10   Something happens that makes you
   remember a moment in the past, e.g., in Carol
   Ann Duffy's poem, the warm rain reminds the
   narrator of blood and his first kill.

Lines 11 & 12   You think of how you've
   changed since then, maybe for the better,
   maybe not.

Verse 4

Lines 13 & 14   You come back to the present
   and react to the people around you.

Lines 15 & 16   If you had a wish or prayer
   right now, what would it be?

b)   When you have written your responses to
   these questions, look through them to see if
   any are unnecessary words or phrases. If so,
   remove them.

c)   Decide where line endings will come
   and if you will rearrange any lines for
   greater effect. You may go through
   several drafts before arriving at your
   final version of the monologue.
   For more on drafting see Unit 1, page 68
   and Unit 3, pages 88-89.

2   To accompany your final draft write a short
   piece describing the attractions and challenges
   of this form for a writer. Considering all three
   monologues in this section and your own
   writing, discuss:

   ● what you can include in monologue
      that writers using other forms cannot
   ● what the reader has to do
   ● what information you cannot give in
      monologue

Poem as pattern

A poet's drafts

In Units 1 and 2 the images a poem can carry and the story-line it creates were considered. Looking at ballads, the patterns of rhyme, rhythm and shape that a poet can choose were also considered.

The following drafts made by W. B. Yeats as he wrote his poem *After long silence* show the notes a poet will use as they think through ideas, feelings, story-line language and pattern to reach their final form. They show his progress from an idea to a story-line and a suitable structure.

Below are printed the four drafts Yeats wrote together with the final version of the poem. ● With a partner, read through all five versions.
  ● Together, jot down the main changes you notice.
  ● Look carefully at each line of the final draft and discuss with your partner why you think the changes have been made.

After long silence

Draft 1

Subject

Your hair is white
My hair is white
Come let us talk of love
What other theme, do we know
When we were young
We were in love with one another
So And therefore ignorant

Draft 2

Those
Your other lovers being dead and gone

friendly light
hair is white
on love descant descant
Upon the sole theme supreme theme of art & song
Wherein there's theme so fitting for the aged; young
we loved each other and were ignorant

Draft 3

It
Once more I have kissed your hand & it is right—
All other lovers being estranged or dead
The heavy curtain drawn—the candle light
Waging a doubtful battle with the shade
We call our wisdom up upon our wisdom & descant discant
Upon the supreme theme of art and song
Decrepitude increases wisdom - young
We loved each other & were ignorant ignor ignorant

For discussion

1 In pairs, consider the following points:
a) How is Draft 1 different to the rest and why?
b) By the end of Draft 3 what progress has been made in terms of structure and ideas?
c) Looking at Draft 4, lines 3 and 4 of the final piece obviously gave Yeats difficulty. How do the final words he chose contribute to the whole?

Below are the annotations around the poem by GCSE student, Robert.

2 Read Robert's notes around the poem. He followed the ideas contained on 'Jotting around a poem' (see page 74) but he had not seen the earlier drafts of the piece.
a) Do your thoughts match his at any point?
b) Do you differ over any points?

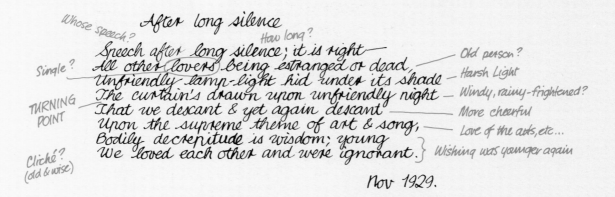

Whose speech?

After long silence

How long?

Single?
Speech after long silence; it is right — — Old person?
All other (lovers) being estranged or dead, — — Harsh Light
Unfriendly lamp-light hid under its shade — Windy, rainy-frightened?

TURNING POINT
The curtain's drawn upon unfriendly night —
That we descant & yet again descant ———— More cheerful
Upon the supreme theme of art & song, — Love of the arts, etc...
Bodily decrepitude is wisdom; young

Cliché?
(old & wise)
We loved each other and were ignorant. } Wishing was younger again

Nov 1929.

Draft 4

Un
~~The~~ friendly lamplight hidden by its shade
~~And shutters clapped upon the deepening night~~
~~The candle hidden by its friendly shade~~
Those curtains drawn upon the deepening night
~~The curtains drawn on the unfriendly night~~
That we descant & yet again descant
Upon the ~~supreme theme~~ of ~~art & song~~ art & song
Bodily decrepitude is wisdom – young

3 Now write your own appraisal of *After long silence*. Include your thoughts arising from discussion and how they compare and contrast with Robert's. You may also want to consider how looking at the drafting process helped or hindered your understanding of the poem.

Final version

After long silence

Speech after long silence; it is right —
All other lovers being estranged or dead,
Unfriendly lamp-light hid under its shade
The curtain's drawn upon unfriendly night —
That we descant & yet again descant
Upon the supreme theme of art & song,
Bodily decrepitude is wisdom; young
We loved each other and were ignorant.

Nov 1929.

89

Patterns of rhyme

The pattern of rhyme in a poem is enjoyed by readers from an early age. In nursery rhymes and limericks matching sounds are used to help readers remember the story and for comic effect.

In the following parodies of well known nursery rhymes, Roald Dahl uses rhyme to provide wit and humour.

Hey diddle diddle

Hey diddle diddle
We're all on the fiddle
And never get up until noon.
We only take cash
Which we carefully stash
And we work by the light of the moon.

Mary, Mary

Mary, Mary, quite contrary,
How does your garden grow?
'I live with my brat in a high-rise flat,
So how in the world would I know.'

Roald Dahl

Writing a parody

Remind yourself of some old nursery rhymes. Using the first line as a starting point, produce an up-to-date version introducing real-life situations. Enter these in your poetry journal.

Another form that combines wit with short story and rhyme is the limerick.

Each night father fills me with dread
When he sits at the foot of my bed
I'd not mind that he speaks
In gibbers and squeaks
But for seventeen years he's been dead.

There was a young man name of Fred,
Who spent every Thursday in bed;
He lay with his feet
Outside of the sheet,
And the pillows on top of his head.

Roger McGough

Taking a closer look

1 You have probably come across favourites of your own. Using anthologies find 2 or 3 limericks that appeal to you and enter them in your poetry journal.
2 Now in a group of 3 or 4 share your limericks.
3 Imagine you had never heard a limerick before. As a group devise a limerick recipe to explain to someone how it works. For example, what about rhyme, shape, number of lines, number of beats in a line and subject matter?
4 Pool your ideas as a class.

More points for the limerick recipe

◆ With a limerick you show that lines 1, 2 and 5 rhyme by labelling them **a**. Lines 3 and 4 share a different rhyme so we label them **b**. This is called the **rhyme scheme** and in this case is **a a b b a**.

◆ How many syllables in each line?

◆ Read your limerick aloud and notice which words you stress. Now try writing out your limerick. Where a syllable is stressed or heavy put a dash ∕ and where it is light or soft put ◡.

⠀⠀⠀⠀◡⠀⠀◡⠀⠀∕⠀⠀◡⠀⠀◡⠀⠀∕⠀⠀◡⠀⠀◡⠀⠀◡⠀⠀∕
⠀⠀There was a young man name of Fred

This rhythm or pattern of stress is called **metre**.

Write out your full limerick recipe in your journal

The following limericks won commendations in *The Observer* 'Great Green Limericks Competition'. As a class, use the same 'green' theme and write your own limericks. Make a display of these and ask a panel of staff and/or pupils to judge them.

Said the seal to the salmon and otters,
'Did God really design us as blotters
To mop up the oil
From the sea and the soil
Spewed out by these corporate rotters?'

Said a woman about to give birth,
'Put his name down for Friends of the Earth.
He must learn to think green,
Keep the waterways clean,
And know what the ozone is worth.'

Full rhyme and half rhyme

Not all rhymes within a poem are as strong or obvious as the **full rhymes** used in limericks and nursery rhymes. While full rhymes match each other in terms of sound, **half rhymes** have just some letters which sound the same.

So while a full rhyme would be 'bread' and 'head', a half rhyme would be 'bread' and 'break' which has *some* sounds in common, the *br* sound and the *ea* sound.

Create a list of words that link in terms of half rhyme. Either continue the chain started by the four words below or make up a half rhyme chain of you own.

⠀⠀Stir⠀⠀⠀⠀⠀⠀Star⠀⠀⠀⠀⠀⠀Armour⠀⠀⠀⠀⠀⠀Mourning

In the two poems on page 92, one piece uses a mixture of half rhyme and full rhyme and the other uses just full rhyme. The poet has deliberately chosen the rhyme pattern to match the story she is relating and the ideas she wants to convey.

Choose one word from each group below and fill in the blanks on your own copies of the poems. In each case consider which word is most suitable for the story and pattern of the poem.

The enemies

Last night they came across the river and
Entered the city. Women were awake
With lights and food. They entertained the band,
Not asking what the men had come to _____
Or what _____ tongue they spoke
Or why they came so suddenly through the land.

Now in the morning all the town is filled
With stories of the swift and _____ invasion;
The women say that not one stranger _____
A reason for his coming. The intrusion
Was not for _____:
Peace is apparent still on hearth and _____.

Yet all the city is a ____ place
Man meeting man speaks _____. Old friends
_____ up the candid looks upon their face
There is no _____ in hands accepting hands;
Each ponders 'Better hide myself in _____
Those strangers have set up their _____ in minds
I used to _____ in. Better draw the _____
Even if the strangers haunt in my own house.

Elizabeth Jennings

1 homes	6 steal	10 blinds
2 haunted quiet desolate	take devour	curtains shutters
3 live walk	7 gain devastation ruin	11 case
		12 close shut lock
4 gave told revealed	8 foreign strange hostile	13 quietly cautiously
5 terrible dark ghastly	9 love warmth	14 doorstep green field

1 eyes smiles	4 sighs sings	6 kept preserved developed
2 sentences letters	5 thought awe kindness	7 glances kisses
3 giving friendship		

Friendship

Such love I cannot analyse;
It does not rest in lips or _____,
Neither in _____ or caress.
Partly, I know, it's gentleness

And understanding in one word
Or in brief ____. It's _____
By trust and by respect and ____
These are the words I'm feeling for.

Two people, yes, two last friends
The _____ comes, the taking ends.
There is no measure for such things.
For this all Nature slows and _____.

Elizabeth Jennings

When you have chosen the words you consider most suitable for each blank, note down the rhyme schemes used in each poem, indicating where half rhyme occurs by underlining the letter(s) in red.

Group discussion

Read the original poems and consider the following questions in a group of 3 or 4.
1 What has happened in the city where *The enemies* takes place?
2 What is disturbing about this event?
3 Who is recalling the incident?
4 'Man meeting man speaks cautiously'. What do you notice about the words and language used to tell this story?
5 In your groups write a short scripted conversation between 3 or 4 women of the city after the invasion. Do they all want to help the soldiers? What do they fear?
6 Role play a conversation between two old friends before the invasion and the same meeting after the invasion. How would their language change?
7 Using examples from your own experience, compile a list of seven or eight qualities that you feel are important in a friend. Rank these qualities from most to least important and work to reach a consensus on this.
8 From your reading of *Friendship*, what does Elizabeth Jennings consider both important and unimportant about this sort of relationship? Make a note of these.
9 Where does your list differ from the poet's and where is it similar?

Considering form

Both full and half rhyme was used in *The enemies* but only full rhyme in *Friendship*. Having looked at both poems in detail, discuss as a class why you think the poet chose these different patterns. What contribution do they make to the overall meaning of both pieces?

For writing

1 Write the following as an inhabitant of the city invaded in *The enemies*.
  a) A diary entry in which you describe the effect of the invasion on yourself, your friends and family, day-to-day life. Fill in missing detail concerning who the invaders are and why they have come.
  b) A letter to your friend outside which is liable to be censored by the invaders. Again touch on the above details but with care.

Compare and contrast

Compare and contrast the two poems looking at both the subjects raised and the way in which the pieces are written.
  Prepare for this by making jottings around both poems considering the areas discussed above.
  In your final write up, you may find the following structure useful:
● a first paragraph looking at the key ideas and patterns in both poems
● several paragraphs that consider the first poem in detail
● several paragraphs that consider the second piece in detail
● a section that looks at differences of message and style
● a section that looks at similarities of message and style
● your preferences and reasons for them

Internal rhyme

Rhyme does not have to come at the end of a line. Poets will often repeat distinctive sounds within a line, or over several lines to create a particular mood or atmosphere.

For example, in the poem below, Wilfred Owen captures the terrible conditions that faced soldiers in the trenches in The First World War. Here, they are assaulted by both the enemy and the weather.

As you read or listen, note down particular words, phrases or lines that convey the harsh, freezing and demoralizing conditions.

Exposure

Our brains ache in the merciless iced east winds that knive us ...
Wearied we keep awake because the night is silent ...
Low, drooping flares confuse our memories of the salient ...
Worried by silence, sentries whisper, curious, nervous,
     But nothing happens.

Watching, we hear the mad gusts tugging on the wire
Like twitching agonies of men among its brambles.
Northward, incessantly the flickering gunnery rumbles
Far off, like a dull rumour of some other war
     What are we doing here?

The poignant memory of dawn begins to grow ...
We only know war lasts, rain soaks, and clouds sag stormy.
Dawn massing in the east her melancholy army
Attacks once more on shivering ranks of grey,
     But nothing happens.

Sudden successive flights of bullets streak the silence.
Less deathly than the air that shudders black with snow.
With sidelong flowing flakes that flock, pause and renew;
We watch them wandering up and down the wind's nonchalance,
     But nothing happens.

Pale flakes with fingering stealth come flickering for our faces –
We cringe in holes, back on forgotten dreams, and stare, snowdazed,
Deep into grassier ditches. So we drowse, sun-dozed,
Littered with blossoms trickling where the blackbird fusses,
     Is it that we are dying?

Slowly our ghosts drag home: glimpsing the sunk fires, glozed
With crusted dark-red jewels; crickets jingle there;
For hours the innocent mice rejoice: the house is theirs;
Shutters and doors all closed: on us the doors are closed –
     We turn back to our dying.

Since we believe not otherwise can kind fires burn
Nor ever suns smile true on child, or field, or fruit.
For God's invincible spring our love is made afraid;
Therefore, not loath, we lie out here; therefore were born
      For love of God seems dying.

Tonight, His frost will fasten on this mud and us
Shrivelling many hands, puckering foreheads crisp.
The burying party, picks and shovels in their shaking grasp,
Pause over half-known faces. All their eyes are ice,
      But nothing happens.

Wilfred Owen

Looking at internal rhyme

In your poetry journal note down the impression of the trenches conveyed by these phrases and words:

- 'the merciless iced east winds that knive us…'
- 'Worried by silence, sentries whisper, curious, nervous,'
- 'gunnery rumbles/Far off,'
- 'rain soaks, and clouds sag stormy'
- 'the air that shudders black with snow'

Alexander Pope wrote 'The sound must seem an echo to the sense.' Here Owen is using the combined sounds of words to convey the sense of cold, nerves and desolation. If you look back at the five quotes on page 95 you will find that:

1 The repeated 'i' and 'e' vowel sounds convey a sense of viciousness and savagery in the first quote. This repetition of vowel sounds in the middle of words is called **assonance**.

2 The repeated 's' consonant sounds at the start and in the middle of words in the second quote mimic the nervous whispers of the men. This repetition of consonants is known as **consonance**.

3 The words 'rumbles' and 'shudders' in the third and fifth quotes echo the sounds they describe. This technique is called **onomatopoeia**.

4 The repeated 's' sounds at the start of words in the fourth quote slow down the piece and convey a mood of stasis and gloom. This repetition of the same letter at the start of a word is known as **alliteration**.

Sound echoing sense

● Read through the poem again and try to find your own examples of these terms and describe the mood or idea conveyed.
● Look at the end of lines in the poem and note down the rhyme scheme. Why do you think Owen uses this pattern?
● In the poem, the gunnery rumbles, bullets streak past, a burying party works and yet the line 'But nothing happens' is repeated four times. What is Owen suggesting here?
● Trace the soldier's feelings about the front line, God and home. What do the following lines suggest?
    'Since we believe not otherwise can kind fires burn...we lie out here'
    'What are we doing here?'
    'We only know war lasts'
    'For love of God seems dying./Tonight, His frost will fasten on this mud and us'
    'on us the doors are closed – /We turn back to our dying.'
● Share your observations and jottings in a group of 3 or 4 and discuss your feelings and thoughts on the poem.

For writing

1 If this poem has made an impact on you, write as fully as you can about it and the feelings it arouses in you. Begin by developing detailed notes around the poem that incorporate your ideas as discussed above. Try to include observations on the poet's use of internal and end rhyme, his mood and the attitude of his narrator, the soldier.

2 Write a letter home from a soldier recently arrived at the front line. The photographs on pages 94 and 95 will provide ideas. Try, as Owen has, to evoke the sense of conditions through the sounds of the words you use. Before you start, read the following poems by Owen to give you further ideas: *Strange meeting, Dulce et decorum est* and *Anthem for doomed youth*.

For more on the First World War see the Forms of Narrative module, pages 42-43 and the Knowledge about Language module in Book 4B, pages 57-58.

Assignment

When a poem is read aloud, the sound of various phrases, the emphasis given by rhyme, the tone of voice and the pauses used can give the listener a much clearer understanding of the piece.

Below are a selection of possible poems that work well in performance. Choose one of the following, or select another that appeals to you, and prepare a reading.

Fern hill – Dylan Thomas
Skating – William Wordsworth: *The Prelude*
Spring – Gerard Manley Hopkins
Digging – Seamus Heaney
Churning day – Seamus Heaney
Blackberry picking – Seamus Heaney
Anthem for doomed youth – Wilfred Owen
The naming of parts – Henry Reed

Bear in mind these points when planning your reading.
- The tone of the poem and whether or not this varies.
- The punctuation; use commas, full stops, dashes and exclamation marks to help your interpretation.
- If there is no pause at the end of a verse or line, read on without a pause.
- Use examples of alliteration, assonance and consonance for stress and use your voice to convey the feeling suggested.
- Use examples of rhyme if they appear to emphasise certain words.
- Is the pace fast or slow? Build this into your reading.

It may help if you write in interpretation notes around your chosen poem to remind you of how you wanted to read each section. The example below provides a guideline for interpretation notes. The extract describes the dramatic moment when Sir Gawain beheads the Green Knight in a modern version of the poem, *Sir Gawain and the green knight*, from Chaucer's period.

- Once you have made your own interpretation notes, record your performance on tape.
- Using your notes write about your understanding of the poem in terms of mood, themes and style.
- Hand in all three pieces as part of the assignment: the notes, the recording and your interpretation written as a critical piece.

Use k and o sounds - long and slow   Pause

Each action should be read slowly

Regretful

Gathers speed gradually
Sound 's' for emphasis

Tone of finality
Emphasise brown of blade

The green knight now kneels down, now lies upon the floor, — *Sound 'l'*
Lowers his head a little, and the white flesh displays. — *Continue to next line*
His lovely long locks he lays over his crown — *'n' sound for alliteration – harsh*
To let his naked neck show to the knight. — *Pause at end of line*
Gawayn grips his great axe and gathers to the swing, — *Gather speed through 'g' sound*
Puts his left foot forward on the floor for balance, — *Pause*
Lets it swing swiftly down, sees it land on the skin — *Vicious, harsh*
So the champion's sharp edge sheared the bone,
And sank through the soft flesh and split it in two,
Till the blade of brown steel bit into the ground: — *Drop voice at end*
The head from its place pitched to the floor.

Whole line slow and low   Jerky, sharp – like action

The whole piece should build in tension. Use punctuation to hold the audience on the edge of their seat. Need to infuse a note of regret/waste in whole piece. End low and slow for pathos.

Syllabic verse

One other pattern poets often use to shape their ideas is a **syllable pattern**, where the number of syllables in each line is fixed. The best known form of this kind is the Japanese Haiku which you may have come across before. The beauty of this pattern is its simplicity and the vivid picture it paints. Here is a reminder of how it works.

◆ A haiku has three lines.
◆ Line one has five syllables, line two has seven, and line three has five.
◆ It tries to capture a mood or express an emotion.
◆ It cuts out all unnecessary words.
◆ The mood is often suggested by a clear picture and/or comparison.

Because of translation from Japanese to English it is often difficult to make syllable count exact. This is the case in some of the following haiku snapshots. Put your favourites in your journal and try and explain why you like them.

The weeping willow

How strong a green
are the strings of willow branches;
the flowing of a stream

Parting

For me who go
For you who stay
Two autumns

Spring

They have the guise
Of being married just today –
Two butterflies

Constancy

Though it be broken
Broken again – still it's there:
The moon on the water.

City people

Towns folk it is plain –
carrying red maple leaves
in the homebound train

It kills people
This kind of mushroom –
Of course it's pretty

Issa

Writing your own haiku

Practise using syllable count by writing two or three haiku of your own.

Aim at creating a precise picture that conveys the mood or feeling you want to show.

The Japanese illustrate their work with prints like the ones shown here. These may give you some ideas.

Single haiku are good practice but now try and extend your initial idea in a haiku sequence – a series of haiku linked by a common theme. This has been done before with the seasons. Below are single haiku by Japanese writers which have been linked in a sequence:

Life-line

Handing back the baby
The wet-nurse finds
Her lap feels empty.

Gathering water-oats
The boy half-asleep
Rowing his boat

Her summer kimono
Loose, untied
Yet somehow trim

A father at last
Like a lizard,
Stopping, starting, stopping.

Water mirror:
Making you suspect
Your own face a bit.

In the old man's eyes
The piercing sun
Looks fuddled.

Like dust swirling
At the height of winter
News of his death.

Group writing

Create your own haiku sequence in a group of 3 or 4, with each person contributing two haiku.

1 Decide on your theme:
   ● months of the year
   ● stages in life
   ● moments from history
2 Agree which people will deal with which part of your theme.
3 Sequence your ideas.
4 Put finished sequences in your own anthologies.

Writing tanka

A natural extension of the haiku form is the tanka. This form is made up of the following pattern of syllables:

Line 1 = 5 syllables
Line 2 = 7 syllables
Line 3 = 5 syllables
Line 4 = 7 syllables
Line 5 = 7 syllables

In old Japanese literary circles, it was the custom to give a haiku to a close friend as a way of sharing your vision of the world around you. The friend would add two additional seven syllable lines to respond to the idea, thus creating a shared poem.

Beyond the back door
Nothing to see
Cold, chilling:
Clouded sun leaning
On withered reeds.

At the roadside
Where a clear stream bubbles
In the shade of the willows.
'Just for a while,' I said,
And still have not gone.

Share a haiku you have written with a partner. Exchange poems and create a tanka for your own collection. Your response should:
● consist of two lines of seven syllables attached to the first three lines
● respond to or develop the first idea

Free verse

Many writers, particularly those of the Twentieth century, have not wanted the restrictions of a regular rhyme scheme or a syllable count. This does not mean, however, that their work is devoid of any kind of pattern. In the pieces that follow, poets use the patterns of repetition, image and shape to help reflect their ideas

I Repetition

The American poet, Walt Whitman was the pioneer of free verse. Read the piece by him below.

I sit and look out

I sit and look out upon all the sorrows of the world, and upon
all oppression and shame.
I hear the secret convulsive sobs from the young men at anguish with
themselves, remorseful after deeds done,
I see in low life the mother misused by her children, dying
neglected, gaunt, desperate,
I see the wife misused by her husband, I see the treacherous
seducer of young women,
I mark the ranklings of jealousy and unrequited love attempted
to be hid, I see these sights on earth.
I see the workings of battle, pestilence, tyranny, I see martyrs
and prisoners,
I observe famine at sea, I observe sailors casting lots who
shall be killed to preserve the lives of the rest,
I observe the slights and degradations cast by arrogant persons
upon labourers, the poor, and upon Negroes, and the like;
All these – all the meaness and agony without end I sitting
look out upon
See, hear, and am silent.

Walt Whitman

Although this poem does not have obvious patterns of rhyme, there is a strong rhythm set up by:
● the repetition of 'I' at the start of lines and within them
● the building up in list form of all the wrongs of the world
● the heavy tone set up by the long sound of words like 'remorseful', 'gaunt', and 'oppression'

Writing your own
Use the pattern of the Whitman piece to develop your 'free verse' version of the world as you see it.
1 Collect clippings from papers and colour supplements on world events as material for your 'I sit and look out'.
2 Arrange these as a collage like the one on page 67.
3 Study the details in your collage and use these to create lines on what you: see, observe, hear, mark, look out on and feel.
4 Use strong opening and closing lines to help 'frame' the poem and create your rhythm through the patterns already mentioned.

II Patterns of imagery

Sometimes a central image or comparison can run through a piece of free verse, linking verses and lines together.

The poem below has been printed out of sequence. With a partner, read through all the numbered sections and decide which order you think they should go in. When you are satisfied with your solution, compare your completed piece with another pair's and justify your choices.

Bedtime stories

1   But I became impatient
    discovered the thrill of speed
    rejected his slow
    unfolding of words
    with all the extra meaning it could bring

2   Travelling for the love of it
    we would never hesitate
    to stop and look around us
    change direction
    start afresh

3   journeyed far and journeyed fast
    missed much
    saw much

4   He reads to my sister now
    and sometimes
    a world-weary nomad
    I sneak into her room
    and lie curled up on the floor

5   made my own way

6   Together we had the main roads
    and the less trod paths:
    With him I learned
    to use the signposts
    read the maps

7   I wanted to set my own pace
    plan my own route

8   We were company

9   At night we were wanderers
    through a world of words

10   Slowly we drifted apart
    went our separate ways
    we travelled together
    less often
    and then not at all

11   In companionable silence

12   I became a solitary explorer.

Jenny Moy

What do you think?

In your pair discuss the following.
- As a reader, what does the poet compare herself to?
- Using this image, explain how her relationship with her father changes.

For writing

With your partner, prepare a scripted conversation between father and daughter now she has grown up. They are looking back at *Bedtime stories* and discussing happy memories and perhaps regrets.

On your own, write up your final version after deciding what areas you want to cover. You could include stories from your own experience as examples of the ones told to the daughter.

III Shape in free verse

In free verse a poet can choose the length of
each line and the overall shape of the verses he
uses. Look carefully at this picture and then read
the poem.

Orchids

They lean over the path
Adder-mouthed,
Swaying close to the face,
Coming out, soft and deceptive,
Limp and damp, delicate as a young bird's tongue,
Their fluttering fledgeling lips
Move slowly,
Drawing in the warm air.

And at night,
The faint moon falling through white-washed glass,
The heat going down
So their musky smell comes even stronger,
Drifting down from their mossy cradles:
So many devouring infants!
Soft luminescent fingers
Lips neither dead nor alive,
Loose ghostly mouths
Breathing.

Theodore Roethke

Taking a closer look

In the piece above, sound, imagery, detail and
shape combine to convey the author's impression
of orchids. On your own, make notes on the
following ideas.

1 Using evidence from the poem, decide where
   the orchids are.
2 The orchids are compared to several things.
   Use the following lines to work out these
   comparisons and explain the similarity:
   - 'Adder-mouthed
     Swaying close to the face,'
   - 'Limp and damp, delicate as a young bird's
       tongue,
       Their fluttering fledgeling lips...'
   - 'So many devouring infants!'
   - 'Loose ghostly mouths'
3 Why has Roethke made line length vary as
   he has? Why are short lines followed by
   longer ones?
4 What impression does the poet give of this
   flower?
5 How does he use sound to underline this
   impression?

In a pair, discuss the way Roethke combines
the shape, imagery and the sound of the poem
to describe an orchid.

Comparing patterns

Below are two poems in which the writers describe their grandmothers. The first is written in free verse, and the second is structured around a regular verse pattern and rhyme scheme. Read the two pieces through.

For my grandmother knitting

There is no need they say
but the needles still move
their rhythms in the working of your hands
as easily
as if your hands
were once again those sure and skilful hands
of the fisher girl

You are old now
and your grasp of things is not so good
but master of your moments then
deft and swift
you slit the still-ticking quick silver fish
Hard work it was too
of necessity.

But now they say there is no need
as the needles move
in the working of your hands
once the hands of a bride
with the hand-span waist
once the hands of the miner's wife
who scrubbed his back
in a tin bath by the coal fire
Once the hands of the mother of
six who made do and mended
scraped and slaved slapped sometimes
when necessary

But now they say there's no need
the kids they say grandma
have too much already
more than they can wear
too many scarves and cardigans
gran you do too much
there's no necessity.

At your window you wave
them goodbye Sunday
with your painful hands
big on shrunken wrists
swollen-jointed. Red. Arthritic. Old.
But the needles still move
their rhythms in the working of your hands
easily
as if your hands remembered
of their own accord the pattern
as if your hands had forgotten
how to stop.

Liz Lochhead

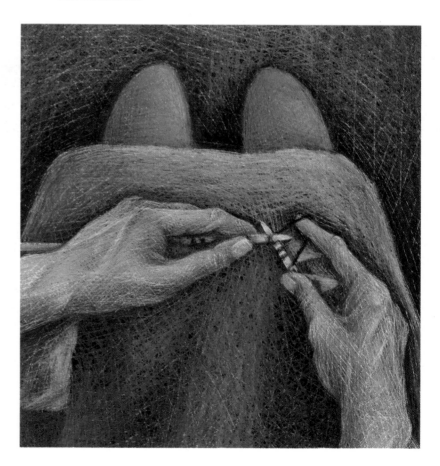

My grandmother

She kept an antique shop – or it kept her.
Among Apostle spoons and Bristol glass,
The faded silks, the heavy furniture,
She watched her own reflections in the brass
Salvers and silver bowls, as if to prove
Polish was all, there was no need of love.

And I remember how I once refused
To go out with her, since I was afraid.
It was perhaps a wish not to be used
Like antique objects. Though she never said
That she was hurt, I still could feel the guilt
Of that refusal, guessing how she felt.

Later, too frail to keep a shop, she put
All her best things in one long narrow room.
The place smelt old, of things too long kept shut
The smell of absences where shadows come
That can't be polished. There was nothing then
To give her own reflection back again.

And when she died I felt no grief at all
Only the guilt of what I once refused.
I walked into her room among the tall
Sideboards and cupboards – things she never used
but needed: and no finger marks were there,
Only the new dust falling through the air.

Elizabeth Jennings

For my grandmother knitting

Note down your thoughts on the following.
1 In your own words describe the grandmother's past.
2 How does Liz Lochhead link these different incidents?
3 As well as a linking image, certain lines and phrases are repeated. Why has the writer chosen to repeat these lines?
4 In your own words describe the poet's feelings for her grandmother. Choose one or two phrases from the poem to help you do this.
5 Why will the grandmother's hands not stop?

My grandmother

Make notes on the following.
1 What details stand out for the poet when she recalls her grandmother?
  ● 'Side-boards and cupboards – things she never used but needed:'

Why were the old lady's antiques so important to her?
2 In your own words describe the poet's feelings towards her grandmother? You may want to pick out some phrases from the poem like:
  ● 'I was afraid.
    It was perhaps a wish not to be used
    Like antique objects.'
  ● 'I still could feel the guilt'
3 In this poem the poet uses full rhyme and half rhyme at the ends of lines. What effect does this have?
Having made your own notes, in a group of 3 or 4 people, discuss the similarities and differences between the poets' feelings about their grandmothers and their different styles of describing them.

Assignments

1 Look back at the section on dramatic monologue on page 84 and read
   A cream cracker under the settee by Alan Bennett in the Media Scripts module, page 154. Reread your notes on one of the two grandmothers studied above and write your own monologue from their point of view.
   a) Try to include the following details:
      ● how they spend their day
      ● the thoughts that go through their minds about their past
      ● thoughts about their family and visitors
      ● what they can see from their windows
      ● worries and fears
   b) Use the Alan Bennett script as a model for layout and write in directions for the speaker.
   c) If you are pleased with your piece prepare it for performance to the class or tape record it to go with your written piece.
2 Compare and contrast the two portraits of the grandmothers in the poems by Liz Lochhead and Elizabeth Jennings.
   a) In what ways are their lives and personalities different? What do they have in common?
   b) Contrast the different styles of writing in both pieces and comment on which piece you prefer and why.
   For more on old age see the Media Scripts module, pages 159-163.

Relative values

The poems and suggestions that follow can be combined to form an autobiographical portfolio of both prose and free verse. Focus on events and particular people and develop ideas in your poetry journal from jottings to notes into free verse through a series of drafts. To remind yourself of the drafting process turn back to the Judith Nicholls poem on page 68.

You might also like to include some of the work you do in Unit 1 of the Forms of Narrative module, which looks at other autobiographical forms.

I A frozen moment

The two poems that follow focus on a moment particularly vivid for the poet. The first is based on a memory, the second on a photograph. As you read, write down any lines you find particularly vivid. In this piece the poet 'freezes' a moment with his young daughter.

Full moon and little Frieda

A cool small evening shrunk to a dog bark and the clank of a bucket –

And you listening.
A spider's web, tense for the dew's touch.
A pail lifted, still and brimming – mirror
To tempt a first start to tremor.

Cows are going home in the lane there, looping the hedges
                    with their warm wreaths of breath –
A dark river of blood, many boulders,
Balancing unspilled milk.

'Moon!' you cry suddenly. 'Moon! Moon!'

The moon has stepped back like an artist gazing amazed at a work
That points at him amazed.

Ted Hughes

In the second poem, a photograph of her father brings back strong feelings for the poet.

On finding an old photograph

Yalding 1912. My father
in an apple orchard, sunlight
patching his stylish bags;

three women dressed in soft
white blouses, skirts that brush the ground;
a child with curley hair.

If they were strangers
it would calm me – half drugged
by the atmosphere – but it does more –

eases a burden
made of all his sadness
and the things I didn't give him.

There he is, happy, and I am unborn.

Wendy Cope

Thinking about the poems

In a pair compare:
● the settings of the two poems
● the feelings evoked in the writer
Share the lines you found most effective and explain why.

Your own frozen moment

1 To call up special memories from your past, assemble a memory bag of four or five objects that evoke strong feelings about events in the past. These may be photographs, a letter, jewellery, a ticket, a map, an item of clothing.

2 In groups of 3 or 4 share your special objects. Group members should select one object from each person's collection and ask them to talk for a few minutes about it.

3 Following your talk, make some rough jottings that describe the time, place, event and your feelings linked to your object. Use your five senses to make this vivid.

4 Now pick out the lines you feel are most striking and start to arrange them in a logical order. Add in any more lines that you think of at this stage and introduce comparisons.

5 Write out a draft copy and share it with a partner. Build up each others' pieces by identifying your favourite parts and commenting on areas that need more work.

6 Take your own piece back and look back at the free verse patterns examined on pages 100-102. Have you repeated any lines or images? Have you used sound in your writing? Consider the shape of your piece. Where will lines begin and end? If it seems appropriate, incorporate some of these techniques in your poem.

7 After negotiation with a partner or teacher, try a final draft.

8 If you are pleased with the piece, you may want to include a prose accompaniment explaining your thoughts at each stage of the poem's development.

II Different worlds

In the following poem a boy compares his childhood in a busy, cold London to the childhood of his parents, brought up in Jamaica, evoking two different worlds.

Mum, dad and me

My parents grew up among palm trees,
in sunshine strong and clear.
I grow in weather that's pale,
misty, watery or plain cold,
around back streets of London.

Dad swam in warm sea, at my age.
I swim in a roofed pool.
Mum – she still doesn't swim.

Mum went to an open village market
at my age. I go to a covered
arcade one with her now.
Dad works most Saturdays.

At my age Dad played
cricket with friends.
Mum helped her mum, or
talked shouting halfway up a hill
Now I read or talk on the phone.

With her friends Mum's mum washed
clothes on a river stone. Now
washing machine washes our clothes
We save time to eat to watch TV
never speaking.

My dad longed for a freedom in Jamaica
I want a greater freedom
Mum prays for us, always.

Mum goes to church
some evenings and Sundays.
I go to the library
Dad goes for his darts at the local.

Mum walked everywhere at my age.
Dad rode a donkey.
Now I take a bus
Or catch the underground train.

James Berry

Thinking about different worlds

1 With a partner, devise a set of questions you could ask someone from a different country or generation about how life was different from yours when they were your age. Ask questions that will encourage them to describe their life-style in detail. Here are some areas you could consider.

 ● Housing: where did they live and did they have as much space as your family do?
 ● Schooling: what did they learn and when did they leave?
 ● Fashion: what kind of clothing was popular?
 ● Money: what did they spend their money on and how did they earn it?
 ● Time: how did they spend leisure time then?
 ● Transport: how did they get from one place to another?
 ● Holidays: where did they go and when?
 ● Plans: what were their plans in life?

2 When you have decided on your questions, arrange them in a logical order and discuss the way you will open your interview. How will you explain what you are doing and the information you are looking for?

3 Think about who you are going to interview. Will it be a relative, a friend or someone from your neighbourhood? Approach them to see if they are willing to talk to you.

4 Conduct the interview, if possible taping it.

5 Using either your tape of the interview or your written record of it, note down the most interesting differences between your two worlds.

6 On your own, look back at the James Berry poem and begin to draft several verses that begin with your interviewee's world, and then contrast this with your own world.

7 Bring in images and repetition to shape your idea and discuss your piece with your partner. Agree on any changes to be made.

8 Write a final draft considering where you will begin and end lines.

III Different views

The following poems explore the relationship between 'sisters'.
Read both pieces through.

Sistahs

...And four five six
different coloured black
women gathered together
to share
our treasures.
We sat in a ring
We put food in the middle
We started around.

Each gave
We were there –
not in our shyness
not in our histories
not in keeping any games up
Each gave
her utter presence that
rare bird that alights
once in a black full dark blood moon.

Each gave
complete hearing –
We heard so hard
We were in danger of becoming one
Letting each other in
was exciting
we were excited
and bubbling
– connected.

We talked black-woman-talk
all the different sides of it
We were so loud
we laughed
     slapped thighs
     hooted and chortled
into the night.

We spoke the words
our mothers divided
     insane
     drunk and
     silenced
could not speak,
– boy we had centuries of
catchin' up to do.

Letting us share their pain
     and questions upon questions
     never asked –
they were watching us
sitting right behind us
slightly bewildered
a bit shocked ...
but smiling in their hearts.

Gabriela Pearse

Poem for my sister

My little sister likes to try my shoes
To strut in them,
admire her spindle thin twelve year old legs
in this season's styles.
She says they fit her perfectly
but wobbles
on their high heels, they're
hard to balance

I like to watch my little sister
playing hopskotch, admire the neat hop and
  skips of her,
their quick peck
never missing their mark, not
over-stepping the line.
She is competent at peever.

I try to warn my little sister
about unsuitable shoes,
point out my own distorted feet, the callouses
odd patches of hard skin.
I should not like to see her
in my shoes.
I wish she should stay
sure-footed,
       sensibly shod.

Liz Lochhead

What do you think?

In a group of 3 or 4 discuss the following:
1 How do the two poets here feel about their
 'sisters'? What qualities do these
 relationships share and how do they differ?
2 If the first poem had been about 'brothers'
 talking together, what issues do you think
 they would discuss and how? Would they be
 similar to the issues the women choose in
 Sistahs?

Writing your own

1 Taking the words brother, sister, mother,
 father in their widest sense to include close
 friends or people from your community,
 choose someone, or a group of people, you
 know very well.
In *Poem for my sister* Liz Lochhead uses a
technique she also uses in *For my grandmother
knitting*. In the first poem she concentrates on
her sister's feet and the way they reflect her
character, and in the second she concentrates
on her grandmother's hands. In both, she
paints pictures of vivid scenes in their lives
where hands and feet show personality.

2 Describe the person or group you have
 chosen through the actions of hands, feet,
 eyes or lips. Again, use vivid moments from
 their life to convey their personality. It may
 help to begin with a prose account before
 you move into your first draft in verse.
   When you begin your later drafts consider
 the following:
 ● take out unnecessary words or lines
 ● you may want to repeat certain lines or
   words that make an impact
 ● use comparisons to bring this person to
   life
 ● choose vivid words and details
3 As you complete your own writing in this
 section, look back through all your *own*
 poems and choose any you would especially
 like to include in the anthology suggestion
 on pages 117–118.
   If friends have a particular piece *you* wish
 to use, negotiate with them so you can include it.

Poetry and precision

Probably one of the most demanding forms a poet can choose is the **sonnet** because of the specific framework within which it requires a writer to work. Below is a Shakespearian or English sonnet, named after its original author.

Sonnet 104

To me, fair friend, you never can be old
For as you were when first your eye I eyed
So seems your beauty still. Three winters cold
Have from the forest shook three summers pride
Three beauteous springs to yellow autumn turned
In process of the seasons have I seen
Three April perfumes in three hot Junes burned,
Since first I saw you fresh, which yet are green.
Ah! yet doth beauty, like a dial-hand
Steal from his figure and no pace perceived;
So your sweet hue, which methinks still doth stand,
Hath motion, and my eye may be deceived:
    For fear of which, hear this, thou age unbred
    Ere you were born was beauty's summer dead.

William Shakespeare

Thinking about the poem

1 Read the piece through several times and then, with a partner work out a set of guidelines to explain the structure of this kind of sonnet.
Consider:
  - number of lines
  - number of syllables in a line
  - rhyme scheme
  - how the line of argument within the piece develops
  - how the argument fits with the rhyme scheme

2 Pool your ideas and write a Shakespearian sonnet guide for someone who is not familiar with the form. Then compare your guidelines with the ones below.

Shakespearian sonnet guidelines

◆ A sonnet has fourteen lines.
◆ Each line has ten syllables and an iambic metre. (Look back at your work on limericks to remind yourself of metre). **Iambic metre** has a pattern of a light stress followed by a heavy stress which repeats five times.

> To me fair friend you never can be old.

The rhyme scheme is as follows:

abab
cdcd   The first twelve lines are made up of three quatrains
efef   (blocks of four lines linked by rhyme).

gg   The last two lines form a rhyming couplet, i.e. a pair of rhyming lines.

◆ Argument: There may be a shift in thought between the first eight lines and the next four, but the couplet usually brings the ideas together or provides a twist.

Group discussion

In the light of your reading of *Sonnet 104* and the work done above on sonnet structure, discuss the following points in a group of 3 or 4.

1 To whom is the poem addressed and what lines convince you of this?
2 How long have these people known each other?
3 What is the speaker saying about their friendship? Consider the idea above that there may be a shift in argument between the first eight lines and the next four.
4 Does the final couplet round off this argument or provide a twist in it?
5 What imagery does the poet use to evoke his ideas?

113

Parody

Many of Shakespeare's sonnets are written seriously on the subjects of love and time. Wendy Cope however has produced parodies of Shakespeare's most well known pieces to mock his style and entertain her readers. Here are two original sonnets that she has parodied and the opening lines of her versions of them.

Sonnet 55

Not marble, nor the gilded monuments
Of princes, shall outlive this powerful rime,
But you shall shine more bright in these contents
Than unswept stone, besmear'd with sluttish time.
When wasteful war shall statues overturn
And broils root out the work of masonry
Nor Mars his sword nor war's quick fire shall burn
The living record of your memory
'Gainst death and all-oblivious enmity
Shall you pace forth; your praise shall still find room,
Even in the eyes of all posterity
That wear this world out to the ending doom.
     So, till the judgement that yourself arise,
     You live in this and dwell in lovers' eyes.

William Shakespeare

From Strugnell's sonnets

(iv)

Not only marble but the plastic toys
From cornflake packets will outlive this rhyme
I can't immortalise you love – our joys
will lie unnoticed in the vault of time...

Wendy Cope

Sonnet 116

Let me not to the marriage of true minds
Admit impediments. Love is not love
Which alters when it alteration finds
Or bends with the remover to remove:
O no! It is an ever-fixed mark
That looks on tempests and is never shaken
It is the star to every wandering bark
Whose worth's unknown although his height be taken,
Love's not Time's fool, though rosy lips and cheeks
Within his bending sickle's compass come;
Love alters not with his brief hours and weeks
But bears it out even to the edge of doom
     If this be error and upon me prov'd
     I never writ, nor no man ever lov'd.

William Shakespeare

(vi)

Let me not to the marriage of true swine
Admit impediments. With his big car
He's won your heart, and you have punctured mine
I have no spare; henceforth I'll bear the scar...

Wendy Cope

Writing your own parody

1 Using your knowledge of the form, work out what Shakespeare is saying in these two pieces and use Wendy Cope's lines as the starting point for your own parodies.
2 Write a short piece to include with your parody explaining what you found easy and/or difficult about this form of writing.

Comparing two sonnets

As well as Shakespearian sonnets there is another sonnet pattern called the Petrarchan or Italian sonnet, named after the writer Petrarch who wrote a series of love sonnets to Laura. Below is a sonnet by Edwin Morgan written in Petrarchan form. Read it through carefully and make a note of which elements are the same as in the Shakespearian sonnet and which differences in form occur.

Glasgow sonnet

A mean wind wanders through the backcourt trash,
Hackles on puddles rise, old mattresses
puff briefly and subside. Play-fortresses
of brick and bric-a-brac spill out some ash.
Four storeys have no windows left to smash
but in the fifth a chipped sill buttresses
mother and daughter the last mistresses
of that black block condemned to stand not crash.
Around them the cracks deepen, the rats crawl.
The kettle whimpers on a crazy hob
Roses of mould grow from ceiling to wall.
A man lies late since he has lost his job,
smokes on one elbow, letting his coughs fall
thinly into an air too poor to rob.

Edwin Morgan

Petrarchan sonnet guidelines

In terms of line number, syllable count and metre, Shakespearian and Petrarchan sonnets are the same. The difference is one of rhyme scheme and thus structure of the argument. The rhyme scheme runs as follows:

abba } The first eight lines (or octave) have two sets of rhyme arranged
abba } in two four-line units. This section usually presents the idea.

c c c
d c d   The last six lines (or sestet) can vary in pattern with two or
c d e   three rhymes used. These final lines complete the idea or
d c c   make a comment.
c c d   (Read down each of these columns for alternative rhyme patterns.)
d d e

Assignment

Using your knowledge of Shakespearian and Petrarchan sonnets compare the two poems below. Many writers of Shakespeare's time wrote very exaggerated love sonnets to their mistresses. These two pieces represent a departure from this style.

- Read each sonnet through several times.
- Using the points given in 'Jotting around a poem' on page 74, make your own notes.
- Write up your ideas, comparing the two poems in terms of their sonnet form, what they say and how they say it.

From Sonnets from the Portuguese

If thou must love me, let it be for naught
Except for love's sake only. Do not say,
'I love her for her smile...her look...her way
Of speaking gently,...for a trick of thought
That falls in well with mine, and certes brought
A sense of pleasant ease on such a day' –
For these things in themselves, Beloved, may
Be changed, or change for thee, – and love so wrought,
May be unwrought so. Neither love me for
Thine own dear pity's wiping my cheeks dry, –
Since one might well forget to weep, who bore
Thy comfort long, and lose thy love thereby!
But love me for love's sake, that evermore
Thou mayst love on through love's eternity.

Elizabeth Barrett Browning

Sonnet 130

My mistresses eyes are nothing like the sun;
Coral is far more red than her lips' red;
If snow be white, why then her breasts are dun;
If hairs be wires, black wires grow on her head.
I have seen roses, damask'd, red and white
But no roses see I in her cheeks;
And in some perfume there is more delight
Than in the breath that from my mistress reeks,
I love to hear her speak, yet well I know
That music hath a far more pleasing sound;
I grant I never saw a goddess go –
My mistress when she walks treads on the ground.
     And yet, by heaven, I think my love as rare
     As any she belied by false compare.

William Shakespeare

116

Creating your own anthology

During your own reading, discussion and writing, you have probably looked at a number of different poetry anthologies: collections of one poet's work, collections of poems on one theme like war or the environment, or collections arranged around a number of themes or authors. Using your experience of these, you can be the writer, editor, designer and illustrator on this project and create an anthology that will appeal to people of your own age.

Finding the poems

You are the expert here because in your poetry journal and in your head you will recall those poems that have made an impact on you.

Hopefully you will want to include some poems you have written yourself. To give your reader an insight into your poems you could include the early drafts and a commentary linking these like Judith Nicholls did on page 68.

Look for poems that have different moods: some funny, some thoughtful, sad, regretful, knowledgeable, joyous, angry, passionate. Try and include a variety of the different forms we have looked at: haiku, ballad, free verse, sonnets, dramatic monologues, song lyrics, poems with strong rhymes and rhythms.

You may want to group them in themes that you think will interest your readers. Some of the themes that occur in this collection are: Family and relationships, Love and friendship, Conflict, Growing up, People and places, and Our future.

Design

Having decided what you want on your pages, you need to decide on: the size and shape of these pages; how you will arrange the poems on the page; how you will bind the pages together. You might want to put it in a ring-binder so that later you can add to your ideas. Browse through other anthologies to give you ideas.

Illustration

Choosing the right illustrations, lettering, drawings and pictures to match the poems is a crucial part of preparing your anthology. You can vary illustration by using collage, frames, drawings in black and white and drawings in colour.

Shops like Athena and places like The National Gallery, The National Portrait Gallery, museums and bookshops with their excellent postcard selections are good sources for illustrations. Remember also to spend time on a front cover design and illustration.

References

Your reader will find it easier to find their way around your collection and their way to the poems you have chosen if you include a contents page and a bibliography.

Introduction

This is where you explain to the reader why you have chosen these poems for your anthology and what poetry means to you. The following section in this module, 'So what is poetry?' will help you plan your introduction. Using two or more quotations from the next section that match your own views, develop your own points on what poetry means to you and how your ideas have changed as you worked on this anthology.

Presentation

When it is completed, arrange to have your anthology displayed either in your classroom or in the library so that your readers are encouraged to browse. You may want to place a comments slip at the back asking for constructive responses.

118

So what is poetry?

In following some of the activities in this module, you will have begun to formulate your own personal ideas of just what represents poetry. With a partner, read through the opinions of various poets below and choose four or five statements that seem to capture some of your own thoughts. Should you have a quotation of your own that you feel is not represented here, add it to these.

‘Poetry begins in delight and ends in wisdom.’

Robert Frost

‘When in public, poetry should take off its clothes and wave to the nearest person in sight; it should be seen in the company of thieves and lovers rather than journalists and publishers.’

Brian Patten

‘People disagree about very important things, things like money, sex, race, bombs, school, parents, work… We must also agree with each other but we won't unless we discuss or argue it out. Poems are ways of beginning such arguments.’

Michael Rosen

‘Poetry is language pared down to its essentials.’

Ezra Pound

‘Poetry is basically entertainment. It is no substitute of political speech.’

L. Kwesi Johnstone

‘Poetry is something essential to you, something you recognise instinctively as a true sounding aspect of yourself and your own experience.’

Seamus Heaney

‘Prose: words in their best order.
Poetry: the best words in their best order.’

Samuel Taylor Coleridge

‘All the poet can do today is to warn. That is why the true poets must be truthful.’

Wilfred Owen

‘A poem should not mean but be.’
Archibald McCleish

‘Poetry is…words with a tune…’
Jon Stallworthy

119

❛ Poetry is the spontaneous overflow of powerful feelings. ❜

William Wordsworth

❛ Poetry is...naked words dancing together. ❜

Adrian Mitchell

❛ A poet is someone who has to see everything freshly as though for the first time...I'm having fun with the world – seeing similarities in things that are different. ❜

Craig Raine

❛ You can't write a poem out of emotion only, there must be insight. ❜

Philip Larkin

❛ Writing free verse is like playing tennis with the net down. ❜

Robert Frost

❛ You can do anything with images. A poet can make anything, do anything, make us see, hear, feel, smell, taste, imagine anything she wants. ❜

Gillian Clarke

❛ What matters most, since we are listening to poetry and not to prose, is that we hear the song and dance in the words. ❜

Ted Hughes

Thinking about poetry

With a partner share the quotations you have chosen and explain why you picked them out. Try to refer to your own poems or poems you have read to illustrate the points made in the quotes you have selected.

Assessing your own progress

It may be that you don't want to assemble an anthology but would like some record of your work and progress. During your GCSE course you will have written a number of responses to various poems. Select a variety of these that you are pleased with. They may be:

- creative responses, such as a letter, newspaper, diary
- your own poems with drafts
- your jottings around a poem and your final written comment

Put these in the order in which you did them and consider your own development as a writer. You may want to consider these questions.

- How has the way you read a poem changed since you started the course?
- Has your confidence grown since your first assignment?
- Has the kind of poetry that appeals to you changed?
- Has keeping a poetry journal and jotting around a poem, followed by group discussion, helped you understand some poems?
- How easy/difficult has it been to write your own poetry? Do you think your work has improved?

Use examples from your own work to make your points. You may want to present your ideas in written form or discuss it with your teacher as part of an oral assessment.

Module 3 Media Scripts

UNIT 1   Radio plays   122
UNIT 2   Screenplay   134
UNIT 3   Devising drama   144
UNIT 4   Monologue   154
UNIT 5   Directing the scene   164
FEATURE   Documentary autobiography   174

Objectives

The materials and activities included in this module aim to help you learn more about script forms by:

◆ offering a selection of different scripts for you to read and gain familiarity with their features
◆ introducing you to a number of practical drama techniques, including role play and simulation
◆ providing the chance for you to write creatively in script forms

121

Radio plays

These listings, taken from the *Radio Times*, show the drama on Radio 4 for one week.

SATURDAY

2.30pm
Saturday Playhouse
Christopher and Columbus
An adaptation of the novel by Elizabeth von Armin. The von Twinkler twins are half German and recently orphaned. They set out for America with some trepidation and find that it's not only the Kaiser's torpedoes that they have to face.
Anna Rose von Twinkler
.......................JANE WHITTENSHAW
Anna Felicitas von Twinkler
.......................PHLLIPPA RITCHIE
Edward Twist.....WILLIAM HOPE
Mrs Wilson/Mrs Ridding
...............................GWEN CHERRELL
Mrs Anderson/Mrs Bilton
...............................JO KENDALL
Mrs Twist............HELEN HORTON
Edith Twist............JENNY HOWE
Mr Ridding
...................MICHAEL GRAHAM COX
Emmeline Heap.......SHEILA REID
John Elliott.........MARK STRAKER
With David Goudge, Stephen Garlick, David Bannerman, Michael Kilgarriff, Emma Gregory, Petra Markham and Auriol Smith.
Dramatised by Barbara Clegg and Olwen Wymark
Director Jane Morgan
Stereo

7.45pm
Classic Serial
The Forsyte Chronicles
John Galsworthy's saga dramatised in 23 episodes, narrated by Dirk Bogarde as Galsworthy.
20: It is 1930. Dinny is still 'a maid in waiting', but for how much longer?

A book of poetry is to decide her fate.
Dinny Cherrell
.......................SOPHIE THOMPSON
Lady Mont...........DOROTHY TUTIN
Sir Lawrence Mont
.......................PAUL DANEMAN
Wilfred Desert........PHILIP SULLY
Jack Muskham
.......................AUBERY WOODS
Fleur................AMANDA REDMAN
Michael Mont...........GARY BOND
Adrian..................JOHN MOFFATT
Sir Conway..........GARARD GREEN
Lady Cherrell........MARY ALLEN
Hilary........................DAVID KING
Hubert....................SIMON TREVES
Jean.....................DANIELLE ALLAN
Stack...............DANNY SCHILLER
Telford Yule
...................CHRISTOPHER SCOTT
Compton Grice...........JOHN BULL
Kit......................JODY MCDONALD
With Nigel Carrington and Leonard Fenton.
Piano Mary Nash.
Episode dramatised by Elspeth Sandys
Director Janet Whitaker
Stereo
(Repeated on Friday at 3.00pm)

SUNDAY

2.30pm
Talking Heads
NEW Alan Bennett's acclaimed series of six monologues on radio for the first time.
1: *A Chip in the Sugar*
A middle-aged man lives with his elderly mother, but who is more dependent? Performed by Alan Bennett.
Music George Fenton.
Director Matthew Walters

MONDAY

3.00pm
Our Family
A love story in three plays by Victor Pemberton.
1: *The Trains Don't Stop Here Any More*
Letty is a determined young girl. When she marries Oliver against the wishes of her family, she is convinced that her love can help him overcome the disabilities of his war-wounds and restore his faith in himself and the world about him.
Time: 1916-1930
Letty Edginton
...............................NERYS HUGHES
Beatrice, her mother
...............................SHEILA GRANT
William, her father
...............................MALCOLM HAYES
Nicky, her younger brother
...............................ADAM GODLEY
Tom, her elder brother
...............................DEREK SEATON
Oliver Hobbs......NIGEL ANTHONY
Violet, his sister
...............................WENDY RICHARD
Bill Brooks.....KENNETH SHANLEY
Mr Cotton...................ERIC ALLAN
Frank O'Malley.........BILL MONKS
Amy Lyall....................EVE KARPF
Mr Pearson........ROBERT TROTTER
Pianist Mary Nash
Director John Tydeman
Stereo (R)

7.45pm
The Monday Play
Flower of Blood
In the desert of Western Australia where the British slew many Aborigines, there grows a scarlet flower. The Spanish monks who also settled there in the 1850s cherished both the flower

and the Aborigines.
Written by Bruce Stewart.
Fr Salvado....MICHAEL WILLIAMS
Fr Serra.........CHRISTIAN RODSKA
Bilagoro................WILLIAM EEDLE
Sister Ursula..........KATE BINCHY
Bishop Brady.......PETER CAFFREY
Teresa........ELIZABETH MANSFIELD
Weld........................BRIAN MILLER
Burgess..............BRUCE STEWART
Landor..........................JOHN BULL
Pianist John Bishop
Music director
Richard Connolly
Director Shaun MacLoughlin
Stereo

TUESDAY

3.00pm *LW only*
Thirty-Minute Theatre
Sweet Reason
Glenda compensates for Lewis's preoccupation with female assistants by becoming a compulsive buyer: electronic guard dogs, underwater torches and atomic alarm clocks are among her more bizarre purchases...
Written by Penny Kline.
Glenda......................JUNE BARRIE
Lewis.......................PETER COPLEY
Vanessa.....CAROLINE BACKHOUSE
Director Shaun MacLoughlin
Stereo

7.45pm
Independence

NEW The first of a four-part drama set in a progressive boarding school on the south coast. Written by Angus Graham-Campbell.
The Wetter Ground
While the school has football and dance scholarships, talented, angry Euan doesn't want to play or allow his girlfriend Jen to dance.

Euan Roberts	JULIAN FRITH
Jen Billington	OONA BEESON
Mrs Fellows	AURIOL SMITH
Charles Fellows	IAN LINDSAY
Peter Billington	ALAN THOMPSON
Julia Billington	JENNY HOWE
Martin	ROSS LIVINGSTONE
Chris	PHIL MCDERMOTT
Jerry	JONATHAN FIRTH
Emma	EMMA GREGORY
Amy	DANIELLE ALLAN
Tasha	JUDY FLYNN
Nick	NICHOLAS GILBROOK
Teacher/Dug	DAVID BANNERMAN
Dance teacher/Voice	VINCENT BRIMBLE

Director Richard Wortley
Stereo

11.00pm
Murder Most Foul

NEW A series of true murder stories from the days when police cars had bells and the men from the Yard wore trilbies.
1:*The Surgeon's Knife*
Two bodies were found in a Scottish ravine. Dr Buck Ruxton's wife and maid were missing.
Written by John Scotney.

Buck Ruxton	MARK ZUBER
Norman Birkett	ANTHONY BATE

With Timothy Carlton, Fraser Kerr, Timothy Bateson, Nigel Carrington, Michael Turner and Danielle Allan.

Producer Mark Savage

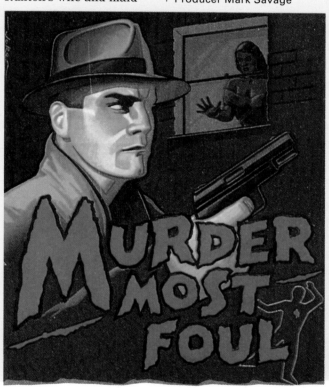

3.00pm *LW only*
The House at No 9 Rue Fleurie

Mr Zilber looks after Mrs Baum's house in Monaco. One day he will have a proper family to look after. Written by Jackie Kohnstamm.

Mr Zilber	HARRY TOWB
Jeanne	JO KENDALL
Rosa	FRANCES JEATER
Count	HAROLD INNOCENT
Giovanni	RONALD HERDMAN
Mario	BEN ONWUKWE
German officer	ALAN BARKER
Driver	NIGEL CARRINGTON
Mrs Baum	MAXINE AUDLEY

Director Janet Whitaker

11.00pm Fear on 4

A series of nerve-tinglers introduced by Edward de Souza, the Man in Black.
Dance in the Underworld
Was Tony really dead when they buried him? Written by Stuart Kerr.

Victor	BRYAN PRINGLE
Doctor	FRASER KERR
Avril	MAGGIE MCCARTHY
Mrs Manners	AURIOL SMITH
Tony	ANGUS WRIGHT
Jenny	JENNY FUNNELL
Scott	SIMON TREVES

Director Martin Jenkins
Stereo

Looking at the listings

1 Can you see a pattern in the timings of these plays?
2 Why do you think these plays are scheduled at these times?
3 Who do you think their audiences are?
4 If you had to choose, which of these plays would you listen to?

Radio versus television

Select and record a radio play from a current Radio 4 listing. In a small group, listen to the recording before starting the following work.

1 Make a list of the differences between radio and television drama.
2 Use your list to help you write a short piece, as if from someone trying to promote radio drama, arguing the benefits of radio drama over television.

For more on argumentative writing see The Process of Writing module in Book 4B, pages 94-99.

Writing for radio

The BBC Radio Drama Script Unit receives on average about two hundred scripts a week from writers wishing to have their plays published. To make the work of considering these plays as easy as possible the BBC issues advice on writing plays for radio. Here is some of this advice.

◆ 'Stage directions' for the producer's benefit are a temptation that should be avoided. If it's important it should be in the dialogue. If it's not, then nobody need ever know.

◆ It should be remembered that listeners will always (quite involuntarily) supply their own mental images in response to what they hear. They should be given enough ideas to work on but never so many that they become restricted or confused.

◆ When deciding on the number of characters in a scene it should be borne in mind that the only ways of establishing someone's presence are either to have them speak or for them to be spoken to by name. If there are too many characters in a scene, the listeners will lose track or become confused.

◆ It is important to construct each individual sequence to provide a variety of sound which will hold the listener's attention. This variety can be achieved in lengths of sequences, number of people speaking, pace of dialogue, volume of sound, background acoustics and location of action.

What do you think?

1 Discuss these points with a partner and decide why each piece of advice is given.
2 Make a list of *dos* and *don'ts* in writing for radio, using the BBC's advice and other points you may have thought of yourself.

The bogeyman

The bogeyman is a play written for radio. In this opening scene three children, Martin and Stuart, who are cousins, and Sarah, a friend of Martin's, are standing at the door of the attic, which they have been forbidden to enter. Bullying, childhood fears and guilty secrets are all themes dealt with in the play.

FADE UP INTERIOR, THE TOP OF A FLIGHT OF STAIRS OUTSIDE AN ATTIC DOOR. THE ATMOSPHERE IS CLOSE AND SECRETIVE, INTENSE.

STUART	1	He's in there. You can hear him.
SARAH	2	Yeah! Listen!
STUART	3	He's moving around. Dragging his feet across the floor.
SARAH	4	Rubbing his hands together.
STUART	5	Laughing.
SARAH	6	Looking for something to eat.
STUART	7	Mice and birds and spiders.
SARAH	8	Listen.
MARTIN	9	I can't hear anything.
SARAH	10	That's 'cos you ain't listening properly. Is he, Stuart?
STUART	11	No. And 'cos he's thick.
SARAH	12	Get closer, Martin.
STUART	13	You have to push your ear right up against the door. Like this.

HE PUSHES MARTIN'S HEAD AGAINST THE DOOR

MARTIN	14	Ow!

STUART AND SARAH LAUGH

STUART	15	Now listen!
MARTIN	16	You're hurting!

– 1 –

STUART	1	Can you hear him?
MARTIN	2	Let go of my head!
SARAH	3	He's in there, Martin.
MARTIN	4	Loose me, Stuart.
		STUART LOOSES HIM
	5	You hurt me then!
SARAH	6	That won't be nothing to what'll happen if the bogeyman gets you.
MARTIN	7	There ain't no such thing.
SARAH	8	Yes, there is.
MARTIN	9	There ain't!
STUART	10	You saying I'm a liar? You saying that me an' Sarah are liars?
SARAH	11	'Cos if you are we'll open the door and shove you in, and then he'll get you.
MARTIN	12	I ain't saying you're liars.
STUART	13	You must believe us then. 'Cos we say there is a bogeyman, and he lives in there.
SARAH	14	In the attic.

STUART	1	Yeah. He lives in there in the day, and he comes out at night when we're asleep. He walks round the house. If you're awake, you can hear his footsteps creaking on the stairs and the landing. And sometimes he comes into your bedroom and stands over you and breathes over your face.
SARAH	2	It smells like the grave.
STUART	3	And that's what gives you nightmares.
SARAH	4	Ain't you never heard the stairs creaking at night, Martin?
MARTIN	5	· Yes...
SARAH	6	You've heard him, then.
STUART	7	And you get nightmares, as well. I know 'cos I've heard you shouting out.
SARAH	8	Does he?
STUART	9	Yeah.
MARTIN	10	Not very often.
STUART	11	He's been in your room and breathed over your face. He's tall and thin and he looks like a skeleton. He wears old rags and you can see the bones through them. He's got long, yellow fingernails like claws, and if he wanted he could tear your heart out and eat it raw. He's got black teeth, and empty holes where his eyes should be.

SARAH	1	And if he thinks you don't believe in him, he'll come out one night and get you and take you back into the attic with him.
STUART	2	Then he'll suck all the blood out of your body like a vampire does, and you'll turn into a bogeyman as well.
SARAH	3	So you'd better believe in him, Martin. Or else.
MARTIN	4	Have you seen him?
STUART	5	No. His face is so horrible that anybody who sees it turns to stone.
MARTIN	6	How do you know what he looks like, then?
STUART	7	What?
MARTIN	8	If you ain't seen him, how'd you know what he looks like?
SARAH	9	You saw him once in the mirror, Stuart. Remember? You told me. You don't turn into stone if you see him in the mirror. It's just his reflection.

– 4 –

David Calcutt

Thinking about the extract

Discuss the following questions with a partner or in a small group:

1 How old are the children in the extract? How do you know they are not adults? Use evidence from the script to show this.
2 What clues early in the extract tell you that Sarah and Stuart are trying to frighten Martin? What finally convinces you that they are deliberately lying to him? Could this be classed as a form of bullying?
3 Why might they wish to frighten Martin in this way? See how many reasons you can suggest.

Your own views

Answer these questions for yourself in writing.

1 What is your impression of these children? Write a short paragraph about each.
2 What can you work out about the relationship between them?
3 From this first scene predict what the rest of the play might be about.

A successful radio play?

In a group decide how well David Calcutt follows the BBC's advice on writing for radio in this brief extract.

Look at:

● his use of stage directions
● whether he has established a clear line of events
● how he introduces and portrays his characters
● whether he uses a variety of sounds, speech lengths and tones

128

Assignment

In a group you are going to record this extract from *The bogeyman* on tape, as a radio play.

1 Before you begin you will need to think carefully about the extract and prepare for the task. The following guidelines may help you to do this.

Ways of working

You will have to make some decisions about the way you work. In your group you may find it useful to have people doing the following jobs.
- **Producer:** to make final decisions about the various things your group has tried out.
- **Performers**: to play the parts of Stuart, Sarah and Martin – and a fourth person to read the title of the play.
- **Recordist**: to operate the tape recorder(s).
- **Sound effects operator**: to create the various sounds/music you may require.

The best way to reach the decisions you have to make about the play is to experiment, to try things out for yourself. For example
- **Music:** will you have introductory music? What will it be? Listen to a number of pieces. Does it convey the right atmosphere?
- **Casting:** ask different people to read the various parts to see who is most suitable.
- **Sound effects:** try various ways of making the sound of someone's head being pushed against a door – without actually using someone's head!
- **Pace/volume:** rehearse the reading before you start to record, to see where speeding up or slowing down the pace of the lines is most effective, and where the volume of the voices needs to be raised or lowered.

2 When you have thought about these guidelines, draw up your own diagram, like the one on page 130, to show the decisions you have made about the questions it raises.
3 Finally, here is a comment on radio drama from Nigel Bryant, who produced *The bogeyman* for BBC Radio 4.

‘In many ways radio is the most real of all media. Nothing comes between the listeners and what they hear. Therefore the listener is acutely aware of any phoneyness or artificiality in a performance. For that reason good radio performance depends on spontaneity – you can't afford to rehearse too much. If it sounds over-rehearsed it's going to sound unreal. As soon as you know, basically, what you are going to do – record it. Remember that even professionals will not get a complete scene a hundred per cent as they want it all in one go, and you can always cut together the best bits from one or two takes, or even re-record a couple of lines you're not happy with and edit those in. Remember, too, that real life speech is not neat and tidy. There's no need to 'speak well' just because you're on radio. As long as fluffs and fumbles sound natural, why not keep them in? In real life people don't speak neatly, one after another. Feel free to interrupt and make background vocal sounds when you feel it's right.’

This diagram shows some of the decisions a radio drama producer would have to make in planning a production.

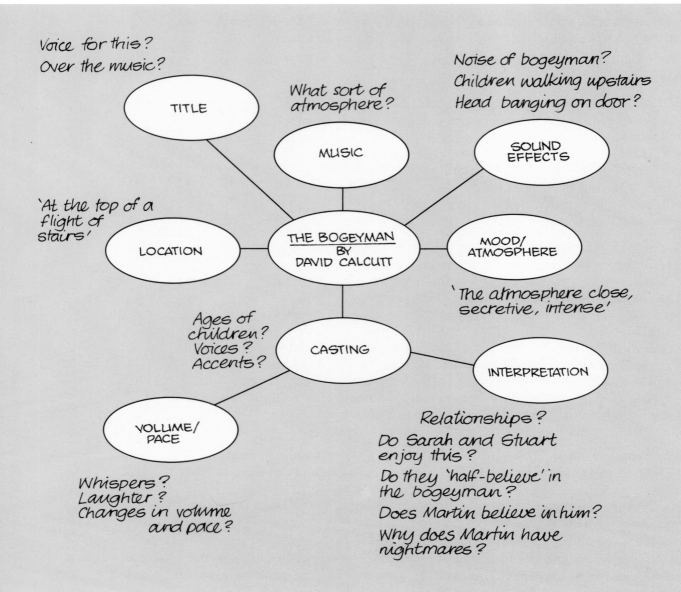

Voice for this?
Over the music?

What sort of atmosphere?

Noise of bogeyman?
Children walking upstairs
Head banging on door?

TITLE

MUSIC

SOUND EFFECTS

'At the top of a flight of stairs'

LOCATION

THE BOGEYMAN BY DAVID CALCUTT

MOOD/ ATMOSPHERE

'The atmosphere close, secretive, intense'

Ages of children?
Voices?
Accents?

CASTING

INTERPRETATION

VOLUME/ PACE

Whispers?
Laughter?
Changes in volume and pace?

Relationships?
Do Sarah and Stuart enjoy this?
Do they 'half-believe' in the bogeyman?
Does Martin believe in him?
Why does Martin have nightmares?

For writing

When you have finished your recording make a written report on the process you went through. You should include in it:
- an account of the stages you followed in preparation
- the decisions you had to make in planning
- how successful you thought your performance was
- whether you followed Nigel Bryant's comments about performance

Follow-up theme: bullying

A theme that David Calcutt often uses in his writing is that of 'bullying' or what is sometimes called 'peer group pressure' – that is, where people behave in a certain way because they feel their friends, or those around them, expect them to. The extract from *The bogeyman* shows an incident where two children seem to enjoy tormenting another, in a way that could be called bullying. This theme is also explored in The Process of Writing module in Book 4B, pages 68-69.

Read the following piece from a newspaper article in which a teacher, who is also a parent, advises parents on how to recognise when children are being bullied.

> ❝We sense something is wrong – there is a sad atmosphere, a clamming up or shrug if we ask about school and friends. Children may want to come home for lunch – or take a variety of routes home to avoid the bully. They may become desperate to own some object which 'all their friends' have. There may be torn clothing, bruises, scratches, or in extreme cases, children steal to meet the bully's demands.❞

Group discussion

1 Can you think of any other signs that might warn a parent that their child was being bullied?
2 Discuss possible reasons why a child might be bullied.

Here is some more advice offered in the same article.

Practical steps you can take

If your child is bullied

◆ Listen calmly and question gently: who is involved, where is it happening? How long has it been going on?
◆ Don't react with hand-wringing horror: your child may then feel responsible for the downfall of family happiness.
◆ Agree that bullying is distressing. Explain that it happens to most children, but it is going to be sorted out.
◆ If you feel that this is more than a short flare-up of quarrelling or teasing, contact the school.
◆ Don't approach the parents of the bully. They might see things in a completely different light.

If your child is a bully

◆ Calmly tell your child what you have heard and listen to his/her story.
◆ If there has been bullying tell him/her it must stop at once, making it clear that it is the behaviour you dislike, not your child.
◆ Is there any obvious reason for your child to be seeking extra attention?
◆ Many bullies feel badly about themselves. Boost their self-confidence, focusing on their feelings and interests.
◆ Show your children how much your friends mean to you – and try to discuss the nature and value of friendship.

What do you think?

In a group of 3 or 4, discuss these questions:
1 Would you disagree with any of the advice offered in 'Practical steps you can take'?
2 Take the sections on the bullied and the bully and try to agree as a group which is the most important piece of advice in each. Rank the points in each section, in order of importance, numbering them from 1 to 5 (1 = most important).

Producing a pamphlet

Using the information you have discussed so far in this unit, design and produce a pamphlet to be sent to the parents of the pupils in your school, advising them on the problems of bullying and how to deal with it.

You will need to consider carefully the best style and tone to adopt in getting information across well on this sensitive subject.

In terms of design and content the pamphlet should:
◆ be brief, use one sheet of A4 paper
◆ be easy to read
◆ be eye-catching, use illustration
◆ contain helpful information
◆ suggest where further information might be found
◆ be capable of being produced by fellow pupils using your school's resources

Some possible ways of presenting your pamphlet are shown below.

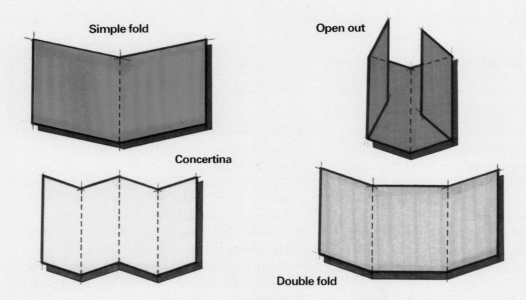

Simple fold

Open out

Concertina

Double fold

For more on leaflets and writing for information, see The Process of Writing module in Book 4B, pages 87-91.

Writing your own views

Write, as a story, a poem, a diary or a letter, about an occasion when either you were part of a group that bullied someone, or when you were bullied. You could write about a real incident, or invent one.

Assignment

1 Use one of the pieces of advice in 'Practical steps you can take' as the starting point for your own scene for a radio play. In this scene a parent is dealing with a child who is a bully *or* who is being bullied. (The parent may or may not be following the advice.)

2 a) You will need to plan and draft first, to decide what will happen in your scene, but in writing your finished script you should take notice of the way *The bogeyman* is set out.

b) You should also look back at the advice on writing radio drama given by the BBC at the beginning of this unit.

Key features of radio script layout are summarised below.

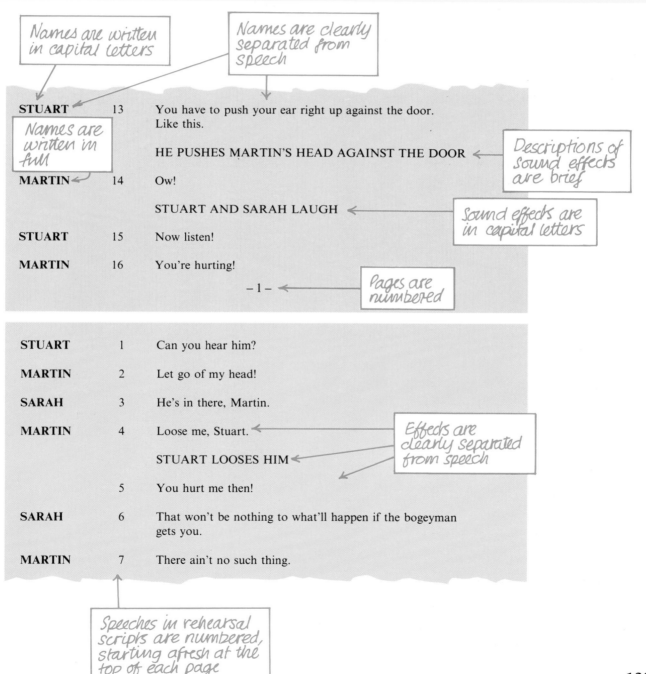

Names are written in capital letters

Names are clearly separated from speech

Names are written in full

Descriptions of sound effects are brief

Sound effects are in capital letters

Pages are numbered

Effects are clearly separated from speech

Speeches in rehearsal scripts are numbered, starting afresh at the top of each page

STUART	13	You have to push your ear right up against the door. Like this.
		HE PUSHES MARTIN'S HEAD AGAINST THE DOOR
MARTIN	14	Ow!
		STUART AND SARAH LAUGH
STUART	15	Now listen!
MARTIN	16	You're hurting!

– 1 –

STUART	1	Can you hear him?
MARTIN	2	Let go of my head!
SARAH	3	He's in there, Martin.
MARTIN	4	Loose me, Stuart.
		STUART LOOSES HIM
	5	You hurt me then!
SARAH	6	That won't be nothing to what'll happen if the bogeyman gets you.
MARTIN	7	There ain't no such thing.

133

Book or film?

Christy Brown, the celebrated painter and writer, overcame the difficulties of being born with cerebral palsy by using his left foot, the only part of his body which he could use with real control.

In this unit you will be comparing the opening of Christy's autobiographical novel with two scenes from the successful film of his early life, *My left foot*.

This extract is taken from the first chapter of his book.

My left foot

I was born in the Rotunda Hospital, on June 5th, 1932. There were nine children before me and twelve after me, so I myself belonged to the middle group. Out of this total of twenty-two, seventeen lived, four died in infancy, leaving thirteen to hold the family fort.

Mine was a difficult birth, I am told. Both mother and son almost died. A whole army of relations queued up outside the hospital until the small hours of the morning, waiting for news and praying furiously that it would be good.

After my birth mother was sent to recuperate for some weeks and I was kept in the hospital while she was away. I remained there for some time, without name, for I wasn't baptised until my mother was well enough to bring me to church.

It was mother who first saw that there was something wrong with me. I was about four months old at the time. She noticed that my head had a habit of falling backwards whenever she tried to feed me. She attempted to correct this by placing her hand on the back of my neck to keep it steady. But when she took it away, back it would drop again. That was the first warning sign. Then she became aware of other defects as I grew older. She saw that my hands were clenched nearly all the time and were inclined to twine behind my back; my mouth couldn't grasp the teat of the bottle because even at that early age my jaws would either lock together tightly, so that it was impossible for her to open them, or they would suddenly become limp and fall loose, dragging my whole mouth to one side. At six months I could not sit up without having a mountain of pillows around me; at twelve months it was the same.

Very worried by this, mother told my father her fears, and they decided to take medical advice without

134

A selection of Christy Brown's paintings, including a self-portrait (bottom)

delay. I was a little over a year old when they began to take me to hospitals and clinics, convinced that there was something definitely wrong with me, something which they could not understand or name, but which was very real and disturbing.

Almost every doctor who saw and examined me, labelled me a very interesting but also a hopeless case. Many told mother very gently that I was mentally defective and would remain so. That was a hard blow to a young mother who had already reared five healthy children. The doctors were so very sure of themselves that mother's faith in me seemed almost an impertinence. They assured her that nothing could be done for me. She refused to accept this truth, the inevitable truth – as it then seemed – that I was beyond cure, beyond saving, even beyond hope. She could not and would not believe that I was an imbecile, as the doctors told her. She had nothing in the world to go by, not a scrap of evidence to support her conviction that, though my body was crippled, my mind was not. In spite of all the doctors and specialists told her, she would not agree. I don't believe she knew why – she just knew without feeling the smallest shade of doubt.

Finding that the doctors could not help in any way beyond telling her not to place her trust in me, or, in other words, to forget I was a human creature, rather to regard me as something to be fed and washed and then put away again, mother decided there and then to take matters into her own hands. I was her child, and therefore part of the family. No matter how dull and incapable I might grow up to be, she was determined to treat me on the same plane as the others, and not as the 'queer one' in the back room who was never spoken of when there were visitors present.

That was a momentous decision as far as my future life was concerned. It meant that I would always have my mother on my side to help me fight all the battles that were to come, and to inspire me with new strength when I was almost beaten. But it wasn't easy for her because now the relatives and friends had decided otherwise. They contended that I should be taken kindly, sympathetically, but not seriously. That would be a mistake. 'For your own sake,' they told her, 'don't look to this boy as you would to the others; it would only break your heart in the end.'

Christy Brown

Thinking about the novel

Answer these questions with a partner.
1 Apart from Christy himself, who is the subject of this extract?
2 What was the first sign that something was wrong with Christy, and when did it occur?
3 a) Draw a time-line from birth to fourteen months, marked off in months, showing the stages by which Christy's parents came to be aware of his disability.
   b) Talk to your parents and then draw another time-line to show your own development for a similar period of time.

Role play

Improvise one or both of the following scenes.
● Mrs Brown takes Christy, aged nine months, for a medical examination and has to face a doctor who has little hope for him. (Christy says: 'Almost every doctor who saw and examined me, labelled me a very interesting but also a hopeless case.')
● Mrs Brown meets two of her neighbours who try to convince her that Christy should be 'taken kindly, sympathetically, but not seriously'.

This extract from Christy's novel comes at the end of the first chapter.

The letter 'A'

In a corner Mona and Paddy were sitting huddled together, a few torn school primers before them. They were writing down little sums on to an old chipped slate, using a bright piece of yellow chalk. I was close to them, propped up by a few pillows against the wall, watching.

It was the chalk that attracted me so much. It was a long, slender stick of vivid yellow. I had never seen anything like it before, and it showed up so well against the black surface of the slate that I was fascinated by it as much as if it had been a stick of gold.

Suddenly I wanted desperately to do what my sister was doing. Then – without thinking or knowing exactly what I was doing, I reached out and took the stick of chalk out of my sister's hand – with my left foot.

I do not know why I used my left foot to do this. It is a puzzle to many people as well as to myself, for, although I had displayed a curious interest in my toes at an early age, I had never attempted before this to use either of my feet in any way. They could have been as useless to me as were my hands. That day, however, my left foot, apparently on its own volition, reached out and very impolitely took the chalk out of my sister's hand.

I held it tightly between my toes, and, acting on an impulse, made a wild sort of scribble with it on the slate. Next moment I stopped a bit dazed, surprised, looking down at the stick of yellow chalk stuck between my toes, not knowing what to do with it next, hardly knowing how it got there. Then I looked up and became aware that everyone had stopped talking and were staring at me silently. Nobody stirred. Mona, her black curls framing her chubby little face, stared at me with great big eyes and open mouth. Across the open hearth, his face lit by flames, sat my father, leaning forward, hands outspread on his knees, his shoulders tense. I felt the sweat break out on my forehead.

My mother came in from the pantry with a steaming pot in her hand. She stopped midway between the table and the fire, feeling the tension flowing through the room. She followed their stare and saw me in the corner. Her eyes looked from my face down to my foot, with the chalk gripped between my toes. She put down the pot.

Then she crossed over to me and knelt down beside me, as she had done so many times before.

'I'll show you what to do with it, Chris,' she said, very slowly and in a queer, jerky way, her face flushed as if with some inner excitement.

Taking another piece of chalk from Mona, she hesitated, then very deliberately drew, on the floor in front of me, the single letter 'A'.

'Copy that,' she said, looking steadily at me. 'Copy it, Christy.'

I couldn't.

I looked about me, looked around at the faces that were turned towards me, tense, excited faces that were at that moment frozen, immobile, eager, waiting for a miracle in their midst.

The stillness was profound. The room was full of flame and shadow that danced before my eyes and lulled my taut nerves into a sort of waking sleep. I could hear the sound of the water-tap dripping in the pantry, the loud ticking of the clock on the mantleshelf, and the soft hiss and crackle of the logs on the open hearth.

I tried again. I put out my foot and made a wild jerking stab with the chalk which produced a very crooked line and nothing more. Mother held the slate steady for me.

'Try again, Chris,' she whispered in my ear. 'Again.'

I did. I stiffened my body and put my left foot out again, for the third time. I drew one side of the letter. I drew half the other side. Then the stick of chalk broke and I was left with a stump. I wanted to fling it away and give up. Then I felt my mother's hand on my shoulder. I tried once more. Out went my foot. I shook, I sweated and strained every muscle. My hands were so tightly clenched that my fingernails bit into the flesh. I set my teeth so hard that I nearly pierced my lower lip. Everything in the room swam till the faces around me were mere patches of white. But – I drew it – the letter 'A'. There it was on the floor before me. Shaky, with awkward, wobbly sides and a very uneven centre line. But it was the letter 'A'. I looked up. I saw my mother's face for a moment, tears on her cheeks. Then my father stooped down and hoisted me on to his shoulder.

Christy Brown

Writing your own versions

Choose one of the following pieces of writing:

1 Write an account of Christy writing the letter 'A' from his sister Mona's point of view.

2 Use one of the pieces of role play you did – or watched – as the basis of a piece of writing that might have been included in *My left foot*. Write as if you were Christy telling the story.

3 In the rest of the novel Christy makes it clear that it was living in such a caring family that helped him to overcome his disability. Write, as one of his brothers or sisters, about the benefits and pleasures of living with Christy. (You will be helped in this if you can read more of the book or see the film of *My left foot*, but if not you could invent details that seem appropriate.)

Same story, different form

The film, *My left foot*, does not start with Christy's birth. Instead, the opening shots show Christy typing with his left foot and then, aged twenty eight, as a successful writer and painter. He is being taken in a white Rolls Royce as a celebrity to a grand charity reception. This is, in fact, where the novel ends.

Why is it important that the writers of the film chose to start the screenplay at this point?

In the film, Christy's life story is revealed in a series of flashbacks as the nurse who is employed to look after him reads his novel. This is how his birth and the discovery of his disability are dealt with in the film:

INT. HOSPITAL. NIGHT
1932 MR BROWN *walks down the corridor of the Rotunda Hospital in Dublin. We hear the sound of a newborn baby crying.*

INT. HOSPITAL WARD. NIGHT
MR BROWN *goes into the ward. The baby stops crying. It is visiting time. The ward is full of happy mothers and their visitors.* MR BROWN *looks for* MRS BROWN. *He can't find her. Ominously, at the end of the ward there is a curtain drawn around one of the beds.* MR BROWN *walks past it, refusing to face it. He continues to near the end of the ward and can't find* MRS BROWN. *He looks back up the ward. A nurse comes towards him and has a word with him. She points to the curtained-off bed.* MR BROWN *nods gravely.*

INT. PUBLIC HOUSE. NIGHT
MR BROWN *stands at the bar.*
MR BROWN: Give me a pint and a chaser there, Brian.
FRIEND: Congratulations.
MR BROWN: On what?
FRIEND: The new boy, Christy.
MR BROWN: Are you trying to make a jackass out of me or what? The child's an imbecile. A moron. A vegetable. I says to the doctor, 'Is there any hope for him?' and the doctor says, 'Well, Mr Brown, there is some movement in his left foot.' His left foot! He'll never be able to pick up a trowel or mend a gable wall.
FRIEND: You might have to put him in a home.
MR BROWN: He'll go into a coffin before any son of mine goes into a home.

Shane Connaughton and *Jim Sheridan*

138

Thinking about the screenplay

1 From whose point of view are these events seen?
2 Make a storyboard showing what happens in this extract from the film. Set it out in three columns, like this:

Picture	Words spoken	Sound effects
1. Artwork (Mr Brown in hospital corridor) 2. Artwork (Mr Brown in ward)		Newborn baby crying Noise of happy conversation

3 What is Mr Brown's attitude towards his newly-born son?
4 Read through this extract again and then discuss the way a screenplay is set out. Here are some points to consider.

- You are told whether the scene is shot inside or outside, by the terms INT. (for INTERIOR) and EXT. (for EXTERIOR), and whether it is NIGHT or DAY. What other piece of information is given with these directions?
- You are told exactly what someone watching the film would see. For example: 'MR BROWN *walks down the corridor of the Rotunda Hospital.*' You are also told about sounds that would be heard: '*We hear the sound of a newborn baby crying.*' What do you notice about these directions?
- Look at the way one event follows on from another. In your discussion, decide what would have happened, in real life, between each of the scenes in the two extracts from the screenplay.

139

This second scene occurs a little later in the film. In the novel there is no direct mention of this incident.

INT. LIVING ROOM. DAY
MRS BROWN *is polishing shoes. There are six pairs of children's and Mr Brown's boots. She polishes away as* CHRISTY *watches her, especially when she holds her back in pain.*

INT. CHILDREN'S BEDROOM. DAY
MRS BROWN *carries* CHRISTY *and the shoes into the room and puts* CHRISTY *onto his bed. She lays the shoes out in their proper places at the foot of each bed. She looks at* CHRISTY's *bare feet.* CHRISTY *looks at them too and smiles.* MRS BROWN *gives him a hug. Then she stands up and puts her hand to her face and rubs her face.*

MRS BROWN: Christy. I have to go outside to make a phone call. You wait here.
(CHRISTY *waits and listens to his mother on the stairs. There is a loud noise.*)

INT. HALLWAY. DAY
CHRISTY *on the landing. At the bottom of the stairs lies his mother, groaning.* CHRISTY *flies down the stairs. At the bottom of the stairs he looks at his mother, puts his foot out to try and awaken her, but she seems unconscious. Suddenly she lets out a huge groan and holds her stomach.* CHRISTY *stands on one foot and leans against the banisters. He tries to get past his fallen mother without hurting her. He flings himself past her and lands on his head on the ground. After a moment he starts to kick the door.*
MRS BROWN: Jesus, Mary and Joseph, where am I?
(*She looks at* CHRISTY, *who is eyeball to eyeball with her*)
CHRISTY, where am I?
(*She goes unconscious again.* CHRISTY *kicks the door. His face throughout is a paroxysm of effort.*)

140

EXT. STREET. DAY

Deserted. Door noise. MAGSO *putting out rubbish. She hears noise, goes over to the door. She looks through the letterbox.*

INT. HALLWAY. DAY

Eyes through the letterbox.

MAGSO's *point of view. She can see* CHRISTY *upside down.*

MAGSO: What's up, Christy?

(MAGSO *hears a moan and looks to the left of the letterbox, where she can see* MRS BROWN *lying on the floor.*)

Jesus, Mary and Joseph.

(*She pulls the key strings up through the letterbox and the door begins to open.*)

EXT. STREET. DAY

CHRISTY *sits alone on the street as all the neighbours crowd around the house. The ambulance pulls away with Christy's mother and* CHRISTY *watches it depart.*

MAGSO: It was the grace of God that door was unlocked.

NAN: What happened?

MAGSO: She was carrying Christy down the stairs when she fell. I heard an unmerciful bang and rushed over to the door. Poor Christy was lying at the bottom of the stairs like a moron.

NAN: He's an awful cross to the poor woman.

MAGSO: It's in a home he ought to be. He has the mind of a three year old.

Shane Connaughton and *Jim Sheridan*

About the extract

What does this scene show about:
- Christy?
- the attitudes of friends and relatives?

Write a section of screenplay

Using the information you have gathered, turn the extract about Christy writing the letter 'A', into a screenplay.

Remember to include these features of screenplay layout in your final version:
- INTERIOR (INT.) or EXTERIOR (EXT.) is specified
- exact LOCATIONS are given for each scene
- DAY or NIGHT is specified
- DIRECTIONS are written in italics
- writers are SELECTIVE about what they show. (One scene does not follow straight after another as it would in real life. Audiences accept jumps in time.)

Assignment

Reread through the extract from the novel on pages 134-135 and the two pieces of screenplay on page 138. Using the work you have already done to help you, write a detailed comparison of these two forms of writing.
- Show how the first scene of screenplay has changed the events of the novel.
- Suggest reasons why these changes have been made.
- Explain what you learn from each one about Christy and the other people in his life.
- Say which account you prefer, and why.

Follow-up theme: disability

Do you think that Christy should have been played in the film as he was by Daniel Day Lewis, an able-bodied person? Would it have been better to have chosen an actor with cerebral palsy to play the part?

Before you discuss this question read the comments which follow. Nigel Skinner, who works for an organisation called 'Stars Organisation for Spastics' was born with cerebral palsy. Nabil Shaban, a successful actor, has been confined to a wheelchair all his life.

Nigel Skinner

'I think there should be more disability in soaps, such as *EastEnders*, *Coronation Street* and the like. It is very rare that you see disability in plays on television, and when you do it makes people pity the disabled. It never shows the positive side to disability. There are many disabled actors and actresses. Why can't we see these people on our screens more? The police series, *The Bill*, has featured actors with disabilities, why can't we see the same on other programmes?

The recent film, *My left foot,* starred Daniel Day Lewis as Christy Brown, the writer who suffered from cerebral palsy, and although Day Lewis was excellent, couldn't the part have been played equally well by an actor with a disability?'

Nabil Shaban

(Interview between Nabil and Jonathon Ross on *The Jonathon Ross Show*.)
J.R. When you first set out to be an actor did people encourage you, or did they look at your disability and try to put you off?
N.S. I wasn't encouraged at all. I wanted to be an actor way back when I was a kid, and I wrote to drama schools when I was about sixteen and explained that I was in a wheelchair and they said: 'Get lost!', basically. 'You haven't got a hope in hell.' So I took them at their word for a while. I worked as an amateur for local am-dram... a guy called Michael Flanders who was in a wheelchair, a singer and a comic actor... suggested the only way you're going to make it is to create a demand for yourself, in other words write your own material and do something only you can do... and eventually I took that advice myself and a friend, Richard Tomlinson, who's able bodied, set up this theatre company... Graeae.

[He goes on in the interview to talk about being the only person he knew of to have played Shakespeare's *Hamlet* in a wheelchair.]

We used it... If you're going to act you've got to be believable. There's no point in trying to say to the audience, 'Look, the wheelchair's not there!' It's stupid to play *Hamlet* set at the time when Hamlet was supposed to be around. And the play, like most Shakespeare, you can do what you like with it. You can set it in 2525 if you want. So we set it in the very near future when Britain...is a Fascist state and I'm a disabled, a deliberately disabled heir to the throne, and that the reason why Claudius marries my mother and kills my father, is because he doesn't want a disabled king to be ruling Denmark. So we used the disability, although we didn't change the text. It's all there in the sub-text. I used an electric wheelchair, purely for the practical reason, for the swordfight. Because it's not easy to have a swordfight doing this... (gestures), but if you've got an electric chair...

J.R. Which was something Shakespeare was stupid enough to overlook, of course, when he wrote...

N.S. Although the great thing about it was that some critic actually thought that Shakespeare might have had a disabled person in mind for the part...putting a disabled person there it suddenly made sense as to why they didn't want Hamlet to be king, why they didn't want him to marry Ophelia...

[Later he spoke about being judged by looks alone.]

In Hollywood and in soap operas if you've got the archetypal beautiful, handsome looks, you're regarded as a good person; a heroine/hero: and if you're ugly or deformed or whatever, you're regarded as evil...we're brainwashed into thinking like that. And it goes right back from childhood when we have stories of Cinderella and the three ugly sisters. All the stories, all the fairy tales, emphasise that... People do judge you by the way you look and if you've got burns and if you've got scars on your face, the first reaction, after having been brainwashed by those things, is to think that person is inherently evil.

Stephen Wiltshire sketching in Moscow

Four years ago, QED discovered the artistic genius of a young autistic boy. Now it goes back to find how fame has changed his life. By Sally Brompton

Brigitte → Nielsen helps a poor unsighted chap across the road. Readers, you saw it here first – *Celebrity Guide Dogs For The Blind!*

Your views

1 From what Nigel Skinner and Nabil Shaban have said, would you agree that it is society that disables people, not their particular physical or mental conditions?

2 a) Conduct your own research and collect examples from film, television, books, comics and magazines showing stereotypes/non-stereotypes of disability.

   b) Write a report agreeing or disagreeing with Nabil Shaban's comments about the links between character and appearance. Include items from your collection of media texts to illustrate your argument. You could begin, as Nabil Shaban suggests, by looking at 'fairy tales'.

For more on argumentative writing see The Process of Writing module in Book 4B, pages 94-99.

Devising drama

Drama techniques

Devising a play involves a number of steps.

> ◆ Deciding what it will be about: the subject.
> ◆ Learning about that subject – through research and through your own improvised drama work.
> ◆ Agreeing how you are going to deal with the material you have.
> ◆ Planning the final form of the play.

Here are the methods which one group of young people used in devising a play about teenage runaways.

You could try out these methods even when no finished production is being planned. They can help you to learn about quite difficult issues, as with homelessness in this case.

I Creating a still picture

A way of capturing and investigating an important moment in a piece of drama.

Two people have been working together in role as father and daughter. They make a still picture of the moment the daughter decides she has to leave home.

● What can you see in this picture?
● What questions would you like to ask these characters?
● Ask two people in your class to take up the positions in the photograph.
● Ask them the questions you have put together.
(You could try the same method with an important moment in your own drama work. Start with an important action and freeze it as a still photograph.)

II Modelling

A way of expressing a group's ideas in a single picture.

Some time after leaving home, the girl regrets what she has done. The group uses one person to show what she is feeling at this point. They decide where she is and tell her how to stand or sit until she looks exactly right.

- What reasons can you think of for a runaway girl regretting her decision?
- As a group choose one reason. Ask one person in your group to freeze into a position that you think expresses the runaway's feelings at that moment. Suggest slight changes of position until you are satisfied that she looks exactly as you would want.
  (Use modelling on other occasions when you want to bring everyone's ideas together at an important moment in your own drama.)

III Thought-tracking

A way of investigating innermost thoughts at certain points in the action.

A group of runaways appears to be having a good time celebrating the finding of a large sum of money. At certain points the action is frozen and we hear the thoughts of different characters. As an alternative, an observer can speak the thoughts of characters in the drama.

- Improvise the scene where the runaways celebrate their find. Interrupt it at different points to hear the true thoughts of individual characters.
- You could, instead, briefly tell the story of this scene as a strip cartoon, where each frame shows the character's thoughts as well as their actions or words.
  (Try this method out when you think that a character's actions or words may be different from his or her thinking in your own improvisations or drama.)

IV Hot seating

A way of investigating a character's motives or feelings after he or she has been involved in a particular piece of action.

One of the runaways asks a teacher at her old school for help with someone who is injured. The teacher refuses to help because he or she does not want to become involved without finding out more about the group. Members of the whole group, as themselves, question the person still in role as the teacher.

● Write down some questions you could ask the person in the role of the teacher.
● Work with someone else to write the answers he or she might give.
● Script your own play scene in which the runaway girl goes back to the group and tells them why the teacher has refused to help. Use the work you have done on the teacher's responses as the basis for this.
(In your own drama work, when your group has watched a piece of dramatic action you could hot seat the person whose actions or attitudes you found most interesting or puzzling.)

V Forum theatre

A way of concentrating on the outcomes of one person's action in a particular situation.

One of the runaways is offered a place in a hostel, but this turns out to be more like a prison. The runaway wants to change the way the hostel is run.

The situation: the runaway tries to persuade the people who run the hostel to change something about it.
   This is acted out while the rest of the group watch. Observers can stop the action at any time and make suggestions about what the runaway could do.
   (You could try this with any situation where one person is trying to persuade another to change something. If you wish, observers can step in to take over roles, or you could add new roles.)
   For more on homelessness see The Process of Writing module in Book 4B, pages 76-78.

If you want to use these methods to make a finished play you could try the following procedure.

1 Agree on the 'story' of your play.
2 Improvise it, scene by scene using some of these drama techniques.
3 Record these improvisations on tape.
4 Transcribe these recordings.
5 Redraft your transcriptions.
   - In doing this always keep your overall story-line in mind and try to make sure the story moves on.
   - Look at how individual characters develop and try to agree the action that will happen each scene.
   - Each member of the group could be responsible for one or two scenes.
6 Read your drafts together and rewrite a final version.
7 As you rehearse the final version do not be afraid to change things if they do not seem to work in performance.

Let her sleep

The following script, devised using the drama techniques on pages 144-146, was finally scripted by a professional writer, Guy Hutchins. *Let her sleep* is about the experiences of some teenagers who have left home and live on the streets of a large city.

During the play we see the teenagers coming together to secretly take over a disused portakabin in a junior school playground. In this scene two fifteen-year-old boys explore the portakabin for the first time.

	NATHAN COMES ON AND CROSSES TOWARDS THE PORTAKABIN AREA
NATHAN	Kevin! Come here!
	KEVIN COMES ON
	What do you think? (INDICATES PORTAKABIN) Home sweet home.
KEVIN	A portakabin? Don't make me laugh.
NATHAN	It's got a roof. It's dry. What's wrong with it?
KEVIN	It's in a school playground for a start.
NATHAN	So?
KEVIN	What about all those little kids? We wouldn't last five minutes.
NATHAN	They're tinies. They wouldn't do anything.
KEVIN	Except run straight home and tell their mums and dads. Or their teachers.
NATHAN	But why should they ever see us?
KEVIN	'Course they would...
NATHAN	No, think it through. What about when you were at junior school? Ever get there too early?
KEVIN	Once or twice...
NATHAN	No one was ever there before eight.
KEVIN	Except the caretaker.
NATHAN	He'd never come over here.
KEVIN	You can't be sure.

NATHAN	Right on the edge of the playing field? Look, he's not even bothered to lock it. So there's nothing for him to want to check up on.
KEVIN	Maybe...
NATHAN	And they've all gone by four. Even the teachers that work hard.
KEVIN	What about parents' evenings?
NATHAN	Prat. It's a gift, look. As long as we're out by eight and stay away till four – then it's our's for life, this place. No one will ever know.
KEVIN	Have you had a look inside?
NATHAN	I've only stuck my head round.
KEVIN	Then how can you be certain no one's using it?
NATHAN	Let's see for ourselves. THEY GO INTO THE PORTAKABIN See? Empty.
KEVIN	What's that pile over there.
NATHAN	(CROSSES AND PICKS THROUGH A SMALL PILE) Nothing much. Sleeping bag. Newspapers. Old poly bag. (UNWRAPS) With a toothbrush in it.
KEVIN	Those are somebody's things!
NATHAN	Nah. (SNIFFS THE SLEEPING BAG) No one'd ever want to sleep in that.
KEVIN	(JOINING HIM) Hey, we could take it to the laundrette.
NATHAN	What with? We need money first.
KEVIN	We could try begging again.
NATHAN	Yeah, and look what we got yesterday. Forty pence.
KEVIN	We'll try a different patch then.
NATHAN	Never give up do you? First things first. We've found our new home. Let's get the moving in sorted.
KEVIN	We are moved in.
NATHAN	Not properly.
KEVIN	We're here. We've got nothing else to move.
NATHAN	We'll go back to that skip we saw. There was a mattress there.
KEVIN	But it's miles!
NATHAN	Want to sleep on the floor instead?
KEVIN	Should we do it in daylight, though?
NATHAN	Mmm. You're right. Let's see if we can blag a cup of tea somewhere first.
KEVIN	Yeah, and some cakes.
NATHAN	(DRY) The way you beg? Never mind. You can share mine. Come on. THEY START TO LEAVE. EMMA MOVES OVER AND BLOCKS THEIR PATH
EMMA	And what the hell are you two doing? THE BOYS TRY TO RUN. EMMA GRABS THEM No you don't. I said what the hell are you doing here?
NATHAN	None of your business.
EMMA	Like hell it isn't! I live here. This is my home. I don't like people snooping round in it.
KEVIN	You mean that stuff's yours?

148

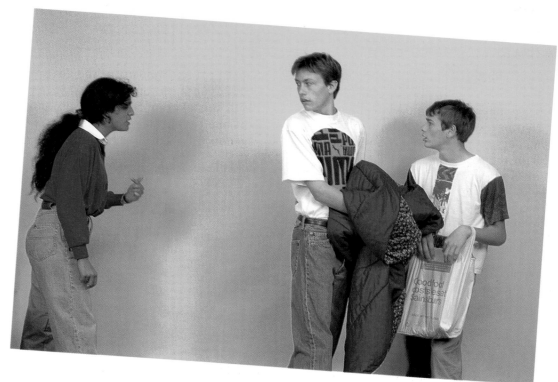

EMMA	Don't you go near it.
NATHAN	We thought the place was empty. Deserted. We didn't think –
EMMA	Well, you can start thinking now.
KEVIN	I mean that stuff over there – we thought – when we...
EMMA	(CROSSES TO HER PILE) You been meddling with it?
	(STARTS TO CHECK THE CONTENTS) What have you taken?
	I should tell me. Easy enough to find out...
NATHAN	Nothing. Honest.
KEVIN	We didn't know it was yours.
NATHAN	We, er – we did think of taking...
EMMA	(STRAIGHTENS. AGGRESSIVE) Yeah?
NATHAN	(LAME) We thought of taking your sleeping bag to the laundrette.
EMMA	Sweetness and light. So you could nick it, eh?
KEVIN	We didn't know it belonged to anybody. And we thought it
	could do with a bit of a clean, before –
	(EMMA SMACKS HIM HARD ACROSS THE MOUTH)
	Ow! What d'you do that for?
EMMA	You come in meddling round where I live – you call me a filthy tart –
	and you try to nick my sleeping bag –
KEVIN	We didn't –
EMMA	Just sod off. Get out. Go back to your nice mummies and daddies and
	your nice warm houses. Go on. Oh, and one more thing. Tell anyone at
	all that you've seen me here, and you're dead. Both of you. Understand?
	THE BOYS STAND EMBARRASSED
	Well? What're you waiting for? (PAUSE) I said get out.
	SHE MOVES TOWARDS THEM. THE BOYS FLINCH. BUT
	STAND THEIR GROUND
EMMA	What's the matter?
KEVIN	We've got nowhere to go.

Getting to know the extract

1 In a group of 3, practise reading the extract aloud.

2 If you have space, work out what movements by the characters would be helpful in acting this scene. Try to put these movements down on paper in the form of diagrams and link them with numbered notes to the script, for example:

NATHAN (1)	(CROSSES AND PICKS THROUGH A SMALL PILE) Nothing much. Sleeping bag. Newspapers. Old poly bag. (UNWRAPS) With a toothbrush in it.
KEVIN	Those are somebody's things!
NATHAN	Nah. (SNIFFS THE SLEEPING BAG) No one'd ever want to sleep in that.
KEVIN (2)	(JOINING HIM) Hey, we could take it to the laundrette.

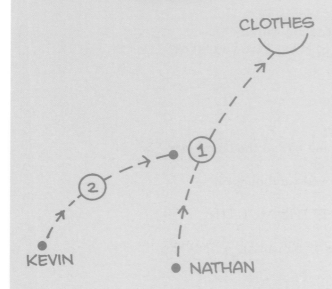

(1) Nathan moves UL to clothes

(2) Kevin moves C

(Terms used in directing movement on stage:
Centre (C) = centre of acting area;
Downstage (D) = towards audience;
Upstage (U) = away from audience;
Right (R) and Left (L) are from the point of view of an actor facing the audience.)

3 In a group, brainstorm the advantages and disadvantages for the runaways of living in this portakabin. Start with those mentioned by the two boys. Have one person in your group list them in a table like the one below.

Advantages of portakabin	Disadvantages of portakabin
It is dry	Junior school children might discover them

4 If the boys are fifteen, how old is Emma? Talk about the evidence in the extract to support your view.

Assignment

Write a script for one or both of the following scenes:

Scene A: Before

The young people in the play had a number of different reasons for leaving home:

● being bullied by an older brother or sister
● having disagreements with parents over boy-friends or girl-friends
● wanting to be with a friend who had run away

1 First list any other reasons you can think of to explain a teenager's leaving home.

2 Then choose one of these reasons and write in playscript form what happens immediately before he or she leaves.

Scene B: After

The extract you have been given ends in the middle of a scene. Set up the end of the scene as a Still picture (see page 144). Question the people in the picture. Improvise the rest of the scene. You could use the Forum theatre technique (see page146) to try different outcomes. Write the rest of the scene in playscript form.

Nathan's case

In this section you are going to take part in a simulation. A simulation is an exercise that allows you to consider a situation from the point of view of people who would have to make a decision about it in real life. People in a class play different roles and all consider the same problem. They have to make a definite decision at the end.

How the simulation works

In this simulation, five people will play the parts of the people involved. The rest of the class will split into small groups – as committees – to interview each of these people in turn. They then consider the case and make their decision.

Those on the committees will probably find it helpful to prepare questions before they start and to keep notes as they conduct the interviews.

Enquiry into the case of Nathan Watts

People involved in the enquiry:

Kevin Field, 15	Nathan's friend
Christine Jones, 27	Nathan's tutor at Three Barns Comprehensive School
Michelle Harrison, 24	A Social Worker, responsible for homeless persons under the age of 17
Emma Noon, 19	A homeless young woman
John Watts, 43	Nathan's father

Background information

For many years Nathan Watts had been bullied by his brother, Dean, who is three years older. His parents had never taken him seriously when he complained and eventually things became too much for him. Six months ago Nathan ran away from home with his friend Kevin Field. The two of them spent three weeks sleeping rough in a city centre, and then made a home in a disused portakabin in a Junior School playground. Emma Noon had already been living there secretly for some time. They were soon joined by a number of other homeless young people, aged from twelve to sixteen.

They only used the portakabin at night so that they would not be discovered, and they were no trouble to anyone else using the site. The group lived together for some time, making money chiefly by begging. One of the younger girls, Jo, was ill when she joined the group. Although the others did their best to look after her, she died one night, of pneumonia. Afraid to be found out the others decided to bury her secretly and hold their own funeral service.

While they were doing this the police caught them. They are now being held in custody until somewhere can be found for them to live. The police do not intend to prosecute Nathan and have asked the Social Services what should happen to him.

Playing the simulation

You are members of the Social Services committee and will make the decision about what will happen to Nathan. You will be able to interview people involved in the case and will then have to decide what is best for him.

The choices you have are:
- to return him to live with his parents
- to place him in a local authority children's home until he is 17
- to find foster parents prepared to look after him until he is 17

When he is past the age of 17 you will no longer have any responsibility for him.

Remember that your decision will affect Nathan for some time to come. You must do what is best for him.

For writing

When you have made your decision, write a letter to Nathan's parents telling them what you have decided and why.

These letters could then be read to the rest of the class.

Role cards

Kevin Field

You are Nathan's best friend. You know that he has been bullied at home by Dean, his brother, for many years. His father is more interested in his work than his family. Nathan is quite clever, but rather immature, in your view. He tends to do things without thinking. Your home life is very unhappy, and is unlikely to improve, but you know that Nathan's could be quite pleasant. The main problem is his brother who is nearly 19 now and could leave home soon.

Christine Jones

You have been Nathan's tutor since he came to this school aged 11. He has been quite successful and particularly likes art and English. Like most adults at the school you were shocked when he disappeared as he never seemed to have any serious problems. You are still not sure how serious his brother's bullying was. If he goes into the children's home he would probably have to move school because of travel difficulties. He has made a good start to his GCSE studies, and despite his absence he could still do well. Any further disruption could have a very serious effect.

John Watts

You are Nathan's father. You and your wife have another son, Dean, who is 18. Nathan has always demanded a lot of attention, unlike Dean who is very independent. You know that Dean is rather boisterous but believe that he would not really harm anyone. Nathan's accusations are an exaggeration. Neither you nor your wife, Anna, believe there is anything wrong in your family, although you admit that both of you have had to work long hours and have sometimes ignored your children's needs. You were relieved when Nathan was found, although you had always thought he would manage, as Kevin was with him.

152

Emma Noon

You left home when you were 15 after many years of neglect. Until recently you had always survived on the streets on your own. You can now cope well and usually manage to stay out of trouble. Originally when Nathan and the others came, you regarded them as a nuisance. Later, though, you began to feel some responsibility for them as they were younger than you and needed to learn to live independently. Eventually, you enjoyed being the 'leader' of this small community. It is the best family you have ever had. You know that young people do not leave home without a good reason, and you are worried that Nathan will not cope unless he has some good friends with him.

Michelle Harrison

You were called in by the police soon after the group of homeless young people were found. Nathan's home problems seem much less serious than those of most young people you meet in your work. However, he seems to have been deeply affected by them and says that he will run away again if he is made to go home. He has refused to see his father, but has spoken to his mother. There seems, though, to be a great distance between them: Nathan believes he has always been 'picked on' in the family. Places at local authority homes are in very short supply and are available only for serious cases. Very few foster parents are willing to take on people of Nathan's age.

Assignment

Once you have tried this simulation you could attempt to write one of your own, following the same procedure, and using the same headings:
- People involved in the enquiry
- Background information
- Playing the simulation

Some hints to help you.

People involved: use characters who will be likely to present different points of view on the matter.

Background information: take care to make your story consistent. Make sure the basic information is clear but allow the people involved to add their own individual pieces of information as well.

Playing the simulation: decide who is conducting the enquiry, its purpose, and what decisions have to be made.

Monologue

This unit begins by asking you to look at the script of a television play by Alan Bennett called *A cream cracker under the settee*, one of six plays first broadcast by the BBC in a television series called *Talking heads*. Each of these plays unfolds the story of one central character by using that person's own spoken thoughts in what is known as a **monologue**.

  In this play Doris, an old lady of seventy-five, is living alone. She has a Home Help but the Social Services would like her to go into a Home. Attempting some dusting, Doris has fallen and broken her hip. She is sitting rather awkwardly on a low chair, rubbing her leg...

A cream cracker under the settee

Shan't let on I was dusting.

> *She shoves the duster down the side of the chair.*

Dusting is forbidden.

> *She looks down at the wedding photo on the floor.*

Cracked the photo. We're cracked, Wilfred.

> *Pause*

The gate's open again. I thought it had blown shut, only now it's blown open. Bang bang bang all morning, it'll be bang bang bang all afternoon.
  Dogs coming in, all sorts. You see Zulema should have closed that, only she didn't.

> *Pause*

The sneck's loose, that's the root cause of it. It's wanted doing for years. I kept saying to Wilfred, 'When are you going to get round to that gate?' But oh no. It was always the same refrain. 'Don't worry, Mother. I've got it on my list.' I never saw no list. He had no list. I was the one with the list. He'd no system at all, Wilfred. 'When I get a minute, Doris.' Well, he's got a minute now, bless him.

> *Pause*

Feels funny this leg. Not there.

> *Pause*

Some leaves coming down now. I could do with trees if they didn't have leaves, going up and down the path. Zulema won't touch them. Says if I want leaves swept I've to contact the Parks Department.

I wouldn't care if they were my leaves. They're not my leaves. They're next-door's leaves. We don't have any leaves. I know that for a fact. We've only got the one little bush and it's an evergreen, so I'm certain they're not my leaves. Only other folks won't know that. They see the bush and they see the path and they think, 'Them's her leaves.' Well, they're not.

I ought to put a note on the gate. 'Not my leaves.' Not my leg either, the way it feels. Gone to sleep.

Pause

I didn't even want the bush, to be quite honest. We debated it for long enough. I said, 'Dad. Is it a bush that will make a mess?' he said, 'Doris. Rest assured. This type of bush is very easy to follow,' and he fetches out the catalogue. '"This labour-saving variety is much favoured by the retired people." Anyway,' he says, 'the garden is my department.' Garden! It's only the size of a tablecloth. I said, 'Given a choice, Wilfred, I'd have preferred concrete.' He said, 'Doris. Concrete has no character.' I said, 'Never mind character, Wilfred, where does hygiene come on the agenda?' With concrete you can feel easy in your mind. But no. He had to have his' little garden even if it was only a bush. Well, he's got his little garden now. Only I bet that's covered in leaves. Graves, gardens, everything's to follow.

I'll make a move in a minute. See if I can't put the kettle on. Come on leg. Wake up.

Go to black.

Come up on Doris sitting on the floor with her back to the wall. The edge of a tiled fireplace also in shot.

Fancy, there's a cream cracker under the settee. How long has that been there? I can't think when I last had cream crackers. She's not half done this place, Zulema.

I'm going to save that cream cracker and show it to her next time she starts going on about Stafford house. I'll say, 'Don't Stafford house me, lady. This cream cracker was under the settee. I've only got to send this cream cracker to the Director of Social Services and you'll be on the carpet. Same as the cream cracker. I'll be in Stafford House, Zulema, but you'll be in the Unemployment Exchange.

I'm en route for the window only I'm not making much headway. I'll bang on it. Alert somebody. Don't know who. Don't know anybody round here now. Folks opposite, I don't know them. Used to be the Marsdens. Mr and Mrs Marsden and Yvonne, the funny daughter. There for years. Here before we were, the Marsdens. Then he died, and she died, and Yvonne went away somewhere. A home, I expect.

Smartish woman after them. Worked for Wheatley and Whiteley, had a three-quarter-length coat. Used to fetch the envelopes round for the blind. Then she went and folks started to come and go. You lose track. I don't think they're married, half of them. You see all sorts. They come in the garden and behave like animals. I find the evidence in the morning.

She picks up the photograph that has fallen from the wall.

Now, Wilfred.

Pause

I can nip this leg and nothing.

Pause

Ought to have had a dog. Then it could have been barking of someone. Wilfred was always hankering after a dog. I wasn't keen. Hairs all up and down, then having to take it outside every five minutes. Wilfred said he would be prepared to undertake the responsibility. The dog would be his province. I said, 'Yes, and whose province would all the little hairs be?' I gave in in the finish, only I said it had to be on the small side. I didn't want one of them great lolloping, lamp post-smelling articles. And we never got one either. It was the growing mushrooms in the cellar saga all over again. He never got round to it. A kiddy'd've solved all that. Getting mad ideas. Like the fretwork, making toys and forts and whatnot. No end of money he was going to make. Then there was his phantom allotment. Oh, he was going to be coming home with leeks and spring cabbage and I don't know what. 'We can be self-sufficient in the vegetable department, Doris.' Never materialised. I was glad. It'd've meant muck somehow.
Hello. Somebody coming. Salvation.

She cranes up towards the window.

Young lad. Hello. Hello.

She begins to wave.

The cheeky monkey. He's spending a penny. Hey.

She shouts.

Hey. Get out. Go on. Clear off. You little demon. Would you credit it? Inside our gate. Broad daylight. The place'll stink.

A pause as she realises what she has done.

He wouldn't have known what to do anyway. Only a kiddy. The policeman comes past now and again. If I can catch him. Maybe the door's a better bet. If I can get there I can open it and wait while somebody comes past.

She starts to heave herself up.

This must be what they give them them frame things for.

Go to black.

Come up on Doris sitting on the floor in the hall, her back against the front door, the letter-box above her head.

This is where we had the pram. You couldn't get past for it. Proper prams then, springs and hoods. Big wheels. More like cars than prams. Not these fold-up jobs. You were proud of your pram. Wilfred spotted it in the Evening Post. I said, 'Don't let's jump the gun, Wilfred.' He said, 'At that price, Doris? This is the chance of a lifetime.'

Pause

Comes under this door like a knife. I can't reach the lock. That's part of the Zulema regime. 'Lock it and put it on the chain, Doris. You never know who comes. It may not be a bona fide caller.

Couple came round last week. Braying on the door. They weren't bona fide callers, they had a Bible. I didn't go. Only they opened the letter-box and started shouting about Jesus. 'Good news,' they kept shouting. 'Good news.' They left the gate open, never mind good news. They ought to get their priorities right. They want learning that on their instruction course. Shouting about Jesus and leaving gates open. It's hypocrisy is that. It is in my book anyway. 'Love God and close all gates.'

She closes her eyes. We hear some swift steps up the path and the letter-box opens as a leaflet comes through. Swift steps away again as she opens her eyes.

Hello, hello.

She bangs on the door behind her.

Help. Help. Oh stink.

She tries to reach the leaflet.

What is it? Minicabs? 'Your roof repaired'?

She gets the leaflet.

'Grand carpet sale.' Carpet sales in chapels now. Else sikhs.

She looks at the place where the pram was.

I wanted him called John. The midwife said he wasn't fit to be called anything and had we any newspaper? Wilfred said, 'Oh yes. She saves newspaper. She saves shoeboxes as well.' I must have fallen asleep because when I woke up she'd gone. I wanted to see him. Wrapping him in newspaper as if he was dirty. He wasn't dirty, little thing. I don't think Wilfred minded. A kiddy. It was the same as the allotment and the fretwork. Just a craze. He said, 'We're better off, Doris. Just the two of us.' It was then he started talking about getting a dog.

If it had lived I might have had grandchildren now. Wouldn't have been in this fix. Daughters are best. They don't migrate.

Pause

I'm going to have to migrate or I'll catch my death.

She nips her other leg.

This one's going numb now.

She picks up the photo.

Come on, Dad. Come on, numby leg.

Go to black.

We were always on our own, me and Wilfred. We weren't gregarious. We just weren't the gregarious type. He thought he was, but he wasn't.

Mix. I don't want to mix. Comes to the finish and they suddenly think you want to mix. I don't want to be stuck with a lot of old lasses. And they all smell of pee. And daft half of them, banging tambourines. You go daft there, there's nowhere else for you to go but daft. Wearing somebody else's frock. They even mix up your teeth. I am H.A.P.P.Y. I am not H.A.P.P.Y. I am un-H.A.P.P.Y. Or I would be.

And Zulema says, 'You don't understand, Doris. You're not up to date. They have lockers, now. Flowerbeds. They have their hair done. They go on trips to Wharfdale.' I said, 'Yes. Smelling of pee.' She said, 'You're prejudiced, you.' I said, 'I am, where hygiene's concerned.'

Alan Bennett

Thinking about the extract

1 In a group discuss and note down what you learn about Doris and:
- her attitude towards her Home Help, Zulema
- her memories involving Wilfred
- her concern with cleanliness and order

2 Look carefully at the extract and then write about Doris' life, as you imagine it, just before her fall. Think about her in relation to the community around her. What do you think about Doris' situation? Why is she so isolated?

3 Write a conversation about Doris between Zulema and another Home Help.

4 The play has a very serious theme, yet it is also intended to be amusing. Which parts, if any, make you smile? Try to explain why these parts amuse you.

Role play

1 In pairs, take on the roles of a student visiting on a community care programme and Doris, and work out a scene which explores the relationship between Doris and Wilfred.

2 As a class discuss the role of Zulema, then hot seat her to discover her feelings about her job and about Doris.

Considering the monologue form

1 What is Alan Bennett able to do by using this form of monologue that he couldn't do in any other form of writing? To answer this consider the following.
- What aspects of the story which unfolds are left to the audience's imagination?
- What information might the playwright have included if he were writing in a different form?

2 Rewrite part of Doris' monologue in the form of an extract from a story. What do you learn about the nature of monologue from doing this?

You may find the work you did in the role play between Doris and the student useful in writing this extract.

3 Write a continuation of this script, as you imagine it might develop. Use this extract as a model for the way you set out your work. (Look, for example, at the way directions are given:

She shoves the duster down the side of the chair.

and the use made of pauses.)
For more on monologue see the Poetry module, pages 84-87, where dramatic monologue is considered.

Follow-up theme: old age

The following extract is from *Frangipani House*, which is set in Guyana. It is the story of Mama King's time in a rest home for 'aged old folk – black women. All relics of work-filled bygone days...waiting for the "call from heaven".'

Frangipani House

She loved the grass. She remembered its feel underfoot as she walked barefoot to school. Her thoughts swung slowly like the pendulum of a weary clock, and touched those memories of the time she lay beside her husband somewhere out there on the grass. They talked and hoped and planned then, but where was that time now? Buried out there? Gone forever? She touched the grass with the tip of a slippered foot, but Matron's voice swept over her like a fly-whisk.

'You walking on the grass Marma King? The sign mean you too, you know!'

The old woman looked up. A strained intensity that became sheer eloquence even as Matron watched, took over her face. 'Don't worry yourself, Marma King. You must feel strange here but you just come... You get used to it!'

'Why you calling me Marma King? I am Mama King. Mama mean mother. Don't call me dat stupid name! Marma King! I ask you! What kinda name dat is?'

'You not happy here?' Matron asked. 'You talkin' so bad? For a old lady you talkin' really bad about everything.'

'Nothin' doin' in here!' The old woman's voice seemed to come from somewhere inside her that had been encrusted with pain.

'I sit down. I rock the chair. I look out. I see the same tree, gasping for breath in the same sun. I see the same cross road where the beggar meet up with them people selling fowl. I see the same scatter of feather and rags like embroidery on the carrion

159

crow bush, where the beggars hang they things. And the time – it nibble away at me life like rat eating cheese. You don't see it going. But you wake up one morning and it all gone. Wha kinda place dis is!'

Mama King suddenly noticed that she was alone – talking to herself. Matron had disappeared. She walked back to her room with discontent biting into her being like a plague of fleas.

Scratching her arm, her leg, her neck, made her conscious of the form of her body. It responded to her in a way that made her aware of being alive in the home, and of the larger awareness of being alive in the world.

Just then Miss Tilley started screaming and as if to ease their own anguish several other old women joined in – their voices blending in guilt, remorse and resentment of old age.

There was nowhere to hide from the screams, they formed an invisible barrier around her. And when at last they stopped she felt compelled to seek out and be grateful for a place of her own. Since her entry into the home, she had begun to see the world through the glass window of her room as was the destiny of many old people. Mr Carey, the druggist, told her once, 'Too often old people get to see the world through window. To make it interesting – they must pretend it's magic.'

Beryl Gilroy

Thinking about the story

1 In groups talk about the picture of life in an old people's home this extract conveys to you. How do you react to it?
2 Look again at Doris's view of Stafford House, in *A cream cracker under the settee*. How do the two views compare?

Assignment

Compose and tape record a monologue for Mama King which reveals her thoughts when alone after she returns from her encounter with Matron to her room. Remember the whole of the extract provides you with information about her life, past and present. Use whatever seems appropriate from this.

Here is a suggestion of how you might go about this.

You may have heard people interviewed on television and radio, who appear to talk easily for quite long periods of time. Often, however, they are actually answering questions which have been edited out. Try this method of composing a monologue.

● Write down ten questions you would like to ask Mama King about her life at present, and when she was younger.
● Use the information from the passage to write the answers she might give.
● Expand and develop these answers, linking them together to make a continuous monologue.
● Finally tape record your monologue in the character of Mama King.

A cream cracker under the settee and *Frangipani House* both give views on old age from an elderly person's point of view. The poem on page 161, about an elderly neighbour, was written by Michelle Rose when she was fourteen. It is based on her own experiences.

160

Elsie

I like going, don't get me wrong
But sometimes I feel torn between conscience and selfishness.
We talk about the weather and how she feels,
The club she goes to on a Monday.
She thinks they're ripping the old ones off
Because they've hardly been anywhere.
I talk about school and my lessons.

I feel sorry for her because she hasn't got any children.
No one to look after her now she's older.
I think it's sad she has to rely on people to help her.
The man a few doors down does do odd jobs for her,
But expects money for it.
I think that's disgusting. It doesn't take much to fit a bulb.
But she does have a niece and nephew who visit her sometimes.

She's the type of person who doesn't like to ask
But I think sometimes in life you have no choice.
Sometimes you have to ask or you don't get anything.
In a way I can understand how she feels.

After we've chatted she sometimes gives me chocolate,
But I don't expect it.
I feel guilty taking it, but she insists.
She says it gives her pleasure.
I feel that maybe she thinks that I only go for the chocolate
But she says that she doesn't think that.

Sometimes I haven't got the time to go.
Or I forget.
I feel guilty when I don't go because I feel it's something
I should do.
After all it's only an hour or so.
Nothing to me,
But she enjoys the chat.
When we do get into a conversation time goes quickly.
Maybe I shouldn't treat it like a torture, because it isn't,
And I do enjoy it.

Sometimes I feel it's hard to get the energy to go,
But once there I feel that it was worth it,
And she does enjoy it.
I think it keeps me in touch with reality
Instead of being in my own little world.
I think I should try and understand how it must be for her.

Michelle Rose

Responding to the poem

1 Make a list of questions you would like to ask:
   a) Elsie
   b) Michelle
2 Write your personal response to the poem. You might consider:
   ● the reason why Michelle wrote it
   ● what you discover from it about Michelle and Elsie
   ● particular parts which you found effective or difficult
   ● whether you liked the poem
3 Write a letter to Michelle, responding to her thoughts and feelings about Elsie.
4 a) In a small group produce short accounts of Elsie from the point of view of each of the following people mentioned directly or indirectly in the poem:
   ● a neighbour
   ● the man a few doors down
   ● someone at her club
   ● the nephew or niece
   ● the shopkeeper who sells her chocolate
   (Share the work by deciding who will write each one before you begin.)
   b) In a similar way write about Michelle from the point of view of:
   ● her mother
   ● a friend
   ● her teacher
5 Write Elsie's poem entitled *Michelle*. Use your work from questions 1 to 4 to help you with ideas for this poem.

Assignments

1 a) In pairs, prepare and then tape a conversation between Elsie and Michelle. Include ideas from the poem or invent things that seem suitable.
   b) Develop the conversation. For example, find ways of including the thoughts of each person as she speaks (perhaps as in Alan Bennett's monologue); introduce an interruption from an outsider; include sound effects.
2 As a class, question various people in role as the people in the story, including Michelle and Elsie.
   a) Discover what each of them feels about the situation. Find out about things that are not clear to you in the poem.
   b) Discuss whether this helps you to understand the poem more.

Developing the theme

Look back over the play, *A cream cracker under the settee*, the extract from *Frangipani House*, the poem, *Elsie* and the work you have produced so far in this unit, before writing your responses to the following questions.

1 All three pieces are about women. Is it easier for a man or for a woman to live alone when they are old? Does it make a difference?

2 Some elderly people live alone through necessity, others choose to live alone. In any case, what measures should be taken to ensure their comfort, safety and happiness? Who is responsible for taking such measures? Research this topic of 'Who is Responsible?' for the care of old people. Then produce a piece of argumentative writing summing up the facts and your views on the issue, in the form of an article for a newspaper.

For more on argumentative writing see the Process of Writing module in Book 4B, pages 94-99.

3 Contact organizations, such as 'Help the Aged', in your area to find what help is available to elderly people. Use the information you gather to produce a pamphlet of advice. For more on putting a pamphlet together see page 132.

4 Write in any way you wish about one of the photographs of young and old people together.

5 Think of your own relationship with an elderly person and write one of the following:
a) your thoughts about this relationship in the form of a poem
b) a monologue script dealing with an event in the elderly person's life

Directing the scene

In this unit you will be looking at several scripted scenes with a romantic theme and thinking about directing them to achieve different results. The first scene is from Shakespeare's *Romeo and Juliet*.

Romeo and Juliet

The plot In the Italian city of Verona, Juliet Capulet and Romeo Montague belong to two wealthy families who are long-standing and bitter enemies. Nevertheless, Mercutio, a relative of the Duke of Verona, persuades Romeo and his cousin Benvolio, to go with him, in disguise, to a party at the Capulets' house. There Romeo meets and falls in love with the fourteen-year-old Juliet, daughter of the house. Later that night, after the party, he discovers that Juliet loves him in return. Knowing that their families will never permit their relationship, Romeo and Juliet, with the help of Juliet's nurse, persuade their confessor, Friar Lawrence, to marry them secretly. Unfortunately their families' feud continues, until, at the end of the play, the suicides of the two young people force their parents to realise what they have done.

> ### *Brainstorm*
>
> In a group or 3 or 4, brainstorm the possible events that could have led to these suicides and then show this sequence in the form of a diagram.

Directing a photo story

Many teenage magazines contain photo stories, in which dialogue accompanies posed photographs. Two pupils were given the following extract from Romeo and Juliet to adapt into a photo story of the type often found in these magazines. (It is taken from the scene where Romeo and Juliet first meet and fall in love.) They decided on the frames (individual pictures) the extract would be broken into and then wrote directions for the photographer which are shown opposite.

Frame no.

Romeo: If I profane with my unworthiest hand,
  This holy shrine, the gentle sin is this,
① —— My lips two blushing pilgrims stand,
  To smooth the rough touch with a gentle kiss.
Juliet: Good pilgrim, you do wrong your hands too much
  Which mannerly devotion shows in this,
② —— For saints have hands, that Pilgrims' hands do touch,
  And palm to palm is holy Palmers' kiss.
Romeo: Have not Saints lips and holy Palmers too?
Juliet: Ay, Pilgrim, lips that they must use in prayer.
③ —— **Romeo:** O then dear Saint, let lips do what hands do,
  They pray, grant thou, lest faith turn to despair.

Juliet: Saints do not move, though grant for prayers' sake.
Romeo: Then move not while my prayers' effect I take,
  Thus from my lips, by thine my sin is purged. ——————— (4)
  (*Kissing her*)
Juliet: Then have my lips the sin that they have took.
Romeo: Sin from my lips, O trespass sweetly urged:
  Give me my sin again. ——————————— (5)
Juliet: You kiss by the book.
Nurse: Madam, your mother craves a word with you. ———— (6)

(Act I Scene 5)

William Shakespeare

Frame no.

Notes for the photographer

Frame no.

1   Romeo: Trying to look into Juliet's eyes, whilst holding her hand.
   Juliet: Blushing and turning away.

2   Romeo: Pulls Juliet round to face him and puts his hand on her whilst with
     his other hand he takes her hand.
   Juliet: Still blushing shyly looks him in the eye, slightly resting her cheek on
     his hand as she smiles.

3   Romeo: Gently runs a finger over Juliet's lips whilst looking at her fondly.
   Juliet: Innocently looks upon him, still smiling, and folds her hands in his
     free one.

4   Romeo: Arms wrapped around Juliet, clasping close, looks straight into her
     eyes.
   Juliet: Arms wrapped around Romeo's neck. Looks straight up at him with
     kind eyes.

5   Romeo: Still with his arms clasped around Juliet, smiling, looks at her with a
     slight look of mock disbelief.
   Juliet: Looks up fondly and teasingly; looks disapprovingly with a glint of
     laughter.

6   Romeo: Now holding hands with Juliet, looks inquisitively at the nurse
   Juliet: Looks away towards her mother with a serious face.
   Nurse: Leaning forward as if in a hurry, slightly exhausted, looks upon Juliet.

What do you think?

1 In pairs, discuss these directions to decide how well the pupils who wrote them have understood the passage.

2 Look carefully at the resulting photo story on page 166 and decide together how well the directions have been followed. How would you have directed the individual shots differently? (For example, the kiss itself is not actually depicted here.)

3 Choose some of each character's words and turn them into speech bubbles to go with each frame.

The photo story

1

2

3

4

5

6

166

This passage follows on from the previous scene, where Romeo and Juliet meet. In it each discovers that the other is a member of an enemy family.

Nurse: Madam, your mother craves a word with you.
Romeo: What is her mother?
Nurse: Marry, bachelor,
    her mother is the Lady of the house,
    And a good Lady, and a wise and virtuous,
    I nurs'd her daughter that you talk'd withal:
    I tell you, he that can lay hold of her
    Shall have the chinks.
Romeo: Is she a Capulet?
    O dear account! my life is my foe's debt.
....

Juliet: What's he that follows there that would not dance?
Nurse: I know not.
Juliet: Go ask his name, if he be married,
    My grave is like to be my wedding bed.
Nurse: His name is Romeo, and a Montague,
    The only son of your great enemy.
Juliet: My only love sprung from my only hate,
    Too early seen, unknown, and known too late,
    Prodigious birth of love it is to me,
    That I must love a loathed enemy.

(Act I Scene 5)

William Shakespeare

Your own photo story

Use the passage (or another of your own choice) to set up your own photo story in a similar way.
- Decide how many frames there will be.
- Describe for each frame what the characters will be doing and how they will be looking and feeling.
- Decide which of the character's words could be used in speech bubbles.

If you have the use of a camera you could arrange your performers and take the photographs. You may then find it helpful to photocopy your photographs to produce the finished photo story.

For more on *Romeo and Juliet* see the Forms of Narrative module, page 41, where an extract from the play is presented as a cartoon.

Action between Romeo and Juliet from different Royal Shakespeare Company productions

Follow-up theme: romance

Look at this advice from a magazine. It is intended to help teenage girls avoid losing their boy-friends.

The seven deadly sins of romance

You've got a new boy-friend and everything's coming along swimmingly. He's devine and you're in lurve! But – oh no! – things suddenly start going a bit wonky... Could it be that you've fallen into the trap of committing one (or more) of romance's Seven Deadly Sins?

1 JEALOUSY

There's hardly anything more likely to damage a relationship than the appearance of the green-eyed monster. Jealousy has the power to turn any perfectly nice, perfectly normal girl into a paranoid, gibbering member of the Spanish Inquisition who drives her boy-friend crazy...

Not only is jealousy a very off-putting trait in a girl-friend, but it also makes you seem like you're incredibly insecure ...

2 Impatience

Trying to take things too fast is an easy way to kill a blossoming relationship.

Boys are notoriously scared of getting 'tied down' however much they adore the person that's trying to tie them down. While girls actually enjoy that feeling of being carried away by their emotions, boys are terrified of losing control.

Given these facts it makes sense to let your boy-friend set the pace of your relationship.

3 GOING POWER MAD

Lads like to be in control, or at least think they are... Being over-possessive is a form of trying to take control. If you try to change the amount of time he spends with his friends or on hobbies...he'll think you're trying to run his life, which he'll hate.

4 Putting yourself DOWN

...sends a subconscious message to your boy-friend saying, 'I don't think much of myself so if you do, you must be potty!'

5 Flirting

It should go without saying that flirting with other guys while your boy-friend is around is the kiss of death to a relationship...

Flirting is for single girls and for you when you're not with your man or anyone he knows.

6 LETTING YOURSELF GO

We wouldn't dream of saying that you should always wear full make-up and a sexy frock but on the other hand it's important not to forget that boys are a fickle bunch heavily influenced by appearances.

7 Being too lighthearted

Everyone loves a girl who enjoys herself but there are times when boys want to get serious, spend a little time with you alone and maybe even get romantic. It's hard to believe because it's something they almost never admit to...

What do you think?

1 According to this article, what are boys like? Make a list of statements, in your own words, each beginning: 'Boys are...'
2 The seven 'sins' are negative points; that is, they say what a girl should *not* do. Try writing, according to this magazine, what a girl *should* do to keep her boy–friend. Do you consider such magazine articles to be genuinely helpful?
3 a) Discuss in a group whether the topic of boy/girl relationships is dealt with seriously in other media. Think about pop records and videos, comics, teenagers' novels, films, soap operas.

b) Make a collage, by collecting examples of both good and bad advice, comments, advertisements, illustrations concerning teenage relationships. Then write a commentary on your collage, explaining what it shows.

For more on the language of the media and the way men and women are presented in advertising see the Non–literary Forms module in Book 4B, pages 139-142 and pages 146-149.

IN A SECLUDED PARADISE...
SURROUNDED BY A CORAL SEA,
A BOY AND A GIRL GREW UP ALONE.

NOW THEY ARE EXPERIENCING
THE FIRST AWAKENINGS OF LOVE.

A LOVE THAT CAN ONLY
BE THREATENED...
BY DISCOVERY.

Affairs Of The Hear

A lover's tiff? The end of an affair? The price of passion is always high... but don't forget, the best part about breaking up is making up!

Top, £17.99 and short
£16.99 both from Snob
Shoes from Faith, £34.99
Earrings and bracelet both model's own.

Shirt from a selection at Debenhams, £12.99.
Trousers £24.99 and Waistcoat £19 both from selected branches of C&A.
Shoes from Shelly's, £34.99.

I CAN'T STOP READING GIRLS' MAGS
I am a 17-year old boy taking A-levels. This may sound stupid, but I am addicted to reading girls magazines such as LOOKS. I spend a lot of money buying them each month and spend my free periods reading magazines that girls at school bring in with them. I daren't tell my mates as they may think I am weird. Also, my mum has saw some of them in my room and asked me about them. I told her I was looking after them for a someone, but I don't think she believed me. I must stop this as it can't be normal (none of my mates do it) and I can no longer afford it.
You'd be surprised how many boys read girls' magazines, and why not? There aren't any similar magazines for boys, and they're often full of interesting things to read. They can even help you to understand girls better! But spending all your time and money on them is a bit over the top - as it would be if a girl did the same thing. Everyone has their own way of escaping from the real world, whether it's through magazines, novels, sport, hobbies or even work. When it starts to take over your life though, it's time to ask what it is you're avoiding. Perhaps you're shy or lonely, unsure of your sexuality or unconfident with people. Try to face up to the things you'd rather not think about, and the magazine obsession will disappear of its own accord.

IF ONLY BOYS KNEW....

They've spent their form... kicking a ball around a ... spiders apart, playing a ... their bedrooms and blatantly picking their noses - and now they expect to walk out into the big wide world and impress the girls... dream on lads! It's no wonder boys make some hideous mistakes - so before they attempt to inflict themselves upon us, why doesn't someone take them aside and point out the following...

Aftershave should not be applied with a hose! If a girl can smell you before she can see you, this is not a good sign.
The golden rule for trousers is too long is better...

If a girl makes a particular reference to an item of your wardrobe that she really likes, and she constantly insists you wear it, it's because...

Never buy her clothes or jewellery you think she'll like unless she's dragged you into a shop and said, "Oooh, I love this one!"
Picking a fight to prove how hard you are will not win her heart - if you attempt to impress her with your macho prowess, she may end up going to the rescue of the other bloke (and she'll probably have a better left hook...)

Experimenting with a new look on a first date is a bad, bad idea - if she agreed to go out with you while you were wearing jeans and a T-shirt, she won't be impressed if you turn up in a white suit and a bow tie.
Ogling Ulrika the weather girl, Mandy Smith, or any Page Three Girl will...

TAURUS
(22nd April -20th May)

Love: Because you're feeling a bit more communicative than usual, make the most of it and tell that special someone how you really feel - for better or for worse! Appealing: 8th.

169

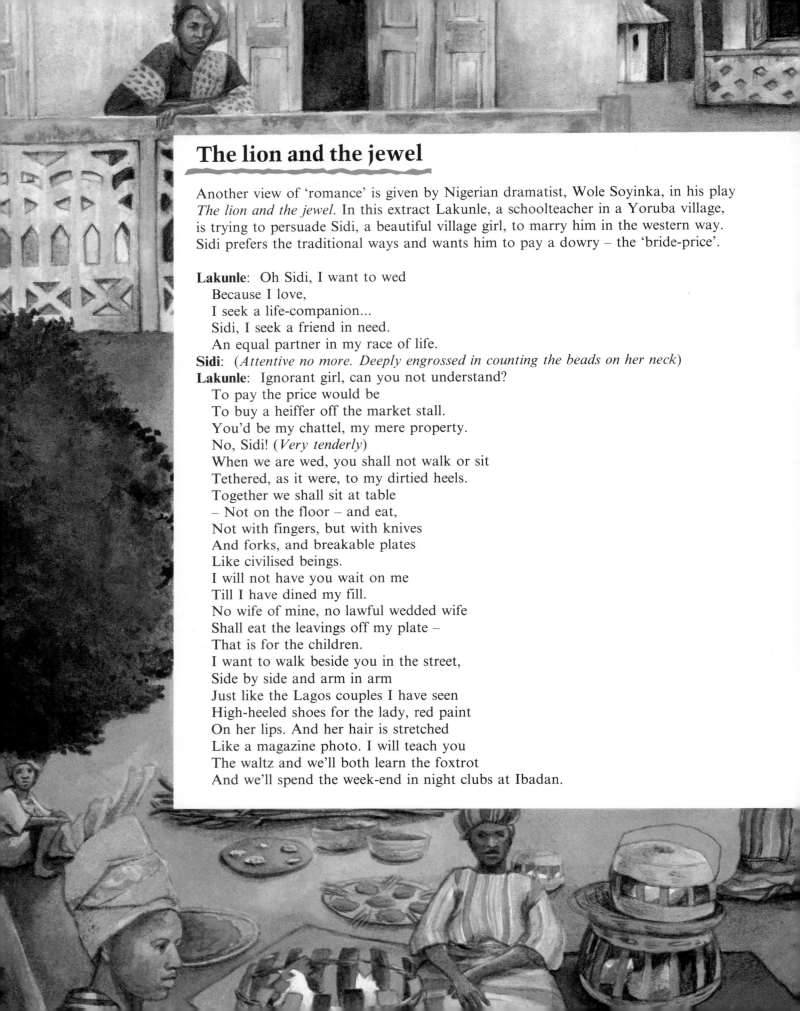

The lion and the jewel

Another view of 'romance' is given by Nigerian dramatist, Wole Soyinka, in his play *The lion and the jewel*. In this extract Lakunle, a schoolteacher in a Yoruba village, is trying to persuade Sidi, a beautiful village girl, to marry him in the western way. Sidi prefers the traditional ways and wants him to pay a dowry – the 'bride-price'.

Lakunle: Oh Sidi, I want to wed
  Because I love,
  I seek a life-companion...
  Sidi, I seek a friend in need.
  An equal partner in my race of life.
Sidi: (*Attentive no more. Deeply engrossed in counting the beads on her neck*)
Lakunle: Ignorant girl, can you not understand?
  To pay the price would be
  To buy a heiffer off the market stall.
  You'd be my chattel, my mere property.
  No, Sidi! (*Very tenderly*)
  When we are wed, you shall not walk or sit
  Tethered, as it were, to my dirtied heels.
  Together we shall sit at table
  – Not on the floor – and eat,
  Not with fingers, but with knives
  And forks, and breakable plates
  Like civilised beings.
  I will not have you wait on me
  Till I have dined my fill.
  No wife of mine, no lawful wedded wife
  Shall eat the leavings off my plate –
  That is for the children.
  I want to walk beside you in the street,
  Side by side and arm in arm
  Just like the Lagos couples I have seen
  High-heeled shoes for the lady, red paint
  On her lips. And her hair is stretched
  Like a magazine photo. I will teach you
  The waltz and we'll both learn the foxtrot
  And we'll spend the week-end in night clubs at Ibadan.

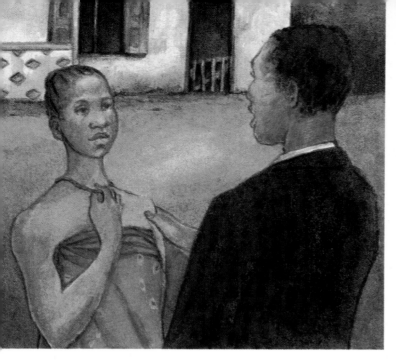

Oh I must show you the grandeur of towns
We'll live there if you like or merely pay visits.
So choose. Be a modern wife, look me in the eye
And give me a little kiss – like this
(*Kisses her*)
Sidi: (*Backs away*)
No don't! I tell you I dislike
This strange unhealthy mouthing you perform.
Every time, your action deceives me
Making me feel that you merely wish
To whisper something in my ear.
Then comes this licking of my lips with yours.
It's so unclean. And then – 'Pyout!'
Are you being rude to me?
Lakunle: (*Wearily*) It's never any use.
Bush-girl you are, bush-girl you'll always be;
Uncivilized and primitive – bush-girl!
I kissed you as all educated men –
And Christians – kiss their wives.
It is the way of civilised romance.
Sidi: (*Lightly*) A way you mean, to avoid
Payment of lawful bride-price
A cheating way, mean and miserly.

Wole Soyinka

Group discussion

1 How does Lakunle try to persuade Sidi to marry him, and how does Sidi counter his argument?
2 Whose side are you on in this argument? Why?
3 Do you think the playwright shows a preference? How?

Role play

Choose someone from your group of 3 or 4 to take on the role of a village counsellor giving advice to both Sidi and Lakunle shortly after this scene.

The counsellor would be someone who would have the wisdom and experience to see the case from both sides.

Assignment

Which qualities would you most value in a marriage partner? Which would you least tolerate? What part should love play in marriage? Is physical attraction important, as it appears to be in *Romeo and Juliet*, or is it more important that two people should share the same sort of views and opinions? Are young people really able to decide for themselves who they should marry? What part should parents play in the process?

Think through these questions carefully and then write your response.

Directing techniques

Here is another extract from *The lion and the jewel*, showing a part of the argument between Lakunle and Sidi which led up to the scene on pages 170-171. It has had notes added as a director might have done, in preparation for directing the scene. The notes show the director's thoughts about the characters, his ideas about their movements, and how he thinks some of the lines should be said.

① Pleading

② Pauses ...

③ Must show contempt for the old ways

④ Simple shake of the head. Simple words
↑
MAKE CONTRAST BETWEEN
↓
⑤ Exaggerated language – 'rhetoric'

⑥ She recognises this

⑦ Brings him down to earth again

⑧ Rejects his 'fine' talk

⑨ 'B..b...p...b' – almost spitting these out to make her point (like talking to a naughty child?)

⑩ Lakunle turns away

⑪ Anger here?

⑫ Lakunle turns back to face her

⑬ Genuine concern at this

Lakunle: ...Sidi, my heart
① Bursts into flowers with my love. ②
③ { But you, you and the dead of this village
Trample it with feet of ignorance.
Sidi: (*Shakes her head in bafflement*)
④ { If the snail finds splinters in his shell
He changes house. Why do you stay?
Lakunle: Faith. Because I have faith.
Oh Sidi, vow to me your own undying love
⑤ { And I will scorn the jibes of these bush minds
Who know no better. Swear, Sidi,
Swear you will be my wife and I will
Stand against earth, heaven, and the nine
Hells...
⑥ **Sidi**: Now there you go again.
One little thing
And you must chirrup like a cockatoo. ⑦
You talk and talk and deafen me.
⑧ { With words that always sound the same
And make no meaning.
I've told you, and I say it again
I shall marry you today, next week
Or any day you name.
⑨ But my bride-price must first be paid. ⑩
Aha, now you turn away.
But I tell you, Lakunle, I must have
The full bride-price. Will you make me
A laughing-stock? Well, do as you please.
But Sidi will not make herself
A cheap bowl for the village spit. } ⑪
⑫ **Lakunle**: On my head let fall their scorn.
Sidi: They will say I was no virgin
That I was forced to sell my shame } ⑬
And marry you without a price.

Wole Soyinka

Working on a double page make your own director's copy of a part of the previous scene, as shown in the example above. On the right-hand side make a copy of the text (use a wordprocessor if possible). On the left add your own thoughts and director's notes.

Set and costume design

An important task for a director is deciding what a production should look like; in other words, what the audience will see in the acting area (the set) and how the characters will be dressed (costume). A designer is then usually responsible for interpreting the director's ideas for these things.

In some plays the writer is very specific about both the set and the costume, giving precise and detailed directions about them. In all cases the set has to be designed to accommodate the events that happen during the play. In *The lion and the jewel*, for example, great use is made of energetic mime and dance. It is important, therefore, that the acting area is large enough to allow for the movements of a number of performers.

In a play where the whole action happens in a single place it is possible to have a permanent set; in another play the scene might change rapidly to different locations. Here is an extract from the opening of *The lion and the jewel* describing the set.

Morning

A clearing on the edge of the market, dominated by an immense 'odan' tree.

It is the village centre. The wall of the bush school flanks the stage on the right, and a rude window opens onto the stage from the wall... Sidi enters from left, carrying a small pail of water on her head. She is a slim girl with plaited hair. A true village belle. She balances the pail on her head with accustomed ease. Around her is wrapped the familiar broad cloth which is folded just above her breasts, leaving her shoulders bare.

...The schoolmaster is dressed in an old-style English suit, threadbare but not ragged, clean but not ironed, obviously a size or two too small. His tie is done in a very small knot, disappearing beneath a shiny black waist-coat. He wears twenty-three-inch bottom trousers, and blanco-white tennis shoes.

Note: an 'odan' is a large, spreading tree something like an oak, common in Yoruba villages.

Creating a set

1 Make a sketch of this set as you would imagine it to be, seen from the audience, and a plan with notes added, of the acting area.
2 Design the schoolmaster's costume, as Sidi's has been done here, with notes drawing attention to the points the writer mentions.

Documentary autobiography

In this unit you will be asked to make a study of events in your own life as they happen to you, over a period of time.

The rock and roll years

What follows is an attempt to describe in words what is happening on a television screen. The writer of this description sat in front of her video, and with the aid of the pause and rewind buttons and a lot of patience, she was able to transcribe (put down in writing) what she saw and heard.

It is an account of an extract from a film in a documentary series called *The rock and roll years*. Using popular songs of the day, comments, news stories and film of current events each programme tries to sum up the history of a particular year. Which year is this?

Group discussion

In groups of 3 or 4, discuss how well you think the chosen music lyrics fit each event described?

Music

Guitar music. Introduction to *The boxer* by Simon and Garfunkel

'I am just a poor boy
Though my story's seldom told
I have squandered my resistance
On a pocketful of mumbles
Such are promises...'

'All lies and jest
Still a man hears what he
wants to hear
And disregards the rest...'

Picture

Man surrounded by police and a lawyer

Sheets of paper with writing which cannot be distinguished. Zoom in and focus on many lines of: 'Kennedy must be assassinated'.

Film of birds flying. They turn out to be helicopters. Zoom in on American soldier in helicopter. It lands and soldiers jump out and squat in the long grass.

Printed/spoken words

Sirhan Sirhan is found guilty of the murder of Senator Robert Kennedy.

Music	Picture	Printed/spoken words
	The helicopter rises and leaves them. The scene is pink, blue, yellow, green: pastel shades as in a tranquil painting. The blades spin and blow the long grass like a breeze.	
'Mmmm...' Instrumental guitar.	The soldiers are creeping, hiding. They listen in on their intercom systems.	
	Close up of a young soldier. Pan out to reveal a line of soldiers waiting.	
'When I left my home and my family I was no more than a boy...' 'In the company of strangers In the quiet of a railway station Running scared.'	Shot of a helicopter with soldiers who appear to be lying down in front of it. They could be dead... ...but people begin pulling them up and dragging them away.	A unit of very young soldiers in South Vietnam... ...goes on strike and refuses to move to orders.
'Laying low'	One of them has a bandage around his eyes and seems to be crying.	
'Seeking out the poorer quarters Where the ragged people go.'	Their young officer appears and a conversation takes place between him and the reporter.	Sergeant Blenkinshipp Alpha Company. 'They felt like they were the only company that was being committed and once I gave them a tactical briefing they understood the situation. I walked away from them and they followed me back up the hill and rejoined the company. That's all there was to it.'
'Lie la lie...'		'They were scared in other words?'
'Lie la lie lie lie la lie.'		'They were scared.'

175

A year in the life of Grace Ndiritu

Having seen the video, *The rock and roll years*, and talked about it with her teacher, fourteen-year-old Grace Ndiritu decided she would use a similar idea to record events in a year of her own life. As it happened, it turned out to be a very eventful year! The following extract is a transcript of part of a tape she made.

January 1st

(Chiming of New Year bells and cheers.)
Happy New Year! Welcome to 1991. This is my year. I'm going to record everything important. Not just in my personal life, but on issues: political, fashion, school, home and music. A year of my life.

Diary 1991: a new beginning. My name is Grace Ndiritu. I'm aged fourteen, nearly fifteen. My life is usually boring, but sometimes something interesting can happen.

January 3rd

National News. A dozen prisoners have escaped from Durham Jail. Two are highly dangerous. Gazza started the year off with a red card and Iron Maiden have knocked Cliff off the number one spot.

'Open your eyes on Saviour's day,
Don't look back or turn away,
Life can be yours if you'll only stay,
He's calling you, calling you,
On a Saviour's day'

'Bring your daughter to the slaughter,
Let her go.'

It marks the beginning of a violent era.
They say that Afros are back. I wish that they'd make new fashions, instead of recycling old ones.

(Musical introduction to 'Kinky Afro'.)

January 6th

Britain is being swept off its feet by strong gales hitting Wales and the South of England quite badly. My relationship with my mother is also quite rocky. Hopefully, everything will blow over and calm down. The trouble is, she favours my brother. I have one brother and one sister. I also happen to be the youngest. He was the first. I want to be me in my own right and not compared to my brother.

176

(*Innuendo* by Queen)
'You can be anything you want to be,
Just turn yourself into anything
You think that you could ever be.
Be free with yourself,
Be free,
Be free.
Surrender your ego,
Be free,
Be free,
To yourself.'

January 7th

Today I started a new term at school. Not exactly the most interesting place to be, but I suppose it went okay. Another major issue in the news is the Gulf crisis. It looks like war will be declared on January 15th. I wonder how Caroline will cope without her brother. I wonder what effect it will have on my life. Will I ever have the chance to grow up or will I die from nuclear bombs? It might seem selfish, but I don't think this war will solve any problems. It'll just create them.

January 8th

The second series of *Twin Peaks* is back on and we're still waiting to find out who killed Laura Palmer. I can't wait to find out who did it. Another new American series is *Beverley Hills 90210* about a group of snotty rich kids who, at the age of sixteen, have nose jobs and drive BMWs. Not very realistic, but it seems okay for dreaming.

January 14th

War is definitely on and from the words of President Bush:

'We're going to kick some ass.'

There is no hope of peace. The mood of the '60s will be back and Woodstock and peace marches will be in.

(*Pretty girls make graves* by The Smiths)
'Upon the sand, upon the bay,
There is a quick and easy way, you say,
Before you will astray,
I'd rather say:
'I'm not the man you think I am,
I'm not the man you think I am.
And sorrow's nature's tongue.
He will not smile for anyone.

And pretty girls make graves.
And of the pair and of the bay,
You take my arm and say:
'Give in to lust, give in to lust,
Oh Heaven knows, we'll soon be dust.'

Also, in Russia, trouble has broken out. They decided to storm the people because they want Lithuania to become an independent country.

On a happier note, there is a new number one. Enigma. It's a very strange tune.

(Music)

January 17th

Today, the war began. Operation Desert Storm. It's gone well. The pilots have gone into combat with Iraqi enemies. British pilots in Jaguars and Tornados have been bombing Iraqi runways and firearms.

An American aircraft has been shot down. President Bush thinks it has gone well. There was little response from the Iraqis. They say that fourteen planes have been shot down.

As for me, I don't feel so well. I think I have the 'flu.

January 18th

The war has gone from bad to worse. The Iraqis have decided to bomb Israel with Scud missiles. Israel is deciding what to do.

I'm stuck in bed.

January 19th

The ground forces have started to move towards the Kuwaiti border. An anxious time. Peace marches have been going on all around the world. In Paris, Glasgow, Rome.

January 21st

Saddam Hussein provoked more outrages today when Iraq revealed it was using prisoners as a human shield against allied air raids. Bush is extremely angry. John Major said it was illegal and inhuman.

Television pictures of the sad and scared prisoners of war were beamed around the western world yesterday. Calls for Saddam Hussein to be overthrown.

Petrol took a turn for the worse in selling prices, but oil prices rose.

January 24th

(Channel 4 News 8.00 p.m.)

'Gulf. Iraq's airforce final attempts to go on the offensive. Minx and the Mirage fly an exocet attack on the allied fleet. It ends with the two Migs shot down and the exocet lost in the desert. As Britain sends further air reinforcements to the Gulf, the RAF loses a sixth Tornado.

Tonight we assess the latest moves in the war, and as independent eye witnesses reach Jordan from Baghdad, they tell us the Iraqi capital is structurally intact, but that most of its services have now been destroyed.

From Washington, we assess how President Bush is handling the war and talk live to former defence secretary Casper Weinberger.

From the occupied territories, we report Palestinian life under an almost permanent Israeli imposed curfew.

And here, we report beyond the war, as the British Chamber of Commerce warns the recession will be longer and deeper.'

Grace Ndiritu

Looking at the transcript

1 Read through the transcript of Grace's diary on your own. As you do so, note down where:
   ● she gives details of her personal life
   ● she links events in her own life with what is happening outside
   ● she uses a record to comment on her own feelings
   ● she shows that world events affect her directly in a personal way
2 From the evidence you have here, what sort of person does Grace seem to be?

179

This is your life

1 Decide on a period of time over which you could produce a piece of work similar to Grace's. It need not be a whole year, as Grace set out to cover. Perhaps a week? A month? Half a term? A term? Whichever you choose make it a firm commitment.

2 Using a portable tape machine, record any of the following for your chosen period:
   ● accounts of things that happen in your own daily life that are important to you
   ● thoughts and feelings about your life at present
   ● thoughts and feelings about what is happening in the outside world
   ● favourite records; those which mean something or are important to you
   ● news items from radio or television which you feel are significant
   ● conversations or 'interviews' with friends and family; others if possible

3 Collect together a scrapbook to go with your tape. In it you could put:
   ● newspaper articles
   ● photographs from newspapers or magazines
   ● your own photographs
   ● letters you receive
   ● copies of letters you write
   ● your own written thoughts and feelings
   ● quotations from your reading which you value

4 At the end of your chosen period select pieces from your tape which you could transcribe, and with the help of your scrapbook, produce a piece of written work which would:
   a) present a picture of a particular period in your life, or
   b) draw out a common theme running through a longer period of time

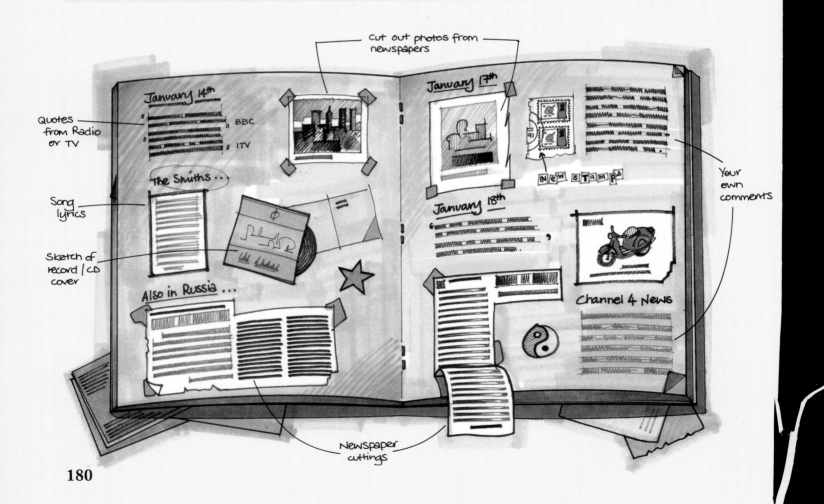

Index of authors and extracts

Allingham, William   Diary extract   2
Angelou, Maya   I know why the caged bird sings   13
Austen, Jane   Emma   52
Bâ, Mariama   Dear Aissatou   16
Ballard, J. G.   Empire of the sun   45
Barr, Pat   A curious life for a lady   20
Barrett Browning, Elizabeth   from 'Sonnets from the Portuguese'   116
Bennett, Alan   A cream cracker under the settee   154
Berry, James   Mum, dad and me   108
Brand, Dionne   Wind   71
Brown, Christy   My left foot   134, 136
Browning, Robert   Porphyria's lover   85
Brunvand, Professor Jan Harold   extracts from 'The vanishing hitchhiker'   34, 35
Calcutt, David   The bogeyman   125
Causley, Charles   extract from The ballad of the bread man;   33
The ballad of Charlotte Dymond   80
Clarke, Gillian   Miracle on St David's Day   76
Connaughton, Shane and Sheridan, Jim
My left foot, screenplay   138, 140
Cope, Wendy   On finding an old photograph;   107
Two extracts from Strugnell's sonnets [iv] and [vi]   114
Crosby Culver, Eloise   Harriet Tubman   83
Dahl, Roald   Hey diddle diddle, and Mary, Mary...   90
de Maupassant, Guy   A Corsican bandit   55
Dickens, Charles   Nicholas Nickleby   51
Duffy, Carol Ann   In Mrs Tilscher's class;   65
Warming her pearls and Too bad   87
du Maurier, Daphne   Frenchman's creek   45
Dunbar, Maureen   Catherine's diary   3
Dunn, Douglas   From the night window   66
Eliot, George   Silas Marner   48
Ende, Michael   The never ending story   27, 49
Franklin, Miles   My brilliant career   52
Gilroy, Beryl   Frangipani House   159
Greene, Graham   Brighton rock   45, 48, 50
Harrison, Harry   The streets of Ashkelon   45
Haselden, John   'Allo, 'allo – The war diaries of René Artois   7
Heaney, Seamus   Boy driving his father to confession;   72
Mid term break   62
Hill, Susan   The magic apple tree   5
Hughes, Glyn   Cold   66
Hughes, Ted   Full moon and little Frieda;   106
The warm and the cold   69
Hunt, Roderick and Brychta, Alex   The lost teddy   37
Hutchins, Guy   Let her sleep   147
Issa   City people, Constancy, Parting, Spring, and The weeping willow   98
Life-line;   99

James, P. D.   Death of an expert witness   45
Jasimuddin   The boatman and the scholar   29
Jennings, Elizabeth   My grandmother;   104
The enemies and Friendship   92
Jonker, Ingrid   The song of the broken reeds   70
Keats, John   Letter to Richard Woodhouse   17
Lee, Laurie   As I walked out one midsummer morning   12
Lester, Helen   A porcupine named Fluffy   38
Lochhead, Liz   For my grandmother knitting;   103
Poem for my sister   111
Malory, Sir Thomas   Le mort d'Arthur   30
McGough, Roger   Each night my father... and There was a young man...;   90
Vinegar   62
McPherson, Ann and MacFarlane, Aidan   I'm a health freak too!   7
Morgan, Edwin   Glasgow sonnet   115
Moy, Jenny   Bedtime stories   101
Murdoch, Iris   An accidental man   14
Ndiritu, Grace   A year in the life of Grace Ndiritu   176
Nicholls, Judith   Orang-utan   68
Nichols, Grace   Praise song for my mother   73
O'Brien, Robert C.   Z for Zachariah   9
O'Hanlon, Redmond   Into the heart of Borneo   22
O'Rourke, P. J.   Holidays in hell   21
Owen, Wilfred   Exposure   94
Pearse, Gabriela   Sistahs   110
Pile, Stephen   The least successful animal rescue   35
Rhys, Jean   from 'Tigers are better looking'   54
Richardson, Samuel   Pamela   15
Rickard, Fred   Early memories of school   10
Rickard, Ken   Free dinners   11
Roethke, Theodore   Orchids   102
Rose, Michelle   Elsie   161
Rowson, Martin   Cartoon version of 'The wasteland'   40
Shakespeare, William   Romeo and Juliet (Act I Sc. 1);   41
Romeo and Juliet (Act I Sc. 5);   164
Sonnet 55;   114
Sonnet 104;   112
Sonnet 116;   114
Sonnet 130   116
Sir Gawain and the green knight   97
Sir Patrick Spens   78
Soyinka, Wole   The lion and the jewel   170, 173
Taylor, Bob   Tale enders   46
Thubron, Colin   Behind the wall   23
Tolkien, J. R. R.   Lord of the rings   26
Treece, Henry   The conquerors   77
Wallington, Mark   500 mile walkies   25
Whitman, Walt   I sit and look out   100
Yeats, W.B.   After long silence   88

Acknowledgements

The authors and publisher are grateful for permission to include the following copyright material:

Module 1: Forms of Narrative

Maya Angelou: from *I Know Why the Caged Bird Sings*. Reprinted by permission of Virago Press. **Marianna Bâ**: 'Dear Aissatou' from *So Long a Letter* (Wm Heinemann Ltd., 1981). **J. G. Ballard**: from *The Empire of the Sun*. Reprinted by permission of Victor Gollancz Ltd. **Pat Barr**: from *A Curious Life For a Lady* (Macmillan & John Murray, 1970/Penguin, 1986). **Charles Causley**: extract from 'Ballad of the Bread Man' from *Collected Poems* (Macmillan). Reprinted by permission of David Higham Associates Ltd. **Daphne du Maurier**: from *Frenchman's Creek*. Copyright the Estate of Daphne du Maurier. Reprinted with permission of Curtis Brown Group Ltd. **Maureen Dunbar**: from *Catherine* (Viking, 1986), ©Maureen Dunbar, 1986. Reprinted by permission of Penguin Books Ltd. **Michael Ende**: from *The Never Ending Story* (Allen Lane, 1983). © K. Thienemanns Verlag, Stuttgart, 1979. Reprinted by permission of Penguin Books Ltd. **Miles Franklin**: from *My Brilliant Career*, published by Angus & Robertson(UK) Ltd, now HarperCollins. Used with permission. **Graham Greene**: from *Brighton Rock* (Heinemann). Reprinted by permission of David Higham Associates Ltd. **Barbara Hambly**: front cover from *Dark Hand of Magic* (Grafton Books). **Harry Harrison**: from *The Streets of Ashkelon*. © 1990 by Harry Harrison. Reprinted by permission of the author. **John Haselden**: from *'Allo, 'Allo - The War Diaries of René Artois*. Reprinted by permission of BBC Enterprises Ltd. **Reginald Hill**: front cover from *Exit Lines* (Grafton books). **Susan Hill**: from *The Magic Apple Tree*. Reprinted by permission of Hamish Hamilton Ltd. **Victoria Holt**: front cover from *The Secret Woman* (Fontana). **Roderick Hunt**: from *The Lost Teddy*, illustrated by Alex Brychta. Reprinted by permission of Oxford University Press. **P. D. James**: from *Death of an Expert Witness*. Reprinted by permission of Faber & Faber Ltd. **Jasimuddin**: 'The Boatman and the Scholar' from *Folk-Tales of Bangladesh* (Oxford University Press, Dhaka). **Laurie Lee**: from *As I Walked Out One Midsummer Morning*. Reprinted by permission of Andre Deutsch Ltd. **Helen Lester**: from *A Porcupine Named Fluffy* (Pan/ Macmillan Children's Books). **Ann McPherson and Aidan MacFarlane**: from *I'm a Health Freak Too!*. Reprinted by permission of Oxford University Press. **Iris Murdoch**: from *An Accidental Man*. Reprinted by permission of Random Century Ltd., on behalf of the author and Chatto & Windus as publishers. **Robert C. O'Brien**: from *Z for Zachariah*. Reprinted by permission of Victor Gollancz Ltd. **Redmond O'Hanlon**: from *Into the Heart of Borneo* (Penguin, 1985). Reprinted by permission of Peters Fraser & Dunlop Ltd. **Ordnance Survey**: extract from *Ordnance Survey Pathfinder Guide to Cornwall*. Published by Ordnance Survey and Jarrold Publishing. © Crown copyright 1990. Used with permission. **P. J. O'Rourke**: from *Holidays in Hell*, © 1988 by P. J. O'Rourke. Used by permission of the Atlantic Monthly Press. **Stephen Pile**: 'Animal Rescue' from *The Book of Heroic Failures* (Routledge, 1979). **Jean Rhys**: from *Tigers are Better Looking*. Reprinted by permission of Andre Deutsch Ltd. **Martin Rowson**: 3rd spread from 'The Fire Sermon' from *The Waste Land* (Penguin Books, 1990). © Martin Rowson, 1990. Used with permission. **Bob Taylor**: from *Tale Enders*. Reprinted by permission of Thomas Nelson & Sons Ltd. **Colin Thubron**: from *Behind the Wall*. Reprinted by permission of William Heinemann Ltd. **J. R. R. Tolkien**: from *The Lord of the Rings*, published by Allen & Unwin, now Unwin Hyman, an imprint of HarperCollins Publishers Ltd. Used with permission.

Module 2: Poetry

James Berry: 'Mum, dad and me' from *When I Dance*, © 1988 James Berry (Hamish Hamilton 1988). Used with permission. **Dionne Brand**: 'Wind' from *Poetry Jump Up*, ed.Grace Nichols. © Dionne Brand. **Charles Causley**: 'The Ballad of Charlotte Dymond'

182

from *Collected Poems* (Macmillan). Reprinted by permission of David Higham Associates Ltd. **Gillian Clarke**: 'Miracle on St. David's Day' from *Letter from a Far Country*. Reprinted by permission of Carcanet Press Ltd. **Wendy Cope**: 'On Finding an Old Photograph' and two extracts from 'Strugnell's Sonnets' [iv] and [vi] from *Making Cocoa for Kingsley Amis*. Reprinted by permission of Faber & Faber Ltd. **Eloise Crosby Culver**: 'Harriet Tubman'. © Eloise Crosby Culver and Associated Publishers Inc. **Roald Dahl**: 'Hey diddle diddle' and 'Mary, Mary... ' from *Rhyme Stew* (Penguin, 1990). Reprinted by permission of Murray Pollinger Literary Agent. **Carol Ann Duffy**: 'In Mrs Tilscher's Class', 'Too Bad' from *The Other Country* and 'Warming Her Pearls' from *Selling Manhattan*. Reprinted by permission of Anvil Press Poetry Ltd. **Douglas Dunn**: 'From the Night Window' from *Terry Street*. Reprinted by permission of Faber & Faber Ltd. **Edward Gorey**: 'Each night... ' from *The Listing Attic*. © 1954 Edward Gorey. **Seamus Heaney**: 'Mid term Break' from *Death of a Naturalist* and 'Boy Driving His Father to Confession'. Reprinted by permission of Faber & Faber Ltd. **Glyn Hughes**: 'Cold' from *Best of Neighbours* (Ceolfrith Press). Reprinted by permission of the author. **Ted Hughes**: 'Full Moon and Little Frieda' from *Wodwo*, 'The Warm and the Cold' from *Season Songs*. Reprinted by permission of Faber & Faber Ltd. **Elizabeth Jennings**: 'The Enemies', 'Friendship' and 'My Grandmother' from *Collected Poems* (Carcanet). Reprinted by permission of David Higham Associates Ltd. **Ingrid Jonker** (trans. Jack Cope and William Plomer): 'The Song of the Broken Reeds' from *Poetry Jump Up*, ed. Grace Nichols. Translation © Jack Cope and William Plomer. **Liz Lochhead**: 'For My Grandmother Knitting' and 'Poem For My Sister' from *Dreaming Frankenstein*. Reprinted by permission of Polygon. **Roger McGough**: 'Vinegar' from *The Mersey Sound* (Penguin, 1967) and 'There Was a Young Man Name of Fred,...' from *Watchwords Three* (Hodder, 1982). Reprinted by permission of Peters Fraser & Dunlop Group Ltd. **Edwin Morgan**: 'Glasgow Sonnet' from *Selected Poems*. Reprinted by permission of Carcanet Press Ltd. **Jenny Moy**: 'Bedtime Stories' from *Wordlife* (Nelson, 1988). **Judith Nicholls**: 'Orang-utan', drafts (and commentary) © Judith Nicholls 1990. Reprinted by permission of the author. 'Orang-utan' is from *Dragonsfire* by Judith Nicholls, published by Faber. **Grace Nichols**: 'Praise Song for My Mother' from *The Fat Black Woman's Poems*. Reprinted by permission of Virago Press. Limericks from *The Observer Book of Great Green Limericks* (W. H. Allen, 1989). Reprinted by permission of the publisher. **Gabriela Pearse**: 'Sistahs' from *Is That The New Room? Poems by Women Poets*, ed. Wendy Cope (Lions Teen Tracks, 1989). **Theodore Roethke**: 'Orchids' from *The Collected Poems of Theodore Roethke*. Reprinted by permission of Faber & Faber Ltd. **Henry Treece**: 'The Conquerors' from *The Haunted Garden*. © Mrs Treece. Reprinted by permission of John Johnson Ltd. **Harriet Tubman** notes: adapted from information in *Yesterday, Today, Tomorrow* (Teacher's activities booklet) The English Media Centre, 1986.

Module 3: Media Scripts

From *BBC Notes on Radio Drama*. Reprinted with permission. This leaflet has now been superseded by *Writing Plays for Radio*. Front cover of *Writing Plays for Radio* reproduced by permission of the BBC. **Alan Bennett**: from 'A Cream Cracker Under the Settee' from *Talking Heads*. Reprinted by permission of BBC Enterprises Ltd. **Christy Brown**: from *My Left Foot*. Reprinted by permission of Martin Secker and Warburg Ltd. **David Calcutt**: extract from *The Bogeyman*. Reproduced by permission of the author. **Shane Connaughton & Jim Sheridan**: from the screenplay of *My Left Foot*. Reprinted by permission of Faber & Faber Ltd. **Beryl Gilroy**: from 'Frangipani House' (Heinemann Caribbean Writers Series, 19486). **Jeff Hooper**: for permission to reproduce photograph on p.23 from his article 'Music Hath Charms ...' in the *Nursing Times*, September 11, Vol.87, No.37, 1991. Photo: Dougie McBride. **Guy Hutchins**: 'Let Her Sleep', scripted by Guy Hutchins from work done by Tony Grady and Les Stringer with a Community Group at Four Dwellings School, Birmingham. Script © 1992 Guy Hutchins. Used by permission of

Cecily Ware Literary Agents. *Just Seventeen*: for 'The Seven Deadly Sins of Romance', *Just Seventeen*, June 6, 1990. *Looks Magazine*: for 'If only Boys Knew...', 'Affairs of the Heart' and 'I can't stop reading Girls' Mags'. Reprinted with permission. From *Radio Times*: drama listings Radio 4, 9-15 February, 1991. Reprinted by permission of BBC Magazines. Photo and caption from 'A Special Way of Seeing', *Radio Times*, 9-15 February, 1991. **Wole Soyinka**: from *The Lion and the Jewel*. © Oxford University Press 1963. Reprinted by permission of Oxford University Press.

Les Stringer would also like to thank **Gail Causer**, **David Dugmore**, **Tony Grady**, and **Lyn Woodey** for the ideas and support they have given during the development of the Media Scripts module.

The illustrations are by: **Mike Allport** p.34, 47, 58, 76, 161; **Tony Ansell** p.75; **John Astrop** p.7; **Hamish Blakely** p.49, 55, 92; **Tony James Chance** p.15, 20, 52, 104, 107, 137; **Gerard Gibson** p.12, 54, 80; **Robin Harris** p.16, 28, 85, 112; **Sarah Hopkins** p.18, 19, 33; **Joanne Hornsby** p.14, 48 (top), 50; **Paul Hunt** p.82, 100; **Mary Kuper** p.73, 86, 87; **Sian Leetham** p.90, 91; **Christopher Logan** p.132, 180; **Katrina Longden** p.41; **Diane Lumley** p.2, 53, 110; **Diana Mayo** p.5, 78/79; **Peter Melnyczuk** p.62, 103, 116; **Nilesh Mistry** p.26, 65, 98, 99, 106; **Nicky Palin** p.30; **Rachel Ross** p.108/109, 159, 170/171, 173; **Susan Scott** p.17; **Michael Sheehy** p.70/71, 117, 118; **Duncan Storr** p.22/3, 48 (bottom), 115, 126/127.

The handwriting and diagrams are by **Elitta Fell**.

The publishers would like to thank the following for permission to reproduce photographs:

Allsport UK Ltd/Budd Symes p.143 top ; **Alpha/Ian Dickson** p.176 right, **Alpha/James Marshall** p.177; **Associated Press** p.179; **BBC Photography Library** p.8, 154; **Biofotos/Heather Angel** p.102; **Mary Brown** p.134 all; **Susan Butler** p.120 right; **Camera Press (UK) Ltd.** p.119 top left, p.178 both; **The J. Allan Cash Photo Library** p.176 left; **Martyn Chillmaid** p.144, 145 both, 146, 149, 166 all; **Christie's Scotland Ltd** p.134 all; **Michael Dudley** p.10, 37 all, 38/9 all, 40, 42/3 all; **Mary Evans Picture Library** p.83, 94, 120 left; **Format Partners - Photo Library/Mo Wilson** p.162, **Format Partners - Photo Library/Maggie Murray** p.163 left; **Granada Films** p.139, 140; **Liz Lockwood** p.10, 42/43; **The Mansell Collection Ltd.** p.119 bottom left; **The National Portrait Gallery, London** p.119 top right, bottom right; **Duncan Phillips** p.64 all; **Photofusion** p.163 right; **Paul Popper Ltd** p.95 bottom, 174; **Topham Picture Source** p.95 top; **Reg Wilson Photography** p.167 all.

The cover photograph is reproduced by permission of the **Science Photo Library**.

Every effort has been made to trace and contact copyright holders prior to printing but in some cases without success. If notified the publisher will be pleased to rectify any errors or omissions at the earliest opportunity.